MICROSOFT® OFFICE
Access 2003

COURSECARD EDITION

Introductory
Concepts and
Techniques

Gary B. Shelly
Thomas J. Cashman
Philip J. Pratt
Mary Z. Last

THOMSON
COURSE TECHNOLOGY

COURSE TECHNOLOGY
25 THOMSON PLACE
BOSTON MA 02210

SHELLY
CASHMAN
SERIES®

Australia • Canada • Denmark • Japan • Mexico • New Zealand • Philippines • Puerto Rico • Singapore
South Africa • Spain • United Kingdom • United States

THOMSON

COURSE TECHNOLOGY

Microsoft Office Access 2003:
Introductory Concepts and Techniques, CourseCard Edition

Gary B. Shelly
Thomas J. Cashman
Philip J. Pratt
Mary Z. Last

Managing Editor:
Alexandra Arnold

Senior Acquisitions Editor:
Dana Merk

Product Manager:
Reed Cotter

Editorial Assistant:
Selena Coppock

Print Buyer:
Laura Burns

Series Consulting Editor:
Jim Quasney

Director of Production:
Patty Stephan

Production Editor:
Catherine G. DiMassa

Production Assistant:
Jill Klaffky

Development Editor:
Ginny Harvey

Copy Editors/Proofreaders:
Ginny Harvey
Nancy Lamm
Lyn Markowicz
Lori Silfen
Lisa Jedlicka
Kim Kosmatka
Marilyn Martin

Interior Design:
Becky Herrington

Cover Design:
Richard Herrera

Illustrators:
Richard Herrera
Andrew Bartel
Ken Russo

Compositors:
Jeanne Black
Andrew Bartel
Kellee LaVars
Kenny Tran
Michelle French

Indexer:
Cristina Haley

Printer:
Banta Menasha

MICROSOFT® OFFICE

Access 2003

Introductory Concepts and Techniques

COURSECARD EDITION

Contents

Preface

The Shelly Cashman Series® offers the finest textbooks in computer education. We are proud of the fact that our series of Microsoft Office 4.3, Microsoft Office 95, Microsoft Office 97, Microsoft Office 2000, and Microsoft Office XP textbooks have been the most widely used books in education. With each new edition of our Office books, we have made significant improvements based on the software and comments made by the instructors and students. The *Microsoft Office 2003* books continue with the innovation, quality, and reliability that you have come to expect from the Shelly Cashman Series.

In this *Microsoft Office Access 2003* book, you will find an educationally sound, highly visual, and easy-to-follow pedagogy that combines a vastly improved step-by-step approach with corresponding screens. All projects and exercises in this book are designed to take full advantage of the Access 2003 enhancements. The popular Other Ways and More About features offer in-depth knowledge of Access 2003. The new Q&A feature offers students a way to solidify important database concepts. The Learn It Online page presents a wealth of additional exercises to ensure your students have all the reinforcement they need. The project material is developed to ensure that students will see the importance of learning Access for future coursework.

Objectives of This Textbook

Microsoft Office Access 2003: Introductory Concepts and Techniques, CourseCard Edition is intended for a course that covers a brief introduction to Access 2003. No experience with a computer is assumed, and no mathematics beyond the high school freshman level is required. The objectives of this book are:

- To teach the fundamentals of Access 2003
- To expose students to practical examples of the computer as a useful tool
- To acquaint students with the proper procedures to create databases
- To develop an exercise-oriented approach that allows learning by doing
- To introduce students to new input technologies
- To encourage independent study and help those who are working alone

The Shelly Cashman Approach

Features of the Shelly Cashman Series *Microsoft Office Access 2003* books include:

- Project Orientation: Each project in the book presents a practical problem and complete solution in an easy-to-understand approach.
- Step-by-Step, Screen-by-Screen Instructions: Each of the tasks required to complete a project is identified throughout the project. Full-color screens accompany the steps.
- Thoroughly Tested Projects: Unparalleled quality is ensured because every screen in the book is produced by the author only after performing a step, and then each project must pass Thomson Course Technology's award-winning Quality Assurance program.
- Other Ways Boxes and Quick Reference Summary: The Other Ways boxes displayed at the end of most of the step-by-step sequences specify the other ways to do the task completed in the steps. Thus, the steps and the Other Ways box make a comprehensive reference unit.
- More About and Q&A Features: These marginal annotations provide background information, tips, and answers to common questions that complement the topics covered, adding depth and perspective to the learning process.
- Integration of the World Wide Web: The World Wide Web is integrated into the Access 2003 learning experience by (1) More About annotations that send students to Web sites for up-to-date information and alternative approaches to tasks; (2) a Microsoft Office Specialist Certification Web page so students can prepare for the certification examinations; (3) an Access 2003 Quick Reference Summary Web page that summarizes the ways to complete tasks (mouse, menu, shortcut menu, and keyboard); and (4) the Learn It Online page at the end of each project, which has project reinforcement exercises, learning games, and other types of student activities.

Microsoft Office
Access 2003

Organization of This Textbook

Microsoft Office Access 2003: Introductory Concepts and Techniques, CourseCard Edition provides basic instruction on how to use Access 2003. The material is divided into three projects, an Integration feature, five appendices, and a Quick Reference Summary.

Project 1 – Creating and Using a Database   In Project 1, students are introduced to the concept of a database and shown how to use Access 2003 to create a database.

Project 2 – Querying a Database Using the Select Query Window   In Project 2, students learn to use queries to obtain information from the data in their databases.

Project 3 – Maintaining a Database Using the Design and Update Features of Access   In Project 3, students learn the crucial skills involved in maintaining a database.

Integration Feature – Sharing Data Among Applications   In the Integration feature, students learn how to embed an Excel worksheet in an Access database and how to link a worksheet to a database. Students also learn how to prepare Access data for use in other applications.

Appendices   The book includes five appendices. Appendix A presents an introduction to the Microsoft Access Help system. Appendix B describes how to use Access's speech and handwriting recognition capabilities. Appendix C explains how to publish Web pages to a Web server. Appendix D shows how to change the screen resolution and reset the menus and toolbars. Appendix E introduces students to Microsoft Office Specialist certification.

Quick Reference Summary   In Access 2003, you can accomplish a task in a number of ways, such as using the mouse, menu, shortcut menu, and keyboard. The Quick Reference Summary at the back of the book provides a quick reference to each task presented.

Access 2003 CourseCard   New! Now includes a free, tear-off Access 2003 CourseCard that provides students with a great way to have Access skills at their fingertips.

End-of-Project Student Activities

A notable strength of the Shelly Cashman Series *Microsoft Access 2003* books is the extensive student activities at the end of each project. Well-structured student activities can make the difference between students merely participating in a class and students retaining the information they learn. The activities in the Shelly Cashman Series *Access 2003* books include the following.

- What You Should Know   A listing of the tasks completed within a project together with the pages on which the step-by-step, screen-by-screen explanations appear.
- Learn It Online   Every project features a Learn It Online page that comprises twelve exercises. These exercises include True/False, Multiple Choice, Short Answer, Flash Cards, Practice Test, Learning Games, Tips and Tricks, Newsgroup usage, Expanding Your Horizons, Search Sleuth, Office Online Training, and Office Marketplace.
- Apply Your Knowledge   This exercise usually requires students to open and manipulate a file on the Data Disk that parallels the activities learned in the project. To obtain a copy of the Data Disk, follow the instructions on the inside back cover of this textbook.
- In the Lab   Three in-depth assignments per project require students to utilize the project concepts and techniques to solve problems on a computer.
- Cases and Places   Five unique real-world case-study situations, including one small-group activity.

Instructor Resources CD-ROM

The Shelly Cashman Series is dedicated to providing you with all of the tools you need to make your class a success. Information on all supplementary materials is available through your Course Technology representative or by calling one of the following telephone numbers: Colleges and Universities, 1-800-648-7450; High Schools,

1-800-824-5179; Private Career Colleges, 1-800-347-7707; Canada, 1-800-268-2222; Corporations with IT Training Centers, 1-800-648-7450; and Government Agencies, Health-Care Organizations, and Correctional Facilities, 1-800-477-3692.

The Instructor Resources for this textbook include both teaching and testing aids. The contents of each item on the Instructor Resources CD-ROM (ISBN 0-619-20048-0) are described below.

INSTRUCTOR'S MANUAL The Instructor's Manual is made up of Microsoft Word files, which include detailed lesson plans with page number references, lecture notes, teaching tips, classroom activities, discussion topics, projects to assign, and transparency references. The transparencies are available through the Figure Files described below.

LECTURE SUCCESS SYSTEM The Lecture Success System consists of intermediate files that correspond to certain figures in the book, allowing you to step through the creation of an application in a project during a lecture without entering large amounts of data.

SYLLABUS Sample syllabi, which can be customized easily to a course, are included. The syllabi cover policies, class and lab assignments and exams, and procedural information.

FIGURE FILES Illustrations for every figure in the textbook are available in electronic form. Use this ancillary to present a slide show in lecture or to print transparencies for use in lecture with an overhead projector. If you have a personal computer and LCD device, this ancillary can be an effective tool for presenting lectures.

POWERPOINT PRESENTATIONS PowerPoint Presentations is a multimedia lecture presentation system that provides PowerPoint slides for each project. Presentations are based on project objectives. Use this presentation system to present well-organized lectures that are both interesting and knowledge based. PowerPoint Presentations provides consistent coverage at schools that use multiple lecturers.

SOLUTIONS TO EXERCISES Solutions are included for the end-of-project exercises, as well as the Project Reinforcement exercises.

RUBRICS AND ANNOTATED SOLUTION FILES The grading rubrics provide a customizable framework for assigning point values to the laboratory exercises. Annotated solution files that correspond to the grading rubrics make it easy for you to compare students' results with the correct solutions whether you receive their homework as hardcopy or via e-mail.

TEST BANK & TEST ENGINE The ExamView test bank includes 110 questions for every project (25 multiple-choice, 50 true/false, and 35 completion) with page number references, and when appropriate, figure references. A version of the test bank you can print also is included. The test bank comes with a copy of the test engine, ExamView, the ultimate tool for your objective-based testing needs. ExamView is a state-of-the-art test builder that is easy to use. ExamView enables you to create paper-, LAN-, or Web-based tests from test banks designed specifically for your Course Technology textbook. Utilize the ultra-efficient QuickTest Wizard to create tests in less than five minutes by taking advantage of Course Technology's question banks, or customize your own exams from scratch.

LAB TESTS/TEST OUT The Lab Tests/Test Out exercises parallel the In the Lab assignments and are supplied for the purpose of testing students in the laboratory on the material covered in the project or testing students out of the course.

DATA FILES FOR STUDENTS All the files that are required by students to complete the exercises are included. You can distribute the files on the Instructor Resources CD-ROM to your students over a network, or you can have them follow the instructions on the inside back cover of this book to obtain a copy of the Data Disk.

ADDITIONAL ACTIVITIES FOR STUDENTS These additional activities consist of Project Reinforcement Exercises, which are true/false, multiple choice, and short answer questions that help students gain confidence in the material learned.

SAM 2003

SAM 2003 helps you energize your class exams and training assignments by allowing students to learn and test important computer skills in an active, hands-on environment.

SAM 2003 ASSESSMENT   With SAM 2003 Assessment, you create powerful interactive exams on critical applications such as Access, Word, Excel, PowerPoint, Outlook, Windows, and the Internet. The exams simulate the application environment, allowing your students to demonstrate their knowledge and think through the skill by performing real-world tasks. Build hands-on exams that allow students to work in the simulated application environment.

SAM 2003 TRAINING   Invigorate your lesson plan with SAM 2003 Training. Using highly interactive text, graphics, and sound, SAM 2003 Training gives your students the flexibility to learn computer applications by choosing the training method that fits them best. Create customized training units that employ various approaches to teaching computer skills.

SAM 2003 ASSESSMENT AND TRAINING   Designed to be used with the Shelly Cashman Series, SAM 2003 Assessment and Training includes built-in page references so students can create study guides that match the Shelly Cashman Series textbooks you use in class. Powerful administrative options allow you to schedule customized exams and assignments, secure your tests, and choose from more than one dozen reports to track testing and learning progress.

Online Content

Course Technology offers textbook-based content for Blackboard, WebCT, and MyCourse 2.1

BLACKBOARD AND WEBCT   As the leading provider of IT content for the Blackboard and WebCT platforms, Course Technology delivers rich content that enhances your textbook to give your students a unique learning experience. Course Technology has partnered with WebCT and Blackboard to deliver our market-leading content through these state-of-the-art online learning platforms. Course Technology offers customizable content in every subject area, from computer concepts to PC repair.

MYCOURSE 2.1   MyCourse 2.1 is Course Technology's powerful online course management and content delivery system. Completely maintained and hosted by Thomson, MyCourse 2.1 delivers an online learning environment that is completely secure and provides superior performance. MyCourse 2.1 allows nontechnical users to create, customize, and deliver World Wide Web-based courses; post content and assignments; manage student enrollment; administer exams; track results in the online gradebook; and more. With MyCourse 2.1, you easily can create a customized course that will enhance every learning experience.

MICROSOFT
Office Access 2003

Office Access 2003

Creating and Using a Database

CASE PERSPECTIVE

Ashton James College (AJC) has a solid reputation in the community, delivers quality computer courses, and has a faculty of highly professional, dedicated instructors. Its graduates are among the top achievers in the state. Recently, at the urging of area businesses that depend on the college-educated workforce, AJC has begun to offer corporate computer training through its Continuing Education department. The programs have proved to be very popular, and the client list is growing rapidly.

AJC employs several trainers to teach these corporate courses. It assigns each client to a specific trainer. The trainer contacts the client to determine the particular course the client requires. The trainer then customizes a program for that particular client. The trainer will schedule all the necessary training sessions.

To ensure that operations run smoothly, Ashton James College needs to maintain data on its trainers and their clients. The AJC administration wants to organize the data in a database, managed by a database management system such as Access. In this way, AJC can keep its data current and accurate while program administrators analyze the data for trends and produce a variety of useful reports. Your task is to help the director of continuing education at Ashton James College, Dr. Robert Gernaey, create and use the database.

As you read through this project, you will learn how to use Access to create a database.

MICROSOFT
Office Access 2003

Creating and Using a Database

Objectives

You will have mastered the material in this project when you can:

- Describe databases and database management systems
- Start Access
- Describe the features of the Access desktop
- Create a database
- Create a table and add records
- Close a table
- Close a database and quit Access
- Open a database
- Print the contents of a table
- Create and use a simple query
- Create and use a simple form
- Create and print a custom report
- Design a database to eliminate redundancy

What Is Microsoft Office Access 2003?

Microsoft Office Access 2003 is a powerful database management system (DBMS) that functions in the Windows environment and allows you to create and process data in a database. Some of the key features are:

- **Data entry and update** Access provides easy mechanisms for adding, changing, and deleting data, including the capability of making mass changes in a single operation.
- **Queries (questions)** Access makes it possible to ask complex questions concerning the data in the database and then receive instant answers.
- **Forms** Access allows the user to produce attractive and useful forms for viewing and updating data.
- **Reports** Access report creation tools make it easy to produce sophisticated reports for presenting data.
- **Web support** Access allows you to save objects, reports, and tables in HTML format so they can be viewed using a browser. You also can import and export documents in XML format. Access's capability of creating data access pages allows real-time access to data in the database via the Internet.

What Is New in Access?

This latest version of Access has many new features to make you more productive. You can view information on dependencies between various database objects. You can enable error checking for many common errors in forms and reports. You can add smart tags to fields in tables, queries, forms, or data access pages. Access now has a command to backup a database. Many wizards provide more options for sorting data. You can export to, import from, or link to a Windows SharePoint Services list. Access now offers enhanced XML support.

Project One — Ashton James College Database

Creating, storing, sorting, and retrieving data are important tasks. In their personal lives, many people keep a variety of records such as names, addresses, and telephone numbers of friends and business associates, records of investments, records of expenses for tax purposes, and so on. For effective use of this data, users must have quick access to it. Businesses also must be able to store and access information quickly and easily.

The term **database** describes a collection of data organized in a manner that allows access, retrieval, and use of that data. A **database management system**, such as Access, is a software tool that allows you to use a computer to create a database; add, change, and delete data in the database; sort the data in the database; retrieve data in the database; and create forms and reports using the data in the database.

In Access, a database consists of a collection of tables. Figure 1-1 shows a sample database for Ashton James College, which consists of two tables. The Client table contains information about the clients to which Ashton James College provides services. The college assigns each client to a specific trainer. The Trainer table contains information about the trainers to whom these clients are assigned.

Client table

fields

CLIENT NUMBER	NAME	ADDRESS	CITY	STATE	ZIP CODE	AMOUNT PAID	CURRENT DUE	TRAINER NUMBER
BS27	Blant and Sons	4806 Park	Lake Hammond	TX	76653	$21,876.00	$892.50	42
CE16	Center Services	725 Mitchell	San Julio	TX	78364	$26,512.00	$2,672.00	48
CP27	Calder Plastics	7300 Cedar	Lake Hammond	TX	76653	$8,725.00	$0.00	48
EU28	Elba's Furniture	1445 Hubert	Tallmadge	TX	77231	$4,256.00	$1,202.00	53
FI28	Farrow-Idsen	829 Wooster	Cedar Ridge	TX	79342	$8,287.50	$925.50	42
FL93	Fairland Lawn	143 Pangborn	Lake Hammond	TX	76653	$21,625.00	$0.00	48
HN83	Hurley National	3827 Burgess	Tallmadge	TX	77231	$0.00	$0.00	48
MC28	Morgan-Alyssa	923 Williams	Crumville	TX	76745	$24,761.00	$1,572.00	42
PS82	PRIM Staffing	72 Crestview	San Julio	TX	78364	$11,682.25	$2,827.50	53
TE26	Telton-Edwards	5672 Anderson	Dunston	TX	77893	$8,521.50	$0.00	48

records

clients of trainer Belinda Perry

Trainer table

TRAINER NUMBER	LAST NAME	FIRST NAME	ADDRESS	CITY	STATE	ZIP CODE	HOURLY RATE	YTD EARNINGS
42	Perry	Belinda	261 Porter	Burdett	TX	76734	$23.00	$27,620.00
48	Stevens	Michael	3135 Gill	Rockwood	TX	78884	$21.00	$23,567.50
53	Gonzalez	Manuel	265 Maxwell	Camino	TX	76574	$24.00	$29,885.00
67	Danville	Marty	1827 Maple	Dunston	TX	77893	$20.00	$0.00

trainer Belinda Perry

FIGURE 1-1

More About

Databases in Access 2003

In some DBMSs, every table, query, form, or report is stored in a separate file. This is not the case in Access 2003, in which a database is stored in a single file on disk. The file contains all the tables, queries, forms, reports, and programs created for this database.

The rows in the tables are called **records**. A record contains information about a given person, product, or event. A row in the Client table, for example, contains information about a specific client.

The columns in the tables are called fields. A **field** contains a specific piece of information within a record. In the Client table, for example, the fourth field, City, contains the city where the client is located.

The first field in the Client table is the Client Number. Ashton James College assigns a number to each client. As is common to the way in which many organizations format client numbers, Ashton James College calls it a *number*, although it actually contains letters. The AJC client numbers consist of two uppercase letters followed by a two-digit number.

These numbers are unique; that is, no two clients are assigned the same number. Such a field can be used as a **unique identifier**. This simply means that a given client number will appear only in a single record in the table. Only one record exists, for example, in which the client number is CP27. A unique identifier also is called a **primary key**. Thus, the Client Number field is the primary key for the Client table.

The next seven fields in the Client table are Name, Address, City, State, Zip Code, Amount Paid, and Current Due. The Amount Paid field contains the amount that the client has paid Ashton James College year-to-date (YTD), but before the current period. The Current Due field contains the amount due to AJC for the current period.

For example, client BS27 is Blant and Sons. The address is 4806 Park in Lake Hammond, Texas. The Zip code is 76653. The client has paid $21,876.00 for training services so far this year. The amount due for the current period is $892.50.

AJC assigns each client a single trainer. The last field in the Client table, Trainer Number, gives the number of the client's trainer.

The first field in the Trainer table, Trainer Number, is the number Ashton James College assigns to the trainer. These numbers are unique, so Trainer Number is the primary key of the Trainer table.

The other fields in the Trainer table are Last Name, First Name, Address, City, State, Zip Code, Hourly Rate, and YTD Earnings. The Hourly Rate field gives the trainer's hourly billing rate, and the YTD Earnings field contains the total amount that AJC has paid the trainer for services so far this year.

For example, Trainer 42 is Belinda Perry. Her address is 261 Porter in Burdett, Texas. The Zip code is 76734. Her hourly billing rate is $23.00, and her YTD earnings are $27,620.00.

The trainer number appears in both the Client table and the Trainer table. It relates clients and trainers. For example, in the Client table, you see that the trainer number for client BS27 is 42. To find the name of this trainer, look for the row in the Trainer table that contains 42 in the Trainer Number field. After you have found it, you know the client is assigned to Belinda Perry. To find all the clients assigned to Belinda Perry, however, you must look through the Client table for all the clients that contain 42 in the Trainer Number field. Her clients are BS27 (Blant and Sons), FI28 (Farrow-Idsen), and MC28 (Morgan-Alyssa).

The last trainer in the Trainer table, Marty Danville, has not been assigned any clients yet; therefore, his trainer number, 67, does not appear on any row in the Client table.

Figure 1-1 on page AC 5 shows the data that must be maintained in the database. The first step is to create the database and the tables it contains. In the process, you must define the fields included in the two tables, as well as the type of data each field will contain. Then, you must add the appropriate records to the tables. Finally, you will print the contents of the tables. After you have completed these tasks, you will create a query, a form, and a report.

Starting Access

If you are stepping through this project on a computer, and you want your screen to agree with the figures in this book, then you should change your computer's resolution to 800 × 600. For more information on how to change the resolution on your computer, see Appendix D. To start Access, Windows must be running. The following steps show how to start Access.

To Start Access

More About

The Access Help System

Need Help? It is no further than the Type a question for help box on the menu bar in the upper-right corner of the window. Click the box that contains the text, Type a question for help (Figure 1-3 on the next page), type help, and then press the ENTER key. Access responds with a list of topics you can click to learn about obtaining help on any Access-related topic. To find out what is new in Access 2003, type what is new in Access in the Type a question for help box.

1

• **Click the Start button on the Windows taskbar, point to All Programs on the Start menu and then point to Microsoft Office on the All Programs submenu.**

Windows displays the Start menu, the All Programs submenu, and the Microsoft Office submenu (Figure 1-2).

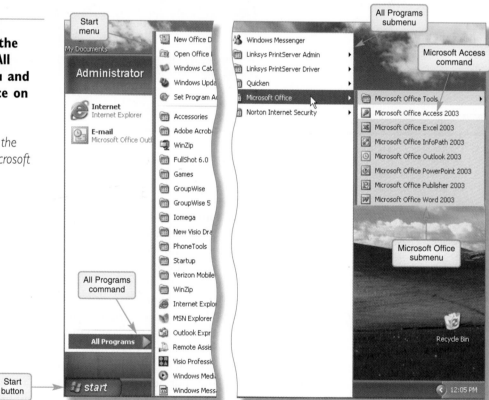

FIGURE 1-2

2

• **Click Microsoft Office Access 2003.**

Access starts. After several seconds, the Access window appears (Figure 1-3).

3

• **If the Access window is not maximized, double-click its title bar to maximize it.**

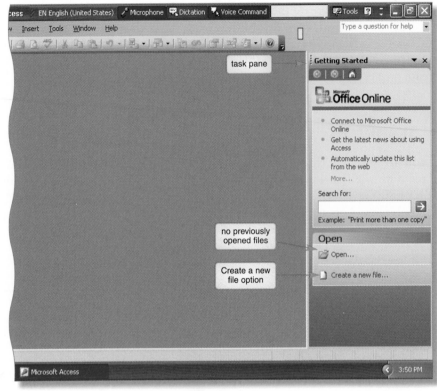

FIGURE 1-3

Microsoft Office
Access 2003

Other Ways

1. Double-click Access icon on desktop
2. Click Microsoft Office Access 2003 on Start menu
3. Click Start button, click All Programs on Start menu, click New Office Document, double-click Blank Database icon

More About

Task Panes

You can drag a task pane title bar to float the pane in your work area or dock it on either the left or right side of a screen, depending on your personal preference.

The screen in Figure 1-3 illustrates how the Access window looks the first time you start Access after installation on most computers. Access displays a task pane on the right side of the screen at startup. A **task pane** is a separate window that enables users to carry out some Access tasks more efficiently. When you start Access, it displays the Getting Started task pane, which is a small window that provides commonly used links and commands that allow you to open files, create new files, or search Office-related topics on the Microsoft Web site. The task pane is used only to create a new database and then it is closed.

If the Office Speech Recognition software is installed and active on your computer, then when you start Access the Language bar is displayed on the screen. The **Language bar** allows you to speak commands and dictate text. It usually is located on the right side of the Windows taskbar next to the notification area and changes to include the speech recognition functions available in Access. In this book, the Language bar is closed. For additional information about the Language bar, see the next page and Appendix B. The following steps show how to close the Language bar if it appears on the screen.

To Close the Language Bar

1

• **Right-click the Language bar to display a list of commands.**

The Language bar shortcut menu appears (Figure 1-4).

2

• **Click Close the Language bar.**
• **Click the OK button.**

The Language bar disappears.

FIGURE 1-4

Speech Recognition

With the **Office Speech Recognition software** installed and a microphone, you can speak the names of toolbar buttons, menus, menu commands, list items, alerts, and dialog box controls, such as OK and Cancel. You also can dictate field entries, such as text and numbers. To indicate whether you want to speak commands or dictate cell entries, you use the Language bar. The Language bar can be in one of three states: (1) **restored**, which means it is displayed somewhere in the Access window (Figure 1-5a); (2) **minimized**, which means it is displayed on the Windows taskbar (Figure 1-5b); or (3) **hidden**, which means you do not see it on the screen. If the Language bar is hidden and you want it to display, then do the following:

1. Right-click an open area on the Windows taskbar at the bottom of the screen.
2. Point to Toolbars and then click Language bar on the Toolbars submenu.

(a) Language Bar in Access Window with Microphone Enabled

(b) Language Bar Minimized on Windows Taskbar

FIGURE 1-5

If the Language bar command is dimmed on the Toolbars submenu or if the Speech command is dimmed on the Tools menu, the Office Speech Recognition software is not installed.

Creating a New Database

In Access, all the tables, reports, form, and queries that you create are stored in a single file called a database. Thus, before creating any of these objects, you first must create the database that will hold them. You can use either the Database Wizard or the Blank database option in the task pane to create a new database. The Database Wizard can guide you by suggesting some commonly used databases. If you choose to create a database using the Database Wizard, you would use the following steps.

To Create a Database Using the Database Wizard

1. Click the New button on the Database toolbar and then click the On my computer link in the New File task pane.
2. When Access displays the Template dialog box, click the Databases tab, and then click the database that is most appropriate for your needs.
3. Follow the instructions in the Database Wizard dialog box to create the database.

Because you already know the tables and fields you want in the Ashton James College database, you would use the Blank database option in the task pane rather than the Database Wizard. The following steps illustrate how to use the Blank database option to create a database on a floppy disk in drive A.

To Create a New Database

1

• **Insert a formatted floppy disk in drive A.**

• **Click the New button on the Database toolbar to display the task pane.**

• **Click the Blank database option in the task pane, and then click the Save in box arrow.**

Access displays the File New Database dialog box and the Save in list appears (Figure 1-6a). Your File name text box may display db1.mdb, rather than db1.

FIGURE 1-6a

2

- **Click 3½ Floppy (A:).**
- **Click the File name text box.**
- **Use the BACKSPACE key or the DELETE key to delete db1 and then type** Ashton James College **as the file name.**

The file name is changed to Ashton James College (Figure 1-6b).

FIGURE 1-6b

3

- **Click the Create button to create the database.**

The Ashton James College database is created. The Ashton James College : Database window appears in the Microsoft Access window (Figure 1-7). The task pane does not appear.

FIGURE 1-7

The Access Window

The Access window (Figure 1-7 on the previous page) contains a variety of features that play important roles when you are working with a database.

Title Bar

The **title bar** is the top bar in the Microsoft Access window. It includes the title of the application, Microsoft Access. The icon on the left is the Control-menu icon. Clicking this icon displays a menu from which you can close the Access window. The button on the right is the Close button. Clicking the Close button closes the Access window.

Menu Bar

The **menu bar** is displayed below the title bar. It is a special toolbar that displays the menu names. Each menu name represents a menu of commands that you can use to retrieve, store, print, and manipulate data. When you point to a menu name on the menu bar, the area of the menu bar is displayed as a selected button. Access shades selected buttons in light orange and surrounds them with a blue outline. To display a menu, such as the Edit menu, click the Edit menu name on the menu bar (Figures 1-8a and 1-8b). A **menu** is a list of commands. If you point to a command on the menu with an arrow to its right, a **submenu** is displayed from which you can choose a command.

(a) **(b)**

FIGURE 1-8

When you click a menu name on the menu bar, Access displays a **short menu** listing the most recently used commands (Figure 1-8a). If you wait a few seconds or click the arrows at the bottom of the short menu, the full menu appears. The **full menu** lists all the commands associated with a menu (Figure 1-8b). You also can display a full menu immediately by double-clicking the menu name on the menu bar. In this book, always have Access display the full menu using one of the following techniques.

1. Click the menu name on the menu bar and then wait a few seconds.
2. Click the menu name and then click the arrows at the bottom of the short menu.

3. Click the menu name and then point to the arrows at the bottom of the short menu.

4. Double-click the menu name.

Both short and full menus display some **dimmed commands** that appear gray, or dimmed, instead of black, which indicates they are not available for the current selection. A command with a medium blue shading to the left of it on a full menu is called a **hidden command** because it does not display on a short menu. As you use Access, it automatically personalizes the short menus for you based on how often you use commands. That is, as you use hidden commands, Access *unhides* them and places them on the short menu.

Toolbars

Below the menu bar is a toolbar. A **toolbar** contains buttons that allow you to perform certain tasks more quickly than using the menu bar. Each button contains a picture, or **icon**, depicting its function. When you move the mouse pointer over a button, the name of the button appears below it in a **ScreenTip**. The toolbar shown in Figure 1-7 on page AC 11 is the Database toolbar. The specific toolbar or toolbars that appear will vary, depending on the task on which you are working. Access routinely displays the toolbar or toolbars you will need for the task. If you want to change these or simply to determine what toolbars are available for the given task, consult Appendix D.

Taskbar

The Windows **taskbar** at the bottom of the screen displays the Start button, any active windows, and the current time.

Status Bar

Immediately above the Windows taskbar is the **status bar**. It contains special information that is appropriate for the task on which you are working. Currently, it contains the word, Ready, which means Access is ready to accept commands.

Database Window

The **Database window**, referred to in Figure 1-7 as the Ashton James College : Database window, is a special window that allows you to access easily and rapidly a variety of objects such as tables, queries, forms, and reports. To do so, you will use the various components of the window.

Shortcut Menus

Rather than use toolbars to accomplish a given task, you also can use **shortcut menus**, which are menus that display the actions available for a particular item. To display the shortcut menu for an item, right-click the item; that is, point to the item and then click the right mouse button. Figures 1-9a and 1-9b on the next page illustrate the use of toolbars and shortcut menus to perform the same task, namely to print the contents of the Client table. In the figure, the tables you will create in this project already have been created.

More About

Toolbars

Normally, the correct Access 2003 toolbar will display automatically. If it does not, click View on the menu bar, and then click Toolbars. On the Toolbars submenu, select the toolbar for the activity in which you are engaged. See Appendix D for additional details.

More About

Shortcut Menus

Shortcut menus contain the most frequently used commands that relate to the object to which the mouse pointer is pointing.

FIGURE 1-9

Before the action illustrated in Figure 1-9a, you would have to select the Client table by clicking it. Then, you would point to the Print button on the toolbar as shown in the figure. When you point to a button on a toolbar, the ScreenTip appears, indicating the purpose of the button, in this case Print. When you click the button, the corresponding action takes place. In this case, Access will print the contents of the Client table.

To use a shortcut menu to perform the same task, you would right-click the Client table, which produces the shortcut menu shown in Figure 1-9b. You then would click the desired command, in this case the Print command, on the shortcut menu. The corresponding action then takes place.

You can use whichever option you prefer. Many professionals who use Access will use a combination. If it is simplest to use the shortcut menu, which often is the case, they will use the shortcut menu. If it is simpler just to click a toolbar button, they will do that. The steps in this text follow this approach; that is, using a combination of both options. The text indicates how to accomplish the task using the other approach, as well. Thus, if the steps use a shortcut menu, the Other Ways box at the end of the steps will indicate how you could accomplish the task using a toolbar button. If the steps use a button, the Other Ways box will indicate how you could accomplish the task with a shortcut menu.

AutoCorrect

Not visible in the Access window, the **AutoCorrect** feature of Access works behind the scenes, correcting common mistakes when you complete a text entry in a cell. AutoCorrect makes three types of corrections for you:

1. Corrects two initial capital letters by changing the second letter to lowercase.
2. Capitalizes the first letter in the names of days.
3. Replaces commonly misspelled words with their correct spelling. For example, it will change the misspelled word *recieve* to *receive* when you complete the entry. AutoCorrect will correct the spelling automatically of more than 400 commonly misspelled words.

Creating a Table

An Access database consists of a collection of tables. After you have created the database, you must create each of the tables within it. In this project, for example, you must create both the Client and Trainer tables shown in Figure 1-1 on page AC 5.

To create a table, you describe the structure of the table to Access by describing the fields within the table. For each field, you indicate the following:

1. **Field name** — Each field in the table must have a unique name. In the Client table (Figure 1-10a and 1-10b on the next page), for example, the field names are Client Number, Name, Address, City, State, Zip Code, Amount Paid, Current Due, and Trainer Number.

Structure of Client table

FIELD NAME	DATA TYPE	FIELD SIZE	PRIMARY KEY?	DESCRIPTION
Client Number	Text	4	Yes	Client Number (Primary Key)
Name	Text	20		Client Name
Address	Text	15		Street Address
City	Text	15		City
State	Text	2		State (Two-Character Abbreviation)
Zip Code	Text	5		Zip Code (Five-Character Version)
Amount Paid	Currency			Amount Paid by Client This Year
Current Due	Currency			Current Due from Client This Period
Trainer Number	Text	2		Number of Client's Trainer

FIGURE 1-10a

Client table

CLIENT NUMBER	NAME	ADDRESS	CITY	STATE	ZIP CODE	AMOUNT PAID	CURRENT DUE	TRAINER NUMBER
BS27	Blant and Sons	4806 Park	Lake Hammond	TX	76653	$21,876.00	$892.50	42
CE16	Center Services	725 Mitchell	San Julio	TX	78364	$26,512.00	$2,672.00	48
CP27	Calder Plastics	7300 Cedar	Lake Hammond	TX	76653	$8,725.00	$0.00	48
EU28	Elba's Furniture	1445 Hubert	Tallmadge	TX	77231	$4,256.00	$1,202.00	53
FI28	Farrow-Idsen	829 Wooster	Cedar Ridge	TX	79342	$8,287.50	$925.50	42
FL93	Fairland Lawn	143 Pangborn	Lake Hammond	TX	76653	$21,625.00	$0.00	48
HN83	Hurley National	3827 Burgess	Tallmadge	TX	77231	$0.00	$0.00	48
MC28	Morgan-Alyssa	923 Williams	Crumville	TX	76745	$24,761.00	$1,572.00	42
PS82	PRIM Staffing	72 Crestview	San Julio	TX	78364	$11,682.25	$2,827.50	53
TE26	Telton-Edwards	5672 Anderson	Dunston	TX	77893	$8,521.50	$0.00	48

FIGURE 1-10b

2. **Data type** — Data type indicates to Access the type of data the field will contain. Some fields can contain only numbers. Others, such as Amount Paid and Current Due, can contain numbers and dollar signs. Still others, such as Name and Address, can contain letters.

3. **Description** — Access allows you to enter a detailed description of the field.

You also can assign field widths to text fields (fields whose data type is Text). This indicates the maximum number of characters that can be stored in the field. If you do not assign a width to such a field, Access assumes the width is 50.

You also must indicate which field or fields make up the primary key; that is, the unique identifier, for the table. In the Ashton James College database, the Client Number field is the primary key of the Client table and the Trainer Number field is the primary key of the Trainer table.

The rules for field names are:

1. Names can be up to 64 characters in length.

2. Names can contain letters, digits, and spaces, as well as most of the punctuation symbols.

3. Names cannot contain periods, exclamation points (!), accent graves (`), or square brackets ([ ]).

4. The same name cannot be used for two different fields in the same table.

Each field has a **data type**. This indicates the type of data that can be stored in the field. The data types you will use in this project are:

1. **Text** — The field can contain any characters. A maximum number of 255 characters is allowed in a field whose data type is Text.

2. **Number** — The field can contain only numbers. The numbers either can be positive or negative. Fields are assigned this type so they can be used in arithmetic operations. Fields that contain numbers but will not be used for arithmetic operations usually are assigned a data type of Text. The Trainer Number field, for example, is a text field because the trainer numbers will not be involved in any arithmetic.

3. **Currency** — The field can contain only monetary data. The values will appear with currency symbols, such as dollar signs, commas, decimal points, and with two digits following the decimal point. Like numeric fields, you can use currency fields in arithmetic operations. Access assigns a size to currency fields automatically.

Table 1-1 shows the other data types that are available.

Table 1-1 Additional Data Types	
DATA TYPE	**DESCRIPTION**
Memo	Field can store a variable amount of text or combinations of text and numbers where the total number of characters may exceed 255.
Number	Field can store numeric data that can be used in mathematical calculations.
Date/Time	Field can store dates and times.
AutoNumber	Field can store a unique sequential number that Access assigns to a record. Access will increment the number by 1 as each new record is added.
Yes/No	Field can store only one of two values. The choices are Yes/No, True/False, or On/Off.
OLE Object	Field can store an OLE object, which is an object linked to or embedded in the table.
Hyperlink	Field can store text that can be used as a hyperlink address.
Lookup Wizard	Field can store a value from another table or from a list of values by using a list box or combo box. Choosing this data type starts the Lookup Wizard, which assists in the creation of the field. The field then is a Lookup field. The data type is set based on the values you selected in the wizard. If the values are text for example, the field is assigned the Text data type.

The field names, data types, field widths, primary key information, and descriptions for the Client table are shown in Figure 1-10a on page AC 15.

With the information in Figures 1-10a and 1-10b, you are ready to begin creating the table. The following steps illustrate how to create a table.

To Create a Table

1

• **Click the New button on the Database window toolbar.**

The New Table dialog box appears (Figure 1-11).

FIGURE 1-11

2

• **Click Design View and then click the OK button.**

The Table1 : Table window appears (Figure 1-12).

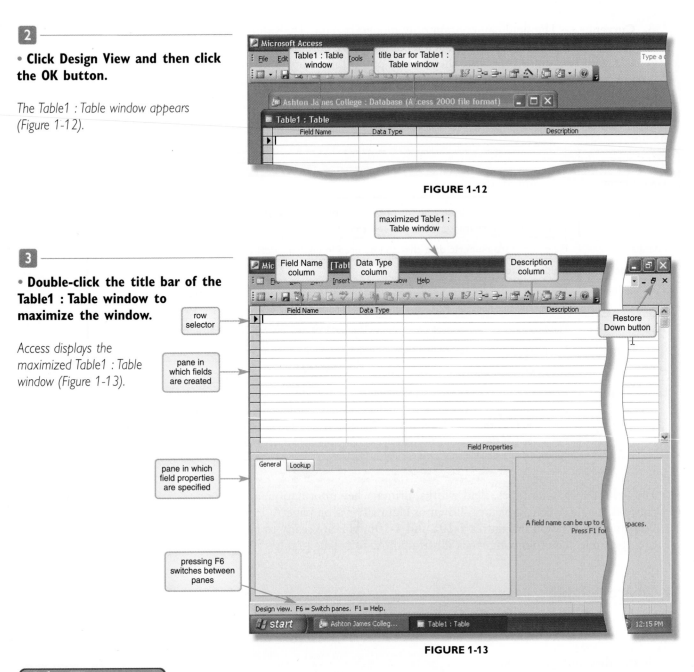

FIGURE 1-12

3

• **Double-click the title bar of the Table1 : Table window to maximize the window.**

Access displays the maximized Table1 : Table window (Figure 1-13).

FIGURE 1-13

Defining the Fields

The next step in creating the table is to define the fields by specifying the required details in the Table window, which include entries in the Field Name, Data Type, and Description columns and additional information in the Field Properties pane in the lower portion of the Table window. You press the F6 key to move from the upper **pane** (portion of the screen), the one where you define the fields, to the lower pane, the one where you define field properties. As you define the fields, the **row selector** (Figure 1-13), the small box or bar that, when you click it, selects the entire row, indicates the field you currently are describing. It is positioned on the first field, indicating Access is ready for you to enter the name of the first field in the Field Name column.

The following steps show how to define the fields in the table.

To Define the Fields in a Table

1

• **Type** Client Number **(the name of the first field) in the Field Name column, and then press the TAB key.**

The words, Client Number, appear in the Field Name column and the insertion point advances to the Data Type column, indicating you can enter the data type (Figure 1-14). The word, Text, one of the possible data types, currently appears. The arrow indicates a list of data types is available by clicking the arrow.

FIGURE 1-14

2

• **Because Text is the correct data type, press the TAB key to move the insertion point to the Description column, type** Client Number (Primary Key) **as the description, and then click the Primary Key button on the Table Design toolbar.**

The Client Number field is the primary key as indicated by the key symbol that appears in the row selector (Figure 1-15). A ScreenTip, which is a description of the button, appears.

FIGURE 1-15

3

• **Press the F6 key.**

The current entry in the Field Size property box (50) is selected (Figure 1-16).

FIGURE 1-16

4

- **Type** 4 **as the size of the Client Number field.**

- **Press the** F6 **key to return to the Description column for the Client Number field, and then press the TAB key to move to the Field Name column in the second row.**

The insertion point moves to the second row just below the field name Client Number (Figure 1-17).

Microsoft Access - [Table1 : Table]

File   Edit   View   Insert   Tools   Window   Help

Type a question fo

Field Name	Data Type	Description
Client Number	Text	Client Number (P Primary Key)

first field entered

insertion point for second field

field properties for first field no longer appear

Field Properties

General   Lookup

FIGURE 1-17

5

- **Use the techniques illustrated in Steps 1 through 4 to make the entries from the Client table structure shown in Figure 1-10a on page AC 15 up through and including the name of the Amount Paid field.**

- **Click the Data Type box arrow.**

The additional fields are entered (Figure 1-18). A list of available data types appears in the Data Type column for the Amount Paid field.

Microsoft Access - [Table1 : Table]

File   Edit   View   Insert   Tools   Window   Help

Type a question fo

Field Name	Data Type	Description
Client Number	Text	Number (Primary Key)
Name	Text	Name
Address	Text	Address
City	Text	City
State	Text	State (Two-Character Abbreviation)
Zip Code	Text	Zip Code (Five-Character Version)
Amount Paid	Text	

Data Type box arrow

six fields entered

seventh field, Amount Paid

Currency data type

Text
Memo
Number
Date/Time
Currency
AutoNumber
Yes/No
OLE Object
Hyperlink
Lookup Wizard...

Field Properties

General   Lookup

Field Size	50
Format	
Input Mask	

list of available data types

FIGURE 1-18

6

- **Click Currency and then press the** TAB **key.**

- **Make the remaining entries from the Client table structure shown in Figure 1-10a.**

All the fields are entered (Figure 1-19).

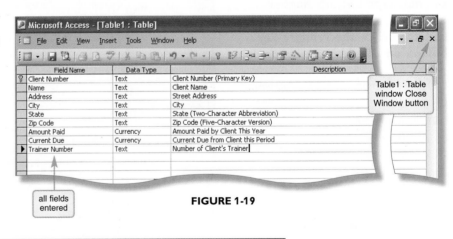

Microsoft Access - [Table1 : Table]

File   Edit   View   Insert   Tools   Window   Help

Field Name	Data Type	Description
Client Number	Text	Client Number (Primary Key)
Name	Text	Client Name
Address	Text	Street Address
City	Text	City
State	Text	State (Two-Character Abbreviation)
Zip Code	Text	Zip Code (Five-Character Version)
Amount Paid	Currency	Amount Paid by Client This Year
Current Due	Currency	Current Due from Client this Period
Trainer Number	Text	Number of Client's Trainer

Table1 : Table window Close Window button

all fields entered

FIGURE 1-19

The description of the table is now complete.

Correcting Errors in the Structure

When creating a table, check the entries carefully to ensure they are correct. If you make a mistake and discover it before you press the TAB key, you can correct the error by repeatedly pressing the BACKSPACE key until the incorrect characters are removed. Then, type the correct characters. If you do not discover a mistake until later, you can click the entry, type the correct value, and then press the ENTER key.

If you accidentally add an extra field to the structure, select the field by clicking the row selector (the leftmost column on the row that contains the field to be deleted). After you have selected the field, press the DELETE key. This will remove the field from the structure.

If you forget a field, select the field that will follow the field you want to add by clicking the row selector, and then press the INSERT key. The remaining fields move down one row, making room for the missing field. Make the entries for the new field in the usual manner.

If you made the wrong field a primary key field, click the correct primary key entry for the field and then click the Primary Key button on the Table Design toolbar.

As an alternative to these steps, you may want to start over. To do so, click the Close Window button for the Table1 : Table window and then click the No button in the Microsoft Office Access dialog box. The initial Microsoft Access window is displayed and you can repeat the process you used earlier.

Closing and Saving a Table

The Client table structure now is complete. The final step is to close and save the table within the database. At this time, you should give the table a name.

Table names are from 1 to 64 characters in length and can contain letters, numbers, and spaces. The two table names in this project are Client and Trainer.

The following steps close and save the table.

To Close and Save a Table

1

• **Click the Close Window button for the Table1 : Table window (see Figure 1-19). (Be sure not to click the Close button on the Microsoft Access title bar, because this would close Microsoft Access.)**

The Microsoft Office Access dialog box appears (Figure 1-20).

Field Name	Data Type	Description
Client Number	Text	Client Number (Primary Key)
Name	Text	Client Name
Address	Text	Street Address
City	Text	City
State	Text	State (Two-Character Abbreviation)
Zip Code	Text	Zip Code (Five-Character Version)
Amount Paid	Currency	Amount Paid by Client This Year
Current Due	Currency	Current Due from Client This Period
Trainer Number	Text	Number of Client's Trainer

Microsoft Office Access dialog box

Microsoft Office Access

Do you want to save changes to the design of table 'Table1'?

Yes button

Yes   No   Cancel

General | Lookup
Field Size   2
Format
Input Mask
Caption

FIGURE 1-20

2

• **Click the Yes button in the Microsoft Office Access dialog box, and then type** Client **as the name of the table.**

The Save As dialog box appears (Figure 1-21). The table name is entered.

3

• **Click the OK button in the Save As dialog box.**

The table is saved. The window containing the table design no longer is displayed.

FIGURE 1-21

Adding Records to a Table

Creating a table by building the structure and saving the table is the first step in a two-step process. The second step is to add records to the table. To add records to a table, the table must be open. When making changes to tables, you work in Datasheet view. In **Datasheet view**, the table is represented as a collection of rows and columns called a **datasheet**. It looks very much like the tables shown in Figure 1-1 on page AC 5.

You often add records in phases. You may, for example, not have enough time to add all the records in one session. To illustrate this process, this project begins by adding the first two records in the Client table (Figure 1-22). The remaining records are added later.

Client table (first 2 records)								
CLIENT NUMBER	NAME	ADDRESS	CITY	STATE	ZIP CODE	AMOUNT PAID	CURRENT DUE	TRAINER NUMBER
BS27	Blant and Sons	4806 Park	Lake Hammond	TX	76653	$21,876.00	$892.50	42
CE16	Center Services	725 Mitchell	San Julio	TX	78364	$26,512.00	$2,672.00	48

FIGURE 1-22

The following steps illustrate how to open the Client table and then add records.

To Add Records to a Table

1

• **Right-click the Client table in the Ashton James College : Database window.**

The shortcut menu for the Client table appears (Figure 1-23). The Ashton James College : Database window is maximized because the previous window, the Client : Table window, was maximized. (If you wanted to restore the Database window to its original size, you would click the Restore Window button.)

FIGURE 1-23

2

• **Click Open on the shortcut menu.**

*Access displays the Client : Table window (Figure 1-24). The window contains the Datasheet view for the Client table. The **record selector**, the small box or bar that, when clicked, selects the entire record, is positioned on the first record. The status bar at the bottom of the window also indicates that the record selector is positioned on record 1.*

FIGURE 1-24

3

• **Type BS27 as the first client number (see Figure 1-22). Be sure you type the letters in uppercase as shown in the table in Figure 1-22 so they are entered in the database correctly.**

The client number is entered, but the insertion point is still in the Client Number field (Figure 1-25). The pencil icon in the record selector column indicates that the record is being edited but changes to the record are not saved yet. Microsoft Access also creates a row for a new record.

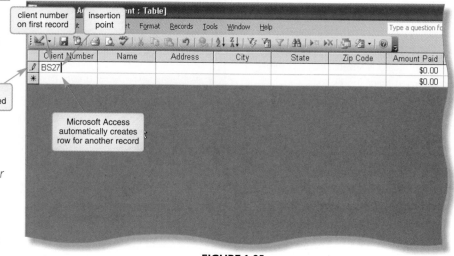

FIGURE 1-25

Microsoft Office
Access 2003

4

• **Press the TAB key to complete the entry for the Client Number field.**

• **Type the following entries, pressing the TAB key after each one:** Blant and Sons **as the name,** 4806 Park **as the address,** Lake Hammond **as the city,** TX **as the state, and** 76653 **as the Zip code.**

The Name, Address, City, State, and Zip Code fields are entered (Figure 1-26).

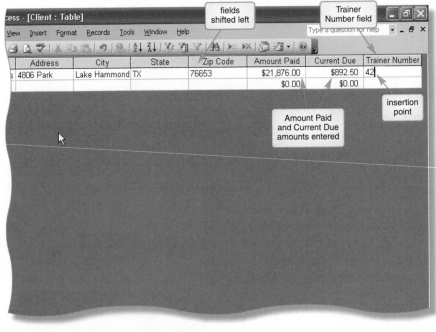

FIGURE 1-26

5

• **Type** 21876 **as the Amount Paid amount and then press the TAB key. (You do not need to type dollar signs or commas. In addition, because the digits to the right of the decimal point are both zeros, you do not need to type either the decimal point or the zeros.)**

• **Type** 892.50 **as the current due amount and then press the TAB key.**

• **Type** 42 **as the trainer number to complete data entry for the record.**

The fields have shifted to the left (Figure 1-27). The Amount Paid and Current Due values appear with dollar signs and decimal points. The insertion point is positioned in the Trainer Number field.

FIGURE 1-27

6

• **Press the TAB key.**

The fields shift back to the right, the record is saved, and the insertion point moves to the client number field on the second row (Figure 1-28).

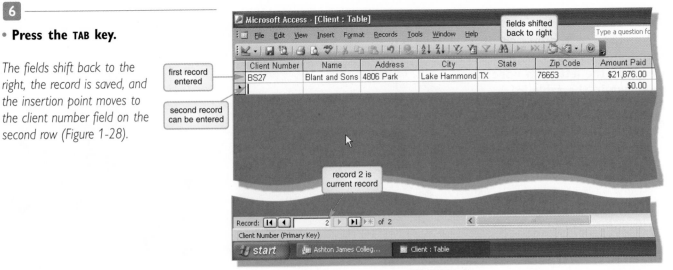

FIGURE 1-28

7

• **Use the techniques shown in Steps 3 through 6 to add the data for the second record shown in Figure 1-22 on page AC 22.**

The second record is added and the insertion point moves to the Client Number field on the third row (Figure 1-29).

first two records entered in Client table

Client : Table window Close Window button

FIGURE 1-29

As soon as you have entered or modified a record and moved to another record, the original record is saved. This is different from other applications. The rows entered in a spreadsheet, for example, are not saved until the entire spreadsheet is saved.

Correcting Errors in the Data

Check your entries carefully to ensure they are correct. If you make a mistake and discover it before you press the TAB key, correct it by pressing the BACKSPACE key until the incorrect characters are removed and then typing the correct characters.

If you discover an incorrect entry later, correct the error by clicking the incorrect entry and then making the appropriate correction. If the record you must correct is not on the screen, use any technique, such as the UP ARROW and DOWN ARROW keys to move to it. If the field you want to correct is not visible on the screen, use the horizontal scroll bar along the bottom of the screen to shift all the fields until the one you want appears. Then make the correction.

If you add an extra record accidentally, select the record by clicking the record selector that immediately precedes the record. Then, press the DELETE key. This will remove the record from the table. If you forget a record, add it using the same procedure as for all the other records. Access will place it in the correct location in the table automatically.

If you cannot determine how to correct the data, you are, in effect, stuck on the record. Access neither allows you to move to any other record until you have made the correction, nor allows you to close the table. If you encounter this situation, simply press the ESC key. Pressing the ESC key will remove from the screen the record you are trying to add. You then can move to any other record, close the table, or take any other action you desire.

Closing a Table and Database and Quitting Access

It is a good idea to close a table as soon as you have finished working with it. It keeps the screen from getting cluttered and prevents you from making accidental changes to the data in the table. If you no longer will work with the database, you should close the database as well. With the creation of the Client table complete, you also can quit Access at this point.

The steps on the next page close the table and the database and then quit Access.

More About

Correcting Errors in the Data

You also can undo changes to a field by clicking the Undo typing button on the Table Datasheet toolbar. If you already have moved to another record and want to delete the record you just added, click Edit on the menu bar and then click Undo Saved Record.

To Close a Table and Database and Quit Access

1

• **Click the Close Window button for the Client : Table window.**

The datasheet for the Client table no longer appears (Figure 1-30).

2

• **Click the Close Window button for the Ashton James College : Database window.**

The Ashton James College : Database window no longer appears.

3

• **Click the Close button for the Microsoft Access window.**

The Microsoft Access window closes and the Windows desktop appears.

FIGURE 1-30

Opening a Database

To work with any of the tables, reports, or forms in a database, the database must be open. The following steps open the database from within Access.

To Open a Database

1

• **Start Access following the steps on pages AC 7 and AC 8.**

• **If the task pane appears, click its Close button.**

• **Click the Open button on the Database toolbar.**

The Open dialog box appears (Figure 1-31).

FIGURE 1-31

2

- **Be sure 3½ Floppy (A:) folder appears in the Look in box. If not, click the Look in box arrow and click 3½ Floppy (A:).**
- **Click Ashton James College.**

Access displays the Open dialog box (Figure 1-32). The 3½ Floppy (A:) folder appears in the Look in box and the files on the floppy disk in drive A are displayed. (Your list may be different.)

3

- **Click the Open button in the Open dialog box.**
- **If a Security Warning dialog box appears, click the Open button.**

The database opens and the Ashton James College : Database window appears.

FIGURE 1-32

Other Ways

1. On File menu click Open
2. In Getting Started task pane, click name of database
3. Press CTRL + O
4. In Voice Command mode, say "Open"

Adding Additional Records

You can add records to a table that already contains data using a process almost identical to that used to add records to an empty table. The only difference is that you place the insertion point after the last data record before you enter the additional data. To do so, use the **Navigation buttons**, which are buttons used to move within a table, found near the lower-left corner of the screen shown in Figure 1-34 on the next page. The purpose of each of the Navigation buttons is described in Table 1-2.

Table 1-2 Navigation Buttons in Datasheet View	
BUTTON	**PURPOSE**
First Record	Moves to the first record in the table
Previous Record	Moves to the previous record
Next Record	Moves to the next record
Last Record	Moves to the last record in the table
New Record	Moves to the end of the table to a position for entering a new record

The steps on the next page add the remaining records (Figure 1-33 on the next page) to the Client table.

Q&A

Q: Why click the New Record button? Could you just click the Client Number on the first open record and then add the record?

A: You could click the Client Number on the first open record, provided that record appears on the screen. With only two records in the table, this is not a problem. Once a table contains more records than will fit on the screen, it is easier to click the New Record button.

Client table (last 8 records)

CLIENT NUMBER	NAME	ADDRESS	CITY	STATE	ZIP CODE	AMOUNT PAID	CURRENT DUE	TRAINER NUMBER
CP27	Calder Plastics	7300 Cedar	Lake Hammond	TX	76653	$8,725.00	$0.00	48
EU28	Elba's Furniture	1445 Hubert	Tallmadge	TX	77231	$4,256.00	$1,202.00	53
FI28	Farrow-Idsen	829 Wooster	Cedar Ridge	TX	79342	$8,287.50	$925.50	42
FL93	Fairland Lawn	143 Pangborn	Lake Hammond	TX	76653	$21,625.00	$0.00	48
HN83	Hurley National	3827 Burgess	Tallmadge	TX	77231	$0.00	$0.00	48
MC28	Morgan-Alyssa	923 Williams	Crumville	TX	76745	$24,761.00	$1,572.00	42
PS82	PRIM Staffing	72 Crestview	San Julio	TX	78364	$11,682.25	$2,827.50	53
TE26	Telton-Edwards	5672 Anderson	Dunston	TX	77893	$8,521.50	$0.00	48

FIGURE 1-33

To Add Additional Records to a Table

1

• **Right-click the Client table in the Ashton James College : Database window, and then click Open on the shortcut menu.**

• **When the Client table appears, maximize the window by double-clicking its title bar.**

The datasheet appears (Figure 1-34).

FIGURE 1-34

2

• **Click the New Record button.**

Access places the insertion point in position to enter a new record (Figure 1-35).

FIGURE 1-35

3
- **Add the records from Figure 1-33 using the same techniques you used to add the first two records.**

The additional records are added (Figure 1-36).

4
- **Click the Close Window button for the datasheet.**

The window containing the table closes and the Ashton James College : Database window appears.

all 10 records entered

Close Window button

FIGURE 1-36

Other Ways

1. Click New Record button on Table Datasheet toolbar
2. On Insert menu click New Record
3. Press CTRL+PLUS SIGN (+)
4. In Voice Command mode, say "Insert, New Record"

Previewing and Printing the Contents of a Table

When working with a database, you often will need to print a copy of the table contents. Figure 1-37 shows a printed copy of the contents of the Client table. (Yours may look slightly different, depending on your printer.) Because the Client table is wider substantially than the screen, it also will be wider than the normal printed page in portrait orientation. **Portrait orientation** means the printout is across the width of the page. **Landscape orientation** means the printout is across the length of the page. Thus, to print the wide database table, use landscape orientation. If you are printing the contents of a table that fit on the screen, you will not need landscape orientation. A convenient way to change to landscape orientation is to preview what the printed copy will look like by using Print Preview. This allows you to determine whether landscape orientation is necessary and, if it is, to change the orientation easily to landscape. In addition, you also can use Print Preview to determine whether any adjustments are necessary to the page margins.

Client   9/15/05

Client Number	Name	Address	City	State	Zip Code	Amount Paid	Current Due	Trainer Number
BS27	Blant and Sons	4806 Park	Lake Hammond	TX	76653	$21,876.00	$892.50	42
CE16	Center Service	725 Mitchell	San Julio	TX	78364	$26,512.00	$2,672.00	48
CP27	Calder Plastics	7300 Cedar	Lake Hammond	TX	76653	$8,725.00	$0.00	48
EU28	Elba's Furniture	1445 Hubert	Tallmadge	TX	77231	$4,256.00	$1,200.00	53
FI28	Farrow-Idsen	829 Wooster	Cedar Ridge	TX	79342	$8,287.50	$925.50	42
FL93	Fairland Lawn	143 Pangborn	Lake Hammond	TX	76653	$21,625.00	$0.00	48
HN83	Hurley National	3827 Burgess	Tallmadge	TX	77231	$0.00	$0.00	48
MC28	Morgan-Alyssa	923 Williams	Crumville	TX	76745	$24,761.00	$1,572.00	42
PS82	PRIM Staffing	72 Crestview	San Julio	TX	78364	$11,682.25	$2,827.50	53
TE26	Telton-Edwards	5672 Anderson	Dunston	TX	77893	$8,521.50	$0.00	48

FIGURE 1-37

The following steps illustrate using Print Preview to preview and then print the Client table.

To Preview and Print the Contents of a Table

1

• **Right-click the Client table.**

The shortcut menu for the Client table appears (Figure 1-38).

FIGURE 1-38

2

• **Click Print Preview on the shortcut menu.**

• **Point to the approximate position shown in Figure 1-39.**

The preview of the report appears. The mouse pointer shape changes to a magnifying glass, indicating you can magnify a portion of the report.

FIGURE 1-39

3

• **Click the magnifying glass mouse pointer in the approximate position shown in Figure 1-39.**

The portion surrounding the mouse pointer is magnified (Figure 1-40). The last field that appears is the Zip Code field. The Amount Paid, Current Due, and Trainer Number fields do not appear. To display the additional fields, you will need to switch to landscape orientation.

Name	Address	City	State	Zip Code
Blant and Sons	4806 Park	Lake Hammon	TX	76653
Center Service	725 Mitchell	San Julio	TX	78364
Calder Plastics	7300 Cedar	Lake Hammon	TX	76653
Elba's Furniture	1445 Hubert	Tallmadge	TX	77231
Farrow-Idsen	829 Wooster	Cedar Ridge	TX	79342
Fairland Lawn	143 Pangborn	Lake Hammon	TX	76653
Hurley National	3827 Burgess	Tallmadge	TX	77231
Morgan-Alyssa	923 Williams	Crumville	TX	76745
PRIM Staffing	72 Crestview	San Julio	TX	78364
Telton-Edward	5672 Anderson	Dunston	TX	77893

FIGURE 1-40

4

• **Click the Setup button on the Print Preview toolbar.**

Access displays the Page Setup dialog box (Figure 1-41).

FIGURE 1-41

5

• **Click the Page tab.**

*The Page sheet appears (Figure 1-42). The Portrait option button currently is selected. (**Option button** refers to the round button that indicates choices in a dialog box. When the corresponding option is selected, the button contains within it a solid circle. Clicking an option button selects it, and deselects all others.)*

FIGURE 1-42

6

• **Click Landscape, and then click the OK button.**

The orientation is changed to landscape as shown by the report that appears on the screen (Figure 1-43). The last field that is displayed is the Trainer Number field; so all fields currently appear. If they did not, you could decrease the left and right margins; that is, the amount of space left by Access on the left and right edges of the report.

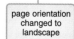

FIGURE 1-43

7

• **Click the Print button to print the report, and then click the Close button on the Print Preview toolbar.**

The report prints. It looks like the report shown in Figure 1-37 on page AC 29. The Print Preview window closes and the Ashton James College : Database window appears.

Creating Additional Tables

A database typically consists of more than one table. The Ashton James College database contains two, the Client table and the Trainer table. You need to repeat the process of creating a table and adding records for each table in the database. In the Ashton James College database, you need to create and add records to the Trainer table. The structure and data for the table are given in Figure 1-44.

Structure of Trainer table

FIELD NAME	DATA TYPE	FIELD SIZE	PRIMARY KEY?	DESCRIPTION
Trainer Number	Text	2	Yes	Trainer Number (Primary Key)
Last Name	Text	10		Last Name of Trainer
First Name	Text	8		First Name of Trainer
Address	Text	15		Street Address
City	Text	15		City
State	Text	2		State (Two-Character Abbreviation)
Zip Code	Text	5		Zip Code (Five-Character Version)
Hourly Rate	Currency			Hourly Rate of Trainer
YTD Earnings	Currency			YTD Earnings of Trainer

Trainer table

TRAINER NUMBER	LAST NAME	FIRST NAME	ADDRESS	CITY	STATE	ZIP CODE	HOURLY RATE	YTD EARNINGS
42	Perry	Belinda	261 Porter	Burdett	TX	76734	$23.00	$27,620.00
48	Stevens	Michael	3135 Gill	Rockwood	TX	78884	$21.00	$23,567.50
53	Gonzalez	Manuel	265 Maxwell	Camino	TX	76574	$24.00	$29,885.00
67	Danville	Marty	1827 Maple	Dunston	TX	77893	$20.00	$0.00

FIGURE 1-44

The following steps show how to create the table.

More About

Printing the Contents of a Table

You can change the margins, paper size, paper source, or the printer that will be used to print the report. To change the margins, select the Margins sheet in the Page Setup dialog box and then enter the appropriate margin size. To change the paper size, paper source, or the printer, select the Page sheet in the Page Setup dialog box, click the appropriate down arrow, and then select the desired option.

To Create an Additional Table

1

• **Make sure the Ashton James College database is open.**

• **Click the New button on the Database window toolbar, click Design View, and then click the OK button.**

• **Enter the data for the fields for the Trainer table from Figure 1-44. Be sure to click the Primary Key button when you enter the Trainer Number field.**

The entries appear (Figure 1-45).

FIGURE 1-45

2

• **Click the Close Window button, click the Yes button in the Microsoft Office Access dialog box when asked if you want to save the changes, and then type** Trainer **as the name of the table.**

The Save As dialog box appears (Figure 1-46). The table name is entered.

3

• **Click the OK button.**

The table is saved in the Ashton James College database. The window containing the table structure no longer appears.

FIGURE 1-46

Adding Records to the Additional Table

Now that you have created the Trainer table, use the steps on the next page to add records to it.

To Add Records to an Additional Table

1

• **Right-click the Trainer table, and then click Open on the shortcut menu. Enter the Trainer data from Figure 1-44 on page AC 32 into the Trainer table.**

The datasheet displays the entered records (Figure 1-47).

2

• **Click the Close Window button for the Trainer : Table window.**

Access closes the table and removes the datasheet from the screen.

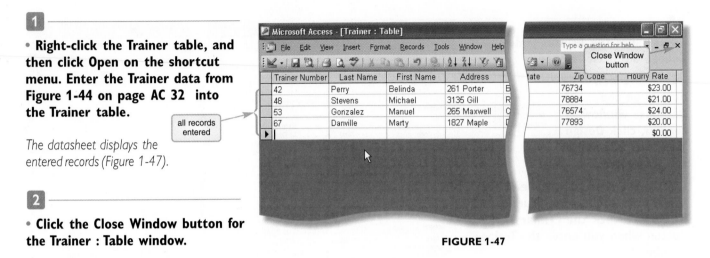

FIGURE 1-47

The records are now in the table.

Using Queries

Queries are simply questions, the answers to which are in the database. Access contains a powerful query feature. Through the use of this feature, you can ask a wide variety of complex questions. For simple requests, however, such as listing the number, name, and trainer number of all clients, you do not need to use the query feature, but instead can use the Simple Query wizard.

The following steps use the Simple Query wizard to create a query to display the number, name, and trainer number of all clients.

To Use the Simple Query Wizard to Create a Query

1

• **With the Tables object selected and the Client table selected, click the New Object button arrow on the Database toolbar.**

A list of objects that can be created is displayed (Figure 1-48).

FIGURE 1-48

2

• **Click Query on the New Object list.**

The New Query dialog box appears (Figure 1-49).

FIGURE 1-49

3

• **Click Simple Query Wizard, and then click the OK button.**

Access displays the Simple Query Wizard dialog box (Figure 1-50). It contains a list of available fields and a list of selected fields. Currently no fields are selected for the query.

FIGURE 1-50

4

• **Click the Add Field button to add the Client Number field.**

• **Click the Add Field button a second time to add the Name field.**

• **Click the Trainer Number field, and then click the Add Field button to add the Trainer Number field.**

The fields are selected (Figure 1-51).

FIGURE 1-51

5

• **Click the Next button, and then type** Client-Trainer Query **as the name for the query.**

The Simple Query Wizard dialog box displays the new query name (Figure 1-52).

FIGURE 1-52

6

• **Click the Finish button to complete the creation of the query.**

Access displays the query results (Figure 1-53). The results contain all records, but only contain the Client Number, Name, and Trainer Number fields.

7

• **Click the Close Window button for the Client-Trainer Query : Select Query window.**

Access closes the query and the Ashton James College : Database window appears.

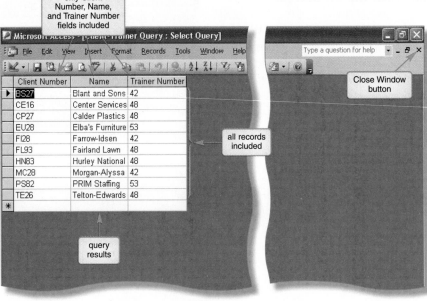

FIGURE 1-53

The query is complete. You can use it at any time you like in the future without needing to repeat the above steps.

Using a Query

After you have created and saved a query, you can use it at any time in the future by opening it. To open a saved query, click the Queries object on the Objects bar, right-click the query, and then click Open on the shortcut menu. To print the results, click the Print button on the toolbar. If you want to change the design of the query, click Design View on the shortcut menu rather than Open. To print the query without first opening it, click Print on the shortcut menu.

You often want to restrict the records that are included. For example, you might only want to include those clients whose trainer number is 42. In such a case, you need to enter the 42 as a **criterion**, which is a condition that the records to be included must satisfy. To do so, you will open the query in Design view, enter the criterion below the appropriate field, and then run the query. The following steps show how to enter a criterion to include only clients of trainer 42 and then run the query.

To Use a Query

1

• **If necessary, click the Queries object. Right-click the Client-Trainer Query.**

The shortcut menu for the Client-Trainer Query is displayed (Figure 1-54).

2

• **Click Design View on the shortcut menu.**

The query appears in Design view (Figure 1-55).

3

• **Click the Criteria row in the Trainer Number column of the grid, and then type 42 as the criterion.**

The criterion is typed (Figure 1-56).

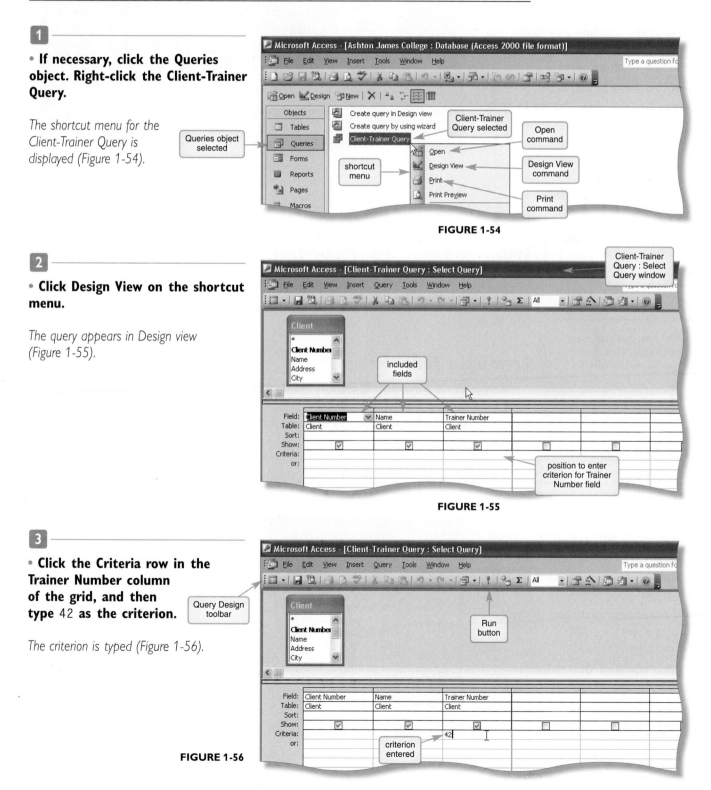

FIGURE 1-54

FIGURE 1-55

FIGURE 1-56

4

- **Click the Run button on the Query Design toolbar.**

Access displays the results (Figure 1-57). Only the clients of trainer 42 are included.

5

- **Close the window containing the query results by clicking its Close Window button.**

- **When asked if you want to save your changes, click the No button.**

The results no longer appear. The changes to the query are not saved.

FIGURE 1-57

Q: If you saved the query, what would happen the next time you ran the query?

A: You would see only clients of trainer 42.

Using a Form to View Data

In creating tables, you have used Datasheet view; that is, the data on the screen appeared as a table. You also can use **Form view**, in which you see data contained in a form.

Creating a Form

To use Form view, you first must create a form. The simplest way to create a form is to use the New Object button on the Database toolbar. The following steps illustrate using the New Object button to create a form for the Client table.

To Use the New Object Button to Create a Form

1

- **Make sure the Ashton James College database is open, the Database window appears, and the Client table is selected.**

- **If necessary, click the Tables object on the Objects bar.**

- **Click the New Object button arrow on the Database toolbar.**

A list of objects that can be created appears (Figure 1-58).

FIGURE 1-58

2

- **Click AutoForm on the New Object list.**

After a brief delay, the form appears (Figure 1-59). If you do not move the mouse pointer after clicking the New Object button, the ScreenTip for the Properties button may appear when the form opens. Access displays the Formatting toolbar when a form is created. (When you close the form, this toolbar no longer appears.)

FIGURE 1-59

Other Ways

1. On Insert menu click AutoForm
2. In Voice Command mode, say "New Object, AutoForm"
3. In Voice Command mode, say "Insert, AutoForm"

Closing and Saving the Form

Closing a form is similar to closing a table. The only difference is that you will be asked if you want to save the form unless you previously have saved it. The following steps close the form and save it as Client.

To Close and Save a Form

1

- **Click the Close Window button for the Client window (see Figure 1-59).**

Access displays the Microsoft Office Access dialog box (Figure 1-60).

FIGURE 1-60

2

- **Click the Yes button.**

The Save As dialog box appears (Figure 1-61). The name of the table (Client) becomes the name of the form automatically. This name could be changed, if desired.

3

- **Click the OK button.**

The form is saved as part of the database and the form closes. The Ashton James College : Database window is redisplayed.

FIGURE 1-61

Opening the Saved Form

After you have saved a form, you can use it at any time in the future by opening it. Opening a form is similar to opening a table. Before opening the form, however, the Forms object, rather than the Tables object, must be selected.

The following steps show how to open the Client form.

To Open a Form

1

• **With the Ashton James College database open and the Database window on the screen, click Forms on the Objects bar, and then right-click the Client form.**

The list of forms appears (Figure 1-62). The shortcut menu for the Client form appears.

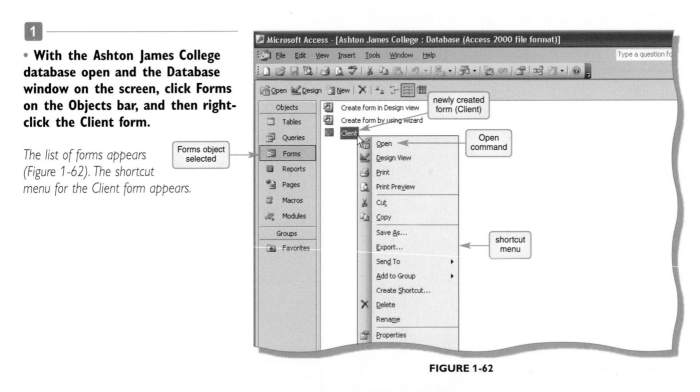

FIGURE 1-62

2

• **Click Open on the shortcut menu.**

The Client form appears (Figure 1-63).

Other Ways

1. Click Forms object, double-click desired form
2. Click Forms object, click desired form, click Open button on Database window toolbar
3. Click Forms object, click desired form, press ALT+O
4. In Voice Command mode, say "Forms, [click desired form], Open"

FIGURE 1-63

Using the Form

You can use the form just as you used Datasheet view. You use the Navigation buttons to move between records. You can add new records or change existing ones. To delete the record appearing on the screen, after selecting the record by clicking its record selector, press the DELETE key. Thus, you can perform database operations using either Form view or Datasheet view.

Because you can see only one record at a time in Form view, to see a different record, such as the fifth record, you must use the Navigation buttons to move to it. The following step illustrates moving from record to record in Form view.

To Use a Form

1

• **Click the Next Record button four times.**

Access displays the fifth record on the form (Figure 1-64).

FIGURE 1-64

Switching Between Form View and Datasheet View

In some cases, after you have seen a record in Form view, you will want to switch to Datasheet view to see the collection of records. The steps on the next page show how to switch from Form view to Datasheet view.

Q: Can you switch between other views, for example, between Datasheet view and Design view?

A: Yes. You also can switch between Form view and Design view using the View button arrow.

To Switch from Form View to Datasheet View

1

- **Click the View button arrow on the Form View toolbar.**

The list of available views appears (Figure 1-65).

FIGURE 1-65

2

- **Click Datasheet View.**

The table appears in Datasheet view (Figure 1-66). The record selector is positioned on the fifth record.

3

- **Click the Close Window button.**

The Client window closes and the datasheet no longer appears.

Client Number	Name	Address	City	State	Zip Code	Amount Paid	Current Due	
BS27	Blant and Sons	4806 Park	Lake Hammond	TX	76653	$21,876.00	$892.50	4
CE16	Center Services	725 Mitchell	San Julio	TX	78364	$26,512.00	$2,672.00	4
CP27	Calder Plastics	7300 Cedar	Lake Hammond	TX	76653	$8,725.00	$0.00	4
EU28	Elba's Furniture	1445 Hubert	Tallmadge	TX	77231	$4,256.00	$1,202.00	5
FI28	Farrow-Idsen	829 Wooster	Cedar Ridge	TX	79342	$8,287.50	$925.50	4
FL93	Fairland Lawn	143 Pangborn	Lake Hammond	TX	76653	$21,625.00	$0.00	4
HN83	Hurley National	3827 Burgess	Tallmadge	TX	77231	$0.00	$0.00	4
MC28	Morgan-Alyssa	923 Williams	Crumville	TX	76745	$24,761.00	$1,572.00	4
PS82	PRIM Staffing	72 Crestview	San Julio	TX	78364	$11,682.25	$2,827.50	5
TE26	Telton-Edwards	5672 Anderson	Dunston	TX	77893	$8,521.50	$0.00	4
*						$0.00	$0.00	

Record: 5 of 10

Client Number (Primary Key)

FIGURE 1-66

Creating a Report

Earlier in this project, you printed a table using the Print button. The report you produced was shown in Figure 1-37 on page AC 29. While this type of report presented the data in an organized manner, the format is very rigid. You cannot select the fields to appear, for example; the report automatically includes all the fields and they appear in precisely the same order as in the table. A way to change the title of the table is not available. Therefore, it will be the same as the name of the table.

In this section, you will create the report shown in Figure 1-67. This report features significant differences from the one in Figure 1-37. The portion at the top of the report in Figure 1-67, called a **page header**, contains a custom title. The contents of this page header appear at the top of each page. The **detail lines**, which are the lines that are printed for each record, contain only those fields you specify and in the order you specify.

Client Amount Report

Client Number	Name	Amount Paid	Current Due
BS27	Blant and Sons	$21,876.00	$892.50
CE16	Center Services	$26,512.00	$2,672.00
CP27	Calder Plastics	$8,725.00	$0.00
EU28	Elba's Furniture	$4,256.00	$1,202.00
FI28	Farrow-Idsen	$8,287.50	$925.50
FL93	Fairland Lawn	$21,625.00	$0.00
HN83	Hurley National	$0.00	$0.00
MC28	Morgan-Alyssa	$24,761.00	$1,572.00
PS82	PRIM Staffing	$11,682.25	$2,827.50
TE26	Telton-Edwards	$8,521.50	$0.00

FIGURE 1-67

The following steps show how to create the report in Figure 1-67.

To Create a Report

1

• **Click Tables on the Objects bar, and then make sure the Client table is selected.**

• **Click the New Object button arrow on the Database toolbar.**

The list of available objects appears (Figure 1-68).

FIGURE 1-68

2

• **Click Report.**

Access displays the New Report dialog box (Figure 1-69).

FIGURE 1-69

3

• **Click Report Wizard, and then click the OK button.**

Access displays the Report Wizard dialog box (Figure 1-70). As you click the Next button in this dialog box, a series of options helps you create the report.

FIGURE 1-70

4

• **Click the Add Field button to add the Client Number field.**

• **Click the Add Field button to add the Name field.**

• **Add the Amount Paid and Current Due fields just as you added the Client Number and Name fields.**

The fields for the report appear in the Selected Fields box (Figure 1-71).

FIGURE 1-71

5

• **Click the Next button.**

The Report Wizard dialog box displays options to specify any grouping that is to take place (Figure 1-72).

FIGURE 1-72

6

- **Because you will not specify any grouping, click the Next button in the Report Wizard dialog box.**
- **Click the Next button a second time because you will not need to change the sort order for the records.**

The Report Wizard dialog box displays options for changing the layout and orientation of the report (Figure 1-73).

FIGURE 1-73

7

- **Make sure that Tabular is selected as the Layout and Portrait is selected as the Orientation, and then click the Next button.**

The Report Wizard dialog box displays options you can select for the style of the report (Figure 1-74).

FIGURE 1-74

8

- **Be sure the Corporate style is selected, click the Next button, and then type** Client Amount Report **as the new title.**

The Report Wizard dialog box displays the new title of the report (Figure 1-75).

FIGURE 1-75

9

• **Click the Finish button.**

Access displays a preview of the report (Figure 1-76). Your report may look slightly different, depending on your printer.

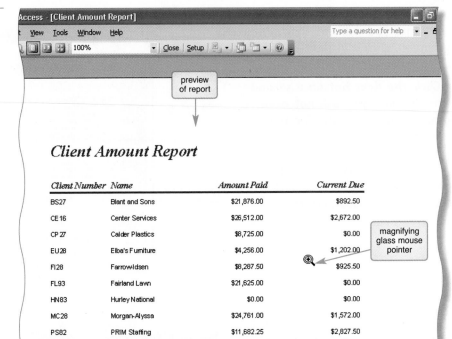

FIGURE 1-76

10

• **Click the magnifying glass mouse pointer anywhere within the report to see the entire report.**

The entire report appears (Figure 1-77).

11

• **Click the Close Window button in the Client Amount Report window.**

The report no longer appears. It has been saved automatically using the name Client Amount Report.

FIGURE 1-77

Other Ways

1. On Objects bar click Reports, double-click Create report by using wizard
2. On Objects bar click Reports, click New on Database window toolbar
3. On Insert menu click Report
4. In Voice Command mode, say "Insert, Report"

Printing the Report

With the report created, you can preview the report to determine if you need to change the orientation or the page margins. You also can print the report. If you want to print specific pages or select other print options, use the Print command on the File menu. The following steps on the next page show how to print a report using the shortcut menu.

To Print a Report

1

• **If necessary, click Reports on the Objects bar in the Database window.**

• **Right-click the Client Amount Report.**

The Client Amount Report is selected and the shortcut menu appears (Figure 1-78).

2

• **Click Print on the shortcut menu.**

The report prints. It should look similar to the one shown in Figure 1-67 on page AC 43.

FIGURE 1-78

Closing the Database

After you have finished working with a database, you should close it. The following step closes the database by closing its Database window.

To Close a Database

1 **Click the Close Window button for the Ashton James College : Database window.**

Access Help System

At any time while you are using Access, you can get answers to questions by using the Access Help system. You can activate the Access Help system by using the Type a question for help box on the menu bar, by clicking the Microsoft Access Help button on the toolbar, or by clicking Help on the menu bar (Figure 1-79 on the next page). Used properly, this form of online assistance can increase your productivity and reduce your frustrations by minimizing the time you spend learning how to use Access.

The section on the next page shows how to get answers to your questions using the Type a question for help box. Additional information about using the Access Help system is available in Appendix A.

Obtaining Help Using the Type a Question for Help Box on the Menu Bar

The Type a question for help box on the right side of the menu bar lets you type in free-form questions, such as *how do I save* or *how do I create a Web page* or, you can type in terms, such as *copy*, *save*, or *formatting*. Access responds by displaying a list of topics related to what you entered. The following steps show how to use the Type a question for help box to obtain information on removing a primary key.

To Obtain Help Using the Type a Question for Help Box

1

• **Click the Type a question for help box on the right side of the menu bar.**

• **Type** how do I remove a primary key **in the box (Figure 1-79).**

FIGURE 1-79

2

• **Press the ENTER key.**

Access displays the Search Results task pane, which includes a list of topics relating to the question, how do I remove a primary key (Figure 1-80). Your list may be different.

FIGURE 1-80

3

• **Point to the Remove the primary key (MDB) topic.**

The mouse pointer changes to a hand indicating it is pointing to a link (Figure 1-81).

FIGURE 1-81

4

• **Click Remove the primary key (MDB).**

Access displays a Microsoft Office Access Help window that provides Help information about removing the primary key (Figure 1-82). Your window may be in a different position.

5

• **Click the Close button on the Microsoft Office Access Help window title bar.**

The Microsoft Access Help window closes.

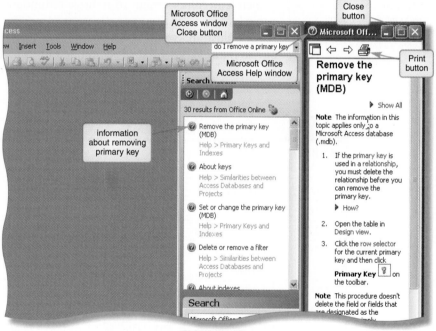

FIGURE 1-82

Use the buttons in the upper-left corner of the Microsoft Office Access Help window (Figure 1-82) to navigate through the Help system, and change the appearance and print the contents of the window.

As you enter questions and terms in the Type a question for help box, Access adds them to its list. Thus, if you click the Type a question for help box arrow, a list of previously asked questions and terms will appear.

Quitting Access

After you close a database, you can open another database, create a new database, or simply quit Access and return to the Windows desktop. The following step quits Access.

To Quit Access

1 Click the Close button in the Microsoft Access window (see Figure 1-82 on the previous page).

Designing a Database

Database design refers to the arrangement of data into tables and fields. In the example in this project, the design is specified, but in many cases, you will have to determine the design based on what you want the system to accomplish.

With large, complex databases, the database design process can be extensive. Major sections of advanced database textbooks are devoted to this topic. Often, however, you should be able to design a database effectively by keeping one simple principle in mind: design to remove redundancy. **Redundancy** means storing the same fact in more than one place.

To illustrate, you need to maintain the following information shown in Figure 1-83. In the figure, all the data is contained in a single table. Notice that the data for a given trainer (number, name, address, and so on) occurs on more than one record.

duplicate trainer names

Client table

CLIENT NUMBER	NAME	ADDRESS	...	CURRENT DUE	TRAINER NUMBER	LAST NAME	FIRST NAME	...
BS27	Blant and Sons	4806 Park	...	$892.50	42	Perry	Belinda	...
CE16	Center Services	725 Mitchell	...	$2,672.00	48	Stevens	Michael	...
CP27	Calder Plastics	7300 Cedar	...	$0.00	48	Stevens	Michael	...
EU28	Elba's Furniture	1445 Hubert	...	$1,202.00	53	Gonzalez	Manuel	...
FI28	Farrow-Idsen	829 Wooster	...	$925.50	42	Perry	Belinda	...
FL93	Fairland Lawn	143 Pangborn	...	$0.00	48	Stevens	Michael	
HN83	Hurley National	3827 Burgess	...	$0.00	48	Stevens	Michael	
MC28	Morgan-Alyssa	923 Williams	...	$1,572.00	42	Perry	Belinda	...
PS82	PRIM Staffing	72 Crestview	...	$2,827.50	53	Gonzalez	Manuel	
TE26	Telton-Edwards	5672 Anderson	...	$0.00	48	Stevens	Michael	

FIGURE 1-83

Storing this data on multiple records is an example of redundancy, which causes several problems, including:

1. Redundancy wastes space on the disk. The name of trainer 42 (Belinda Perry), for example, should be stored only once. Storing this fact several times is wasteful.

2. Redundancy makes updating the database more difficult. If, for example, Belinda Perry's name changes, her name would need to be changed in several different places.

3. A possibility of inconsistent data exists. If, for example, you change the name of Belinda Perry on client FI28's record to Belinda Martin, but do not change it on client BS27's record, the data is inconsistent. In both cases, the trainer number is 42, but the names are different.

The solution to the problem is to place the redundant data in a separate table, one in which the data no longer will be redundant. If, for example, you place the data for trainers in a separate table (Figure 1-84), the data for each trainer will appear only once.

More About

Database Design: Normalization

A special technique, called normalization, identifies and eliminates redundancy. For more information about normalization, visit the Access 2003 More About Web page (scsite.com/ac2003/more) and click Normalization.

trainer data is in separate table

Trainer table

TRAINER NUMBER	LAST NAME	FIRST NAME	ADDRESS	CITY	STATE	ZIP CODE	HOURLY RATE	YTD EARNINGS
42	Perry	Belinda	261 Porter	Burdett	TX	76734	$23.00	$27,620.00
48	Stevens	Michael	3135 Gill	Rockwood	TX	78884	$21.00	$23,567.50
53	Gonzalez	Manuel	265 Maxwell	Camino	TX	76574	$24.00	$29,885.00

Client table

CLIENT NUMBER	NAME	ADDRESS	CITY	STATE	ZIP CODE	AMOUNT PAID	CURRENT DUE	TRAINER NUMBER
BS27	Blant and Sons	4806 Park	Lake Hammond	TX	76653	$21,876.00	$892.50	42
CE16	Center Services	725 Mitchell	San Julio	TX	78364	$26,512.00	$2,672.00	48
CP27	Calder Plastics	7300 Cedar	Lake Hammond	TX	76653	$8,725.00	$0.00	48
EU28	Elba's Furniture	1445 Hubert	Tallmadge	TX	77231	$4,256.00	$1,202.00	53
FI28	Farrow-Idsen	829 Wooster	Cedar Ridge	TX	79342	$8,287.50	$925.50	42
FL93	Fairland Lawn	143 Pangborn	Lake Hammond	TX	76653	$21,625.00	$0.00	48
HN83	Hurley National	3827 Burgess	Tallmadge	TX	77231	$0.00	$0.00	48
MC28	Morgan-Alyssa	923 Williams	Crumville	TX	76745	$24,761.00	$1,572.00	42
PS82	PRIM Staffing	72 Crestview	San Julio	TX	78364	$11,682.25	$2,827.50	53
TE26	Telton-Edwards	5672 Anderson	Dunston	TX	77893	$8,521.50	$0.00	48

FIGURE 1-84

Notice that you need to have the trainer number in both tables. Without it, no way exists to tell which trainer is associated with which client. The remaining trainer data, however, was removed from the Client table and placed in the Trainer table. This new arrangement corrects the problems of redundancy in the following ways:

1. Because the data for each trainer is stored only once, space is not wasted.
2. Changing the name of a trainer is easy. You have only to change one row in the Trainer table.
3. Because the data for a trainer is stored only once, inconsistent data cannot occur.

Designing to omit redundancy will help you to produce good and valid database designs.

More About

Microsoft Certification

The Microsoft Office Specialist Certification program provides an opportunity for you to obtain a valuable industry credential — proof that you have the Access 2003 skills required by employers. For more information, see Appendix E, or visit the Access 2003 Certification Web page (scsite.com/ac2003/cert).

Project Summary

In Project 1, you learned about databases and database management systems. You learned how to create a database and how to create the tables within a database. You saw how to define the fields in a table by specifying the characteristics of the fields. You learned how to open a table, how to add records to it, and how to close it. You also printed the contents of a table. You learned how to use the Simple Query wizard to create a query that included columns from a table as well as how to enter a criterion to restrict the rows that were included. You created a form to view data on the screen and also created a custom report. You learned how to use Microsoft Access Help. Finally, you learned how to design a database to eliminate redundancy.

> **SAM** If you have a SAM user profile, you may have access to hands-on instruction, practice, and assessment of the skills covered in this project. Log in to your SAM account and go to your assignments page to see what your instructor has assigned.

What You Should Know

Having completed this project, you should be able to perform the tasks below. The tasks are listed in the same order they were presented in this project. For a list of the buttons, menus, toolbars, and commands introduced in this project, see the Quick Reference Summary at the back of this book and refer to the Page Number column.

1. Start Access   (AC 7)
2. Close the Language Bar   (AC 9)
3. Create a New Database   (AC 10)
4. Create a Table   (AC 17)
5. Define the Fields in a Table   (AC 19)
6. Close and Save a Table   (AC 21)
7. Add Records to a Table   (AC 23)
8. Close a Table and Database and Quit Access (AC 26)
9. Open a Database   (AC 26)
10. Add Additional Records to a Table   (AC 28)
11. Preview and Print the Contents of a Table (AC 30)
12. Create an Additional Table   (AC 33)
13. Add Records to an Additional Table   (AC 34)
14. Use the Simple Query Wizard to Create a Query (AC 34)
15. Use a Query   (AC 37)
16. Use the New Object Button to Create a Form (AC 38)
17. Close and Save a Form   (AC 39)
18. Open a Form   (AC 40)
19. Use a Form   (AC 41)
20. Switch from Form View to Datasheet View (AC 42)
21. Create a Report   (AC 43)
22. Print a Report   (AC 47)
23. Close a Database   (AC 47)
24. Obtain Help Using the Type a Question for Help Box   (AC 48)
25. Quit Access   (AC 50)

Learn It Online

Instructions: To complete the Learn It Online exercises, start your browser, click the Address bar, and then enter the Web address scsite.com/ac2003/learn. When the Access 2003 Learn It Online page is displayed, follow the instructions in the exercises below. Each exercise has instructions for printing your results, either for your own records or for submission to your instructor.

1 Project Reinforcement TF, MC, and SA

Below Access Project 1, click the Project Reinforcement link. Print the quiz by clicking Print on the File menu for each page. Answer each question.

2 Flash Cards

Below Access Project 1, click the Flash Cards link and read the instructions. Type 20 (or a number specified by your instructor) in the Number of playing cards text box, type your name in the Enter your Name text box, and then click the Flip Card button. When the flash card is displayed, read the question and then click the ANSWER box arrow to select an answer. Flip through Flash Cards. If your score is 15 (75%) correct or greater, click Print on the File menu to print your results. If your score is less than 15 (75%) correct, then redo this exercise by clicking the Replay button.

3 Practice Test

Below Access Project 1, click the Practice Test link. Answer each question, enter your first and last name at the bottom of the page, and then click the Grade Test button. When the graded practice test is displayed on your screen, click Print on the File menu to print a hard copy. Continue to take practice tests until you score 80% or better.

4 Who Wants To Be a Computer Genius?

Below Access Project 1, click the Computer Genius link. Read the instructions, enter your first and last name at the bottom of the page, and then click the PLAY button. When your score is displayed, click the PRINT RESULTS link to print a hard copy.

5 Wheel of Terms

Below Access Project 1, click the Wheel of Terms link. Read the instructions, and then enter your first and last name and your school name. Click the PLAY button. When your score is displayed, right-click the score and then click Print on the shortcut menu to print a hard copy.

6 Crossword Puzzle Challenge

Below Access Project 1, click the Crossword Puzzle Challenge link. Read the instructions, and then enter your first and last name. Click the SUBMIT button. Work the crossword puzzle. When you are finished, click the Submit button. When the crossword puzzle is redisplayed, click the Print Puzzle button to print a hard copy.

7 Tips and Tricks

Below Access Project 1, click the Tips and Tricks link. Click a topic that pertains to Project 1. Right-click the information and then click Print on the shortcut menu. Construct a brief example of what the information relates to in Access to confirm you understand how to use the tip or trick.

8 Newsgroups

Below Access Project 1, click the Newsgroups link. Click a topic that pertains to Project 1. Print three comments.

9 Expanding Your Horizons

Below Access Project 1, click the Expanding Your Horizons link. Click a topic that pertains to Project 1. Print the information. Construct a brief example of what the information relates to in Access to confirm you understand the contents of the article.

10 Search Sleuth

Below Access Project 1, click the Search Sleuth link. To search for a term that pertains to this project, select a term below the Project 1 title and then use the Google search engine at google.com (or any major search engine) to display and print two Web pages that present information on the term.

11 Access Online Training

Below Access Project 1, click the Access Online Training link. When your browser displays the Microsoft Office Online Web page, click the Access link. Click one of the Access courses that covers one or more of the objectives listed at the beginning of the project on page AC 4. Print the first page of the course before stepping through it.

12 Office Marketplace

Below Access Project 1, click the Office Marketplace link. When your browser displays the Microsoft Office Online Web page, click the Office Marketplace link. Click a topic that relates to Access. Print the first page.

Apply Your Knowledge

1 Changing Data, Creating Queries, and Creating Reports

Instructions: Start Access. Open the database Begon Pest Control from the Data Disk. See the inside back cover for instructions for downloading the Data Disk or see your instructor for information about accessing the files required in this book.

Begon Pest Control is a company that performs pest control services for commercial businesses. Begon has a database that keeps track of its technicians and customers. The database has two tables. The Customer table contains data on the customers who use the services of Begon. The Technician table contains data on the individuals employed by Begon. The structure and data are shown for the Customer table in Figure 1-85 and for the Technician table in Figure 1-86.

Structure of Customer table

FIELD NAME	DATA TYPE	FIELD SIZE	PRIMARY KEY?	DESCRIPTION
Customer Number	Text	4	Yes	Customer Number (Primary Key)
Name	Text	20		Customer Name
Address	Text	15		Street Address
City	Text	15		City
State	Text	2		State (Two-Character Abbreviation)
Zip Code	Text	5		Zip Code (Five-Character Version)
Balance	Currency			Amount Owed by Customer
Technician Number	Text	3		Number of Customer's Technician

Customer table

CUSTOMER NUMBER	NAME	ADDRESS	CITY	STATE	ZIP CODE	BALANCE	TECHNICIAN NUMBER
AT23	Atlas Repair	220 Beard	Kady	TN	42514	$335.00	203
AZ01	AZ Auto	412 Beechwood	Conradt	TN	42547	$300.00	210
BL35	Blanton Shoes	443 Chedder	Kady	TN	42514	$290.00	210
CJ45	C Joe Diner	87 Fletcher	Carlton	TN	52764	$0.00	214
CM90	Cramden Co.	234 Fairlawn	Conradt	TN	42546	$355.00	203
HI25	Hill Crafts	245 Beard	Kady	TN	42514	$334.00	210
KL50	Klean n Dri	378 Stout	Carlton	TN	52764	$365.00	210
MC10	Moss Carpet	109 Fletcher	Carlton	TN	52764	$398.00	203
PV83	Prime Video	734 Lanton	Conradt	TN	42547	$0.00	214
SE05	Servete Mfg Co.	879 Redfern	Kady	TN	42515	$343.00	210

FIGURE 1-85

Apply Your Knowledge

Structure of Technician table

FIELD NAME	DATA TYPE	FIELD SIZE	PRIMARY KEY?	DESCRIPTION
Technician Number	Text	3	Yes	Technician Number (Primary Key)
Last Name	Text	10		Last Name of Technician
First Name	Text	8		First Name of Technician
Address	Text	15		Street Address
City	Text	15		City
State	Text	2		State (Two-Character Abbreviation)
Zip Code	Text	5		Zip Code (Five-Character Version)
Hourly Rate	Currency			Hourly Pay Rate

Technician table

TECHNICIAN NUMBER	LAST NAME	FIRST NAME	ADDRESS	CITY	STATE	ZIP CODE	HOURLY RATE
203	Estevez	Miguel	467 Clay	Kady	TN	42517	$11.50
210	Hillsdale	Rachel	78 Parkton	Conradt	TN	42547	$11.75
214	Liu	Chou	897 North	Carlton	TN	52764	$11.65
220	Short	Chris	111 Maple	Conradt	TN	42547	$11.50

FIGURE 1-86

Instructions: Perform the following tasks:

1. Open the Customer table and change the Technician Number for customer KL50 to 214.
2. Print the Customer table.
3. Use the Simple Query Wizard to create a new query to display and print the customer number, name, and technician number for records in the Customer table as shown in Figure 1-87 on the next page.
4. Save the query as Customer-Technician Query and then close the query.
5. Open the Customer-Technician Query in Design View and restrict the query results to only those customers whose technician number is 210.
6. Print the query but do not save the changes.
7. Create the report shown in Figure 1-88 on the next page for the Customer table.
8. Print the report.

(continued)

Microsoft Office
Access 2003

Changing Data, Creating Queries, and Creating Reports *(continued)*

Microsoft Access - [Customer-Technician Query :

File   Edit   View   Insert   Format   Records   Tools

Customer Numb	Name	Technician Num
AT23	Atlas Repair	203
AZ01	AZ Auto	210
BL35	Blanton Shoes	210
CJ45	C Joe Diner	214
CM90	Cramden Co.	203
HI25	Hill Crafts	210
KL50	Klean n Dri	214
MC10	Moss Carpet	203
PV83	Prime Video	214
SE05	Servete Mfg Co.	210
*		

FIGURE 1-87

Customer Amount Report

Customer Number	Name	Balance
AT23	Atlas Repair	$335.00
AZ01	AZ Auto	$300.00
BL35	Blanton Shoes	$290.00
CJ45	C Joe Diner	$0.00
CM90	Cramden Co.	$355.00
HI25	Hill Crafts	$334.00
KL50	Klean n Dri	$365.00
MC10	Moss Carpet	$398.00
PV83	Prime Video	$0.00
SE05	Servete Mfg Co.	$343.00

FIGURE 1-88

1 Creating the Birds2U Database

Problem: Birds2U is a new online retailer. The company specializes in products for bird and nature enthusiasts. The database consists of two tables. The Item table contains information on items available for sale. The Supplier table contains information on the companies that supply the items.

Instructions: Perform the following tasks:

1. Create a new database in which to store all the objects related to the items for sale. Call the database Birds2U.
2. Create the Item table using the structure shown in Figure 1-89. Use the name Item for the table.
3. Add the data shown in Figure 1-89 to the Item table.
4. Print the Item table.

Structure of Item table

FIELD NAME	DATA TYPE	FIELD SIZE	PRIMARY KEY?	DESCRIPTION
Item Code	Text	4	Yes	Item Code (Primary Key)
Description	Text	20		Description of Item
On Hand	Number			Number of Units On Hand
Cost	Currency			Cost of Item
Selling Price	Currency			Selling Price of Item
Supplier Code	Text	2		Code of Item's Supplier

Item table

ITEM CODE	DESCRIPTION	ON HAND	COST	SELLING PRICE	SUPPLIER CODE
BA35	Bat House	14	$43.50	$45.50	21
BB01	Bird Bath	2	$82.10	$86.25	13
BE19	Bee Box	7	$39.80	$42.50	21
BL06	Bluebird House	9	$14.35	$15.99	13
BU24	Butterfly Box	6	$36.10	$37.75	21
GF12	Globe Feeder	12	$14.80	$16.25	05
HF01	Hummingbird Feeder	5	$11.35	$14.25	05
PM05	Purple Martin House	3	$67.10	$69.95	13
SF03	Suet Feeder	7	$8.05	$9.95	05
WF10	Window Feeder	10	$14.25	$15.95	05

FIGURE 1-89

5. Create the Supplier table using the structure shown in Figure 1-90 on the next page. Use the name Supplier for the table.
6. Add the data shown in Figure 1-90 to the Supplier table.
7. Print the Supplier table.
8. Create a form for the Supplier table. Use the name Supplier for the form.
9. Open the form you created and change the address for Supplier Code 17 to 56 Beechwood.
10. Create and print the report shown in Figure 1-91 on the next page for the Item table.

(continued)

Creating the Birds2U Database *(continued)*

Structure of Supplier table

FIELD NAME	DATA TYPE	FIELD SIZE	PRIMARY KEY?	DESCRIPTION
Supplier Code	Text	2	Yes	Supplier Code (Primary Key)
Name	Text	20		Supplier Name
Address	Text	15		Street Address
City	Text	15		City
State	Text	2		State (Two-Character Abbreviation)
Zip Code	Text	5		Zip Code (Five-Character Version)
Telephone Number	Text	12		Telephone Number (999-999-9999 Version)

Supplier table

SUPPLIER CODE	NAME	ADDRESS	CITY	STATE	ZIP CODE	TELEPHONE NUMBER
05	All Birds Supply	234 Southward	Elgin	AZ	85165	602-555-6756
13	Bird Casa Ltd	38 Junction	Grandber	TX	78628	512-555-3402
17	Lawn Fixtures	56 Beecham	Holligan	CA	95418	707-555-4545
21	Natural Woods	67 Main	Ghostman	MI	49301	610-555-3333

FIGURE 1-90

Inventory Report

Item Code	Description	On Hand	Cost
BA35	Bat House	14	$43.50
BB01	Bird Bath	2	$82.10
BE19	Bee Box	7	$39.80
BL06	Bluebird House	9	$14.35
BU24	Butterfly Box	6	$36.10
GF12	Globe Feeder	12	$14.80
HF01	Hummingbird Feeder	5	$11.35
PM05	Purple Martin House	3	$67.10
SF03	Suet Feeder	7	$8.05
WF10	Window Feeder	10	$14.25

FIGURE 1-91

2 Creating the Babbage Bookkeeping Database

Problem: Babbage Bookkeeping is a local company that provides bookkeeping services to several small businesses in the area. The database consists of two tables. The Client table contains information on the businesses that use Babbage's services. The Bookkeeper table contains information on the bookkeeper assigned to the business.

Instructions: Perform the following tasks:

1. Create a new database in which to store all the objects related to the bookkeeping data. Call the database Babbage Bookkeeping.
2. Create and print the Client table using the structure and data shown in Figure 1-92. Then, create and print the Bookkeeper table using the structure and data shown in Figure 1-93 on the next page.

Structure of Client table

FIELD NAME	DATA TYPE	FIELD SIZE	PRIMARY KEY?	DESCRIPTION
Client Number	Text	3	Yes	Client Number (Primary Key)
Name	Text	20		Name of Client
Address	Text	15		Street Address
City	Text	15		City
Zip Code	Text	5		Zip Code (Five-Character Version)
Balance	Currency			Amount Currently Owed for Services
Bookkeeper Number	Text	2		Number of Client's Bookkeeper

Client table

CLIENT NUMBER	NAME	ADDRESS	CITY	ZIP CODE	BALANCE	BOOKKEEPER NUMBER
A54	Afton Mills	612 Revere	Grant City	58120	$315.50	22
A62	Atlas Suppliers	227 Dandelion	Empeer	58216	$525.00	24
B26	Blake-Scripps	557 Maum	Grant City	58120	$229.50	24
D76	Dege Grocery	446 Linton	Portage	59130	$485.75	34
G56	Grand Cleaners	337 Abelard	Empeer	58216	$265.00	22
H21	Hill Shoes	247 Fulton	Grant City	58121	$228.50	24
J77	Jones Plumbing	75 Getty	Portage	59130	$0.00	24
M26	Mohr Crafts	665 Maum	Empeer	58216	$312.50	22
S56	SeeSaw Ind.	31 Liatris	Portage	59130	$362.50	34
T45	Tate Repair	824 Revere	Grant City	58120	$254.00	24

FIGURE 1-92

(continued)

Creating the Babbage Bookkeeping Database *(continued)*

Structure of Bookkeeper table

FIELD NAME	DATA TYPE	FIELD SIZE	PRIMARY KEY?	DESCRIPTION
Bookkeeper Number	Text	2	Yes	Bookkeeper Number (Primary Key)
Last Name	Text	10		Last Name of Bookkeeper
First Name	Text	8		First Name of Bookkeeper
Address	Text	15		Street Address
City	Text	15		City
Zip Code	Text	5		Zip Code (Five-Character Version)
Hourly Rate	Currency			Hourly Rate
YTD Earnings	Currency			Year-to-Date Earnings

Bookkeeper table

BOOKKEEPER NUMBER	LAST NAME	FIRST NAME	ADDRESS	CITY	ZIP CODE	HOURLY RATE	YTD EARNINGS
22	Lewes	Johanna	26 Cotton	Portage	59130	$14.50	$18,245.00
24	Rodriguez	Mario	79 Marsden	Grant City	58120	$13.50	$17,745.50
34	Wong	Choi	263 Topper	Empeer	58216	$14.00	$16,750.25

FIGURE 1-93

3. Change the Bookkeeper Number for client J77 to 34.
4. Use the Simple Query Wizard to create a new query to display and print the Client Number, Name, and Bookkeeper Number for all clients where the bookkeeper number is 24.
5. Create and print the report shown in Figure 1-94 for the Client table.

Balance Due Report

Client Number	Name	Balance
A54	Afton Mills	$315.50
A62	Atlas Suppliers	$525.00
B26	Blake-Scripps	$229.50
D76	Dege Grocery	$485.75
G56	Grand Cleaners	$265.00
H21	Hill Shoes	$228.50
J77	Jones Plumbing	$0.00
M26	Mohr Crafts	$312.50
S56	SeeSaw Ind.	$362.50
T45	Tate Repair	$254.00

FIGURE 1-94

In the Lab

3 Creating the City Guide Database

Problem: The local chamber of commerce publishes a guide for newcomers. To help finance the guide, the chamber includes advertisements from local businesses. Advertising representatives receive a commission based on the advertising revenues they generate. The database consists of two tables. The Advertiser table contains information on the businesses that advertise in the guide. The Ad Rep table contains information on the advertising representative assigned to the account.

Instructions Part 1: Using the data shown in Figures 1-95 and 1-96 on the next page create the City Guide database, the Advertiser table, and the Ad Rep table. Note that the Ad Rep table uses the number data type. Print the tables. Then, create a form for the Advertiser table.

Structure of Advertiser table

FIELD NAME	DATA TYPE	FIELD SIZE	PRIMARY KEY?	DESCRIPTION
Advertiser Number	Text	4	Yes	Advertiser Number (Primary Key)
Name	Text	20		Name of Advertiser
Address	Text	15		Street Address
Zip Code	Text	5		Zip Code (Five-Character Version)
Telephone Number	Text	8		Telephone Number (999-9999 Version)
Balance	Currency			Amount Currently Owed
Amount Paid	Currency			Amount Paid Year-to-Date
Ad Rep Number	Text	2		Number of Advertising Representative

Data for Advertiser table

ADVERTISER NUMBER	NAME	ADDRESS	ZIP CODE	TELEPHONE NUMBER	BALANCE	AMOUNT PAID	AD REP NUMBER
A228	Adam's Music	47 Berton	19363	555-0909	$90.00	$565.00	26
B103	Barbecue Joint	483 Cantor	19363	555-8990	$185.00	$825.00	29
C048	Chloe's Salon	10 Main	19362	555-2334	$0.00	$375.00	29
C135	Creative Toys	26 Jefferson	19362	555-1357	$130.00	$865.00	32
D217	Dog Groomers	33 Maple	19362	555-2468	$290.00	$515.00	26
G346	Gold's Clothes	196 Lincoln	19364	555-3579	$0.00	$805.00	29
M321	Meat Shoppe	234 Magnolia	19363	555-6802	$215.00	$845.00	29
P124	Palace Theatre	22 Main	19364	555-8024	$65.00	$180.00	26
S111	Suds n Spuds	10 Jefferson	19365	555-5791	$465.00	$530.00	32
W456	Western Wear	345 Oaktree	19363	555-7913	$105.00	$265.00	26

FIGURE 1-95

(continued)

Creating the City Guide Database (continued)

Structure for Ad Rep table

FIELD NAME	DATA TYPE	FIELD SIZE	PRIMARY KEY?	DESCRIPTION
Ad Rep Number	Text	2	Yes	Advertising Rep Number (Primary Key)
Last Name	Text	10		Last Name of Advertising Rep
First Name	Text	8		First Name of Advertising Rep
Address	Text	15		Street Address
City	Text	15		City
Zip Code	Text	5		Zip Code (Five-Character Version)
Comm Rate	Number	Double		Commission Rate on Advertising Sales
Commission	Currency			Year-to-Date Total Commissions

Data for Ad Rep table

AD REP NUMBER	LAST NAME	FIRST NAME	ADDRESS	CITY	ZIP CODE	COMM RATE	COMMISSION
26	Febo	Jen	57 Barton	Crescent	19111	0.09	$6,500.00
29	Martinson	Kyle	87 Pearl	Newton	19124	0.08	$6,250.00
32	Rogers	Elena	45 Magret	San Luis	19362	0.09	$7,000.00

FIGURE 1-96

Instructions Part 2: Correct the following error. The ad rep assigned to the Meat Shoppe account should be Elena Rogers. Use the form you created to make the correction, and then print the form showing the corrected record. To print the form, open the form, click File on the menu bar, and then click Print. Click Selected Records(s) as the Print Range. Click the OK button.

Instructions Part 3: Create a query to find which accounts Kyle Martinson represents. Print the results. Prepare an advertiser status report that lists the advertiser's number, name, balance currently owed, and amount paid to date.

Cases and Places

The difficulty of these case studies varies:
■ are the least difficult and ■■ are more difficult. The last exercise is a group exercise.

1 ■ To help finance your college education, you formed a small business. You provide dog-walking services to local residents. Dog walkers are paid by the walk for each dog they walk. The business has grown rapidly and you now have several other students working for you. You realize that you need to computerize your business.

Design and create a database to store the data that College Dog Walkers needs to manage its business. Then create the necessary tables and enter the data from the Case 1-1 College Dog Walkers Word document on the Data Disk. Print the tables. See the inside back cover of this book for instructions for downloading the Data Disk or see your instructor for information on accessing the files required in this book.

2 ■ The Health and Physical Education department at your college recognized early that personal training would be a growth field. One of your friends graduated from the program and has started a company, InPerson Fitness Company. The company specializes in personal training in the comfort of the customer's home. It designs exercise programs for clients based on each person's health history, abilities, and fitness objectives. The company is expanding rapidly and you have been hired to computerize the business.

Design and create a database to store the data that InPerson Fitness needs to manage its business. Then create the necessary tables and enter the data from the Case 1-2 InPerson Fitness Word document on the Data Disk. Print the tables. See the inside back cover of this book for instructions for downloading the Data Disk or see your instructor for information on accessing the files required in this book.

3 ■■ Regional Books is a local bookstore that specializes in books that are of local interest. These are books that are set in the region or are written by authors who live in the area. The owner has asked you to create and update a database that she can use to keep track of the books she has in stock.

Design and create a database to store the book data. To create the Books table, use the Table Wizard and select the Books table. You do not need to select all the fields the Table Wizard provides and you can rename the fields in the table. (*Hint*: See More About Creating a Table: The Table Wizard on page AC 15.) Enter the data from the Case 1-3 Regional Books Word document on the Data Disk. Print the tables. Prepare a sample query and a sample report to illustrate to the owner the types of tasks that can be done with a database management system. See the inside back cover of this book for instructions for downloading the Data Disk or see your instructor for information on accessing the files required in this book.

Cases and Places

4　■■　The Campus Housing office at the local university provides a listing of available off-campus rentals by private owners. The office would like to make this listing available on the campus Web site. The administrator has asked you to create and update a database that can store information about available off-campus housing. The housing list is in the Case 1-4 Campus Housing Word document on the Data Disk. A listing that has 0 bedrooms is either an efficiency apartment or a room for rent in a home. Distance indicates the rental unit's distance in miles from the university. Parking signifies whether reserved parking is available with the unit.

Design and create a database to meet the needs of the Campus Housing office. Then create the necessary tables, enter the data from the Case 1-4 Campus Housing Word document on the Data Disk. Print the tables. Prepare a sample form, sample query, and sample report to illustrate to the office the types of tasks that can be done with a database management system. See the inside back cover of this book for instructions for downloading the Data Disk or see your instructor for information on accessing the files required in this book.

5　■■　**Working Together**　Conducting a job search requires careful preparation. In addition to preparing a resume and cover letter, you will need to research the companies for which you are interested in working and contact these companies to let them know of your interest and qualifications. Microsoft Access can help you manage the job search process. The Database Wizard includes a Contact Management template that can create a database that will help you keep track of your job contacts.

Have each member of your team explore the features of the Database Wizard and determine individually which fields should be included in a Contact Management database. As a group, review your choices and decide on one common design. Prepare a short paper for your instructor that explains why your team chose those particular fields to include in the database.

After agreeing on the database design, assign one member to create the database using the Database Wizard. Every other team member should research a company and add the data to the database. Print the alphabetical contact listing that the Database Wizard creates. Turn in the short paper and the report to your instructor.

Querying a Database Using the Select Query Window

CASE PERSPECTIVE

Dr. Gernaey and his colleagues are eager for Ashton James College (AJC) to obtain the benefits they anticipated when they set up the database of client and trainer data. One immediate benefit they expect is the capability of easily asking questions such as the following concerning the data in the database and rapidly getting the answers.

1. What are the name, the amount paid, and the current due of client CP27?

2. Which clients' names begin with Fa?

3. Which clients are located in Lake Hammond?

4. Which clients have a current due of $0.00?

5. Which clients have an amount paid that is more than $20,000.00?

6. Which clients of trainer 48 have an amount paid that is more than $20,000.00?

7. In what cities are all the clients located?

8. How many hours has each trainer worked so far this year?

9. What is the client number and name of each client, and what is the number and name of the trainer to whom each client is assigned?

AJC needs to find information about clients located in a specific city, but they want to enter a different city each time they ask the question. A parameter query would enable this. They also have a special way they want to summarize their data and a crosstab query will present the data in the desired form.

Your task is to assist the administration of AJC in obtaining answers to these and other questions using Access query features.

As you read through this project, you will learn how to query a database and use the Select Query window.

MICROSOFT

Querying a Database Using the Select Query Window

PROJECT

2

Objectives:

You will have mastered the material in this project when you can:

- Create and run queries
- Print query results
- Include fields in the design grid
- Use text and numeric data in criteria
- Create and use parameter queries
- Save a query and use the saved query
- Use compound criteria in queries
- Sort data in queries
- Join tables in queries
- Perform calculations in queries
- Use grouping in queries
- Create crosstab queries

Introduction

A database management system such as Access offers many useful features, among them the capability of answering questions such as those posed by the administration of Ashton James College (Figure 2-1). The answers to these questions, and many more, are found in the database, and Access can find the answers quickly. When you pose a question to Access, or any other database management system, the question is called a query. A **query** is simply a question represented in a way that Access can understand.

Thus, to find the answer to a question, you first create a corresponding query using the techniques illustrated in this project. After you have created the query, you instruct Access to run the query; that is, to perform the steps necessary to obtain the answer. Access then will display the answer in Datasheet view.

Project Two — Querying the Ashton James College Database

The steps in this project obtain answers to the questions posed by the administration of Ashton James College. These include the questions shown in Figure 2-1, as well as many other questions that may be deemed important.

What are the name, the amount paid, and the current due for client CP27?

Which clients' names begin with Fa?

In what cities are all the clients located?

Which clients are located in Lake Hammond?

Which clients of trainer 48 have an amount paid that is more than $20,000.00?

Client table

CLIENT NUMBER	NAME	ADDRESS	CITY	STATE	ZIP CODE	AMOUNT PAID	CURRENT DUE	TRAINER NUMBER
BS27	Blant and Sons	4806 Park	Lake Hammond	TX	76653	$21,876.00	$892.50	42
CE16	Center Services	725 Mitchell	San Julio	TX	78364	$26,512.00	$2,672.00	48
CP27	Calder Plastics	7300 Cedar	Lake Hammond	TX	76653	$8,725.00	$0.00	48
EU28	Elba's Furniture	1445 Hubert	Tallmadge	TX	77231	$4,256.00	$1,202.00	53
FI28	Farrow-Idsen	829 Wooster	Cedar Ridge	TX	79342	$8,287.50	$925.50	42
FL93	Fairland Lawn	143 Pangborn	Lake Hammond	TX	76653	$21,625.00	$0.00	48
HN83	Hurley National	3827 Burgess	Tallmadge	TX	77231	$0.00	$0.00	48
MC28	Morgan-Alyssa	923 Williams	Crumville	TX	76745	$24,761.00	$1,572.00	42
PS82	PRIM Staffing	72 Crestview	San Julio	TX	78364	$11,682.25	$2,827.50	53
TE26	Telton-Edwards	5672 Anderson	Dunston	TX	77893	$8,521.50	$0.00	48

CLIENT NUMBER	NAME	AMOUNT PAID	CURRENT DUE
FI28	Farrow-Idsen	$8,287.50	$925.50
FL93	Fairland Lawn	$21,625.00	$0.00

CLIENT NUMBER	NAME	ADDRESS
BS27	Blant and Sons	4806 Park
CP27	Calder Plastics	7300 Cedar
FL93	Fairland Lawn	143 Pangborn

CLIENT NUMBER	NAME	AMOUNT PAID	CURRENT DUE
CP27	Calder Plastics	$8,725.00	$0.00

CITY
Cedar Ridge
Crumville
Dunston
Lake Hammond
Tallmadge

CLIENT NUMBER	NAME	AMOUNT PAID	CURRENT DUE	TRAINER NUMBER
CE16	Center Services	$26,512.00	$2,672.00	48
FL93	Fairland Lawn	$21,625.00	$0.00	48

FIGURE 2-1

More About

Queries: Query Languages

Before the advent of query languages in the mid-1970s, obtaining answers to questions concerning data in a database was very difficult, requiring that someone write lengthy (several hundred line) programs in languages such as COBOL. Query languages made it easy to obtain answers to such questions.

More About

The Access Help System

Need Help? It is no further than the Type a question for help box on the menu bar in the upper-right corner of the window. Click the box that contains the text, Type a question for help (Figure 2-5), type help, and then press the ENTER key. Access responds with a list of topics you can click to learn about obtaining help on any Access-related topic. To find out what is new in Access 2003, type what is new in Access in the Type a question for help box.

Opening the Database

If you are stepping through this project on a computer, and you want your screen to agree with the figures in this book, then you should change your computer's resolution to 800 × 600. For more information on how to change the resolution on your computer, see Appendix D. Before creating queries, first you must open the database. The following steps summarize the procedure to complete this task, once you have started Access.

To Open a Database

1 Click the Open button on the Database toolbar.

2 If necessary, click the Look in box arrow and then click 3½ Floppy (A:). Click Ashton James College, the database created in Project 1. (If you did not complete the steps in Project 1, see your instructor for a copy of the database.)

3 Click the Open button in the Open dialog box. If a Security Warning dialog box appears, click the Open button.

The database opens and the Ashton James College : Database window appears.

Creating and Running Queries

You create a query by making entries in a special window called a **Select Query window**. Once the database is open, the first step in creating a query is to select the table for which you are creating a query in the Database window. Then, you use the New Object button to design the new query in the Select Query window. It typically is easier to work with the Select Query window if it is maximized. Thus, as a standard practice, maximize the Select Query window as soon as you have created it. In addition, it often is useful to resize both panes within the window. This enables you to resize the field list that appears in the upper pane so more fields appear.

The following steps initiate creating a query.

To Create a Query

1

• **Be sure the Ashton James College database is open, the Tables object is selected, and the Client table is selected.**

• **Click the New Object button arrow on the Database toolbar.**

The list of available objects appears (Figure 2-2).

FIGURE 2-2

2

• **Click Query.**

Access displays the New Query dialog box (Figure 2-3).

FIGURE 2-3

3

• **With Design View selected, click the OK button.**

The Query1 : Select Query window appears (Figure 2-4).

FIGURE 2-4

4

• **Maximize the Query1 : Select Query window by double-clicking its title bar, and then drag the line separating the two panes to the approximate position shown in Figure 2-5.**

*The Query1 : Select Query window is maximized. The upper pane contains a field list for the Client table. The lower pane contains the **design grid**, which is the area where you specify fields to be included, sort order, and the criteria the records you are looking for must satisfy. The mouse pointer shape indicates you can drag the line.*

FIGURE 2-5

5

• **Drag the lower edge of the field box down far enough so all fields in the Client table are displayed (Figure 2-6).**

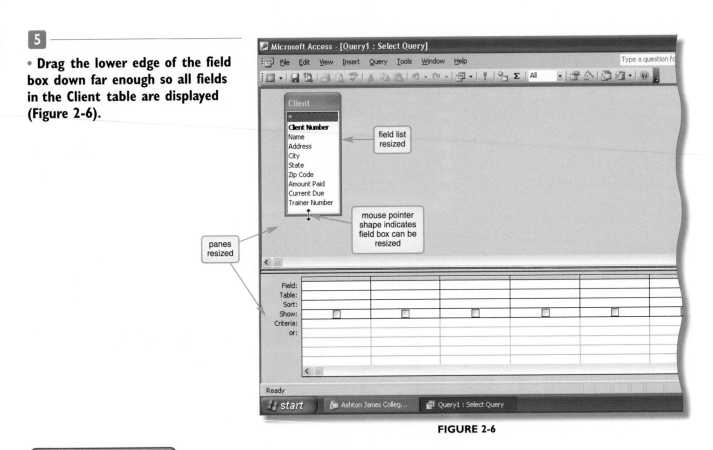

FIGURE 2-6

Using the Select Query Window

Once you have created a new Select Query window, you are ready to create the actual query by making entries in the design grid in the lower pane of the window. You enter the names of the fields you want included in the Field row in the grid. You also can enter criteria, such as the fact that the client number must be a specific number, such as CP27, in the Criteria row of the grid. When you do so, only the record or records that match the criterion will be included in the answer.

Displaying Selected Fields in a Query

Only the fields that appear in the design grid will be included in the results of the query. Thus, to include only certain fields, place only these fields in the grid, and no others. If you place the wrong field in the grid inadvertently, click Edit on the menu bar and then click Delete to remove it. Alternatively, you could click Clear Grid on the Edit menu to clear the entire design grid and then start over.

The following step creates a query to show the client number, name, and trainer number for all clients by including only those fields in the design grid.

To Include Fields in the Design Grid

1

• If necessary, maximize the **Query1 : Select Query** window containing the field list for the Client table in the upper pane of the window and an empty design grid in the lower pane.

• Double-click the **Client Number** field in the field list to include it in the query.

• Double-click the **Name** field to include it in the query, and then double-click the **Trainer Number** field to include it as well.

The Client Number, Name, and Trainer Number fields are included in the query (Figure 2-7).

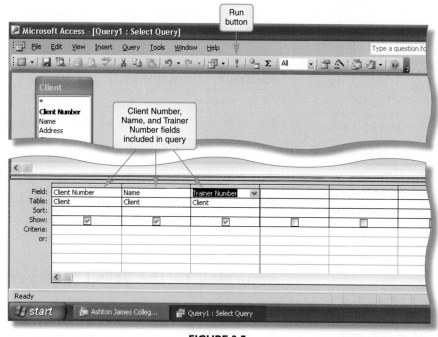

FIGURE 2-7

Running a Query

Once you have created the query, you run the query to produce the results using the Run button on the Query Design toolbar. Access performs the steps necessary to obtain and display the answer. The set of records that makes up the answer will be displayed in Datasheet view. Although it looks like a table that is stored on your disk, it really is not. The records are constructed from data in the existing Client table. If you were to change the data in the Client table and then rerun this same query, the results would reflect the changes. The following step runs the query.

To Run the Query

1

• Click the **Run button** on the Query Design toolbar (see Figure 2-7).

The query is executed and the results appear (Figure 2-8).

FIGURE 2-8

Microsoft Office
Access 2003

More About

Queries: SQL

The most widespread of all the query languages is a language called SQL. In SQL, users type commands such as SELECT CURRENT DUE FROM CUSTOMER WHERE CITY = "Tallmadge" to find the current due amounts of all customers located in Tallmadge. Many database management systems, including Access, offer SQL as one option for querying databases. For more information, visit the Access 2003 More About Web page (scsite.com/ac2003/more) and click SQL.

Printing the Results of a Query

To print the results of a query, use the same techniques you learned in Project 1 on page AC 29 to print the data in the table. The following step prints the current query results.

To Print the Results of a Query

1 **Click the Print button on the Query Datasheet toolbar (see Figure 2-8 on the previous page).**

The results print.

If the results of a query require landscape orientation, switch to landscape orientation before you click the Print button as indicated in Project 1 on page AC 31.

Returning to the Select Query Window

You can examine the results of a query on your screen to see the answer to your question. You can scroll through the records, if necessary, just as you scroll through the records of any other table. You also can print a copy of the table. In any case, once you are finished working with the results, you can return to the Select Query window to ask another question. The following steps illustrate how to return to the Select Query window.

To Return to the Select Query Window

1

• **Click the View button arrow on the Query Datasheet toolbar.**

The Query View list appears (Figure 2-9).

FIGURE 2-9

2

• **Click Design View.**

The Query1 : Select Query window is redisplayed (Figure 2-10).

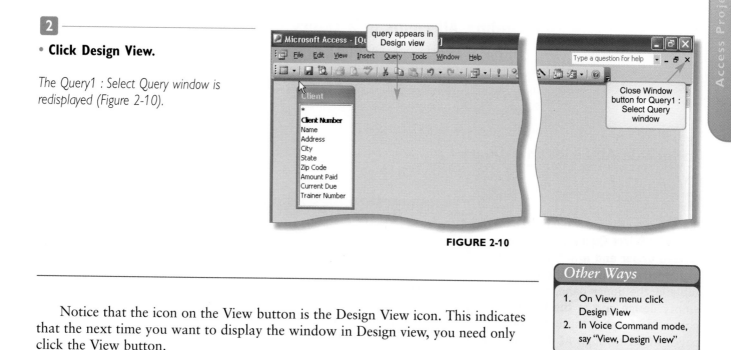

FIGURE 2-10

Other Ways

1. On View menu click Design View
2. In Voice Command mode, say "View, Design View"

Notice that the icon on the View button is the Design View icon. This indicates that the next time you want to display the window in Design view, you need only click the View button.

Closing a Query

To close a query, close the Select Query window. When you do so, Access displays the Microsoft Office Access dialog box asking if you want to save your query for future use. If you think you will need to create the same exact query often, you should save the query. For now, you will not save any queries. You will see how to save them later in the project. The following steps close a query without saving it.

To Close the Query

1

• **Click the Close Window button for the Query1 : Select Query window (see Figure 2-10).**

Access displays the Microsoft Office Access dialog box (Figure 2-11). Clicking the Yes button saves the query and clicking the No button closes the query without saving.

2

• **Click the No button in the Microsoft Office Access dialog box.**

The Query1 : Select Query window closes. The query is not saved.

FIGURE 2-11

Other Ways

1. On File menu click Close
2. In Voice Command mode, say "File, Close"

Including All Fields in a Query

If you want to include all fields in a query, you could select each field individually. A simpler way to include all fields is available, however. By selecting the asterisk (*) in the field list, you are indicating that all fields are to be included. The following steps use the asterisk to include all fields.

To Include All Fields in a Query

1

• **Be sure you have a maximized Query1 : Select Query window with resized upper and lower panes, an expanded field list for the Client table in the upper pane, and an empty design grid in the lower pane. (See Steps 1 through 5 on pages AC 68 through AC 70 to create the query and resize the window.)**

• **Double-click the asterisk at the top of the field list.**

The maximized Query1 : Select Query window displays two resized panes. The table name, Client, followed by a period and an asterisk is added to the design grid, indicating all fields are included (Figure 2-12).

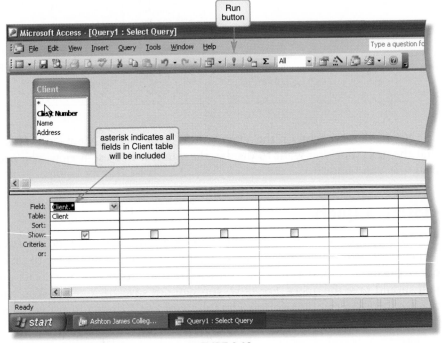

FIGURE 2-12

2

• **Click the Run button.**

The results appear and all fields in the Client table are included (Figure 2-13).

3

• **Click the View button on the Query Datasheet toolbar to return to the Query1 : Select Query window.**

The Query1 : Select Query window replaces the datasheet.

FIGURE 2-13

Clearing the Design Grid

If you make mistakes as you are creating a query, you can fix each one individually. Alternatively, you simply may want to clear the query; that is, clear out the entries in the design grid and start over. One way to clear out the entries is to close the Select Query window and then start a new query just as you did earlier. A simpler approach, however, is to use the Clear Grid command on the Edit menu. The following steps clear the design grid.

To Clear the Design Grid

1

• **Click Edit on the menu bar.**

The Edit menu appears (Figure 2-14).

2

• **Click Clear Grid.**

Access clears the design grid so you can enter your next query.

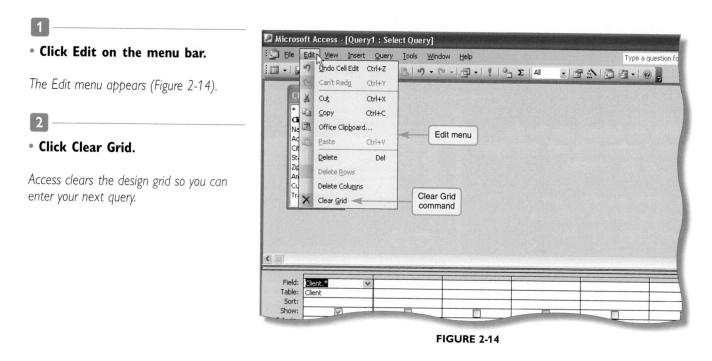

FIGURE 2-14

Entering Criteria

When you use queries, usually you are looking for those records that satisfy some criterion. You might want the name, amount paid, and current due amounts of the client whose number is CP27, for example, or of those clients whose names start with the letters, Fa. To enter criteria, enter them in the Criteria row in the design grid below the field name to which the criterion applies. For example, to indicate that the client number must be CP27, you first must add the Client Number field to the design grid. You then would type CP27 in the Criteria row below the Client Number field.

The next examples illustrate the types of criteria that are available.

Using Text Data in Criteria

To use **text data** (data in a field whose data type is Text) in criteria, simply type the text in the Criteria row below the corresponding field name. The steps on the next page query the Client table and display the client number, name, amount paid, and current due amount of client CP27.

To Use Text Data in a Criterion

1

• **One by one, double-click the Client Number, Name, Amount Paid, and Current Due fields to add them to the query.**

The Client Number, Name, Amount Paid, and Current Due fields are added to the design grid (Figure 2-15).

Client Number, Name, Amount Paid, and Current Due fields included

Criteria row for Client Number field

FIGURE 2-15

2

• **Click the Criteria row for the Client Number field and then type** CP27 **as the criterion.**

The criterion is entered (Figure 2-16). When the mouse pointer is in the Criteria box, its shape changes to an I-beam.

client number must be CP27

FIGURE 2-16

3

• **Click the Run button to run the query.**

The results appear (Figure 2-17). Only client CP27 is included. (The extra blank row contains $0.00 in the Amount Paid and Current Due fields. Unlike text fields, which are left blank, number and currency fields in the extra row contain 0. Because the Amount Paid and Current Due fields are currency fields, the values are displayed as $0.00.)

only Client Number, Name, Amount Paid, and Current Due fields included

only client CP27 included

results of query

FIGURE 2-17

Using Wildcards

Two special wildcards are available in Microsoft Access. **Wildcards** are symbols that represent any character or combination of characters. The first of the two wildcards, the **asterisk** (*), represents any collection of characters. Thus Fa* represents the letters, Fa, followed by any collection of characters. The other wildcard symbol is the **question mark** (?), which represents any individual character. Thus t?m represents the letter, T, followed by any single character followed by the letter, m, such as Tim or Tom.

The following steps use a wildcard to find the number, name, and address of those clients whose names begin with Fa. Because you do not know how many characters will follow the Fa, the asterisk is appropriate.

To Use a Wildcard

1

- **Click the View button on the Query Datasheet toolbar to return to the Query1 : Select Query window.**

- **If necessary, click the Criteria row below the Client Number field.**

- **Use the DELETE or BACKSPACE key as necessary to delete the current entry (CP27).**

- **Click the Criteria row below the Name field.**

- **Type Fa* as the criterion.**

The criterion is entered (Figure 2-18).

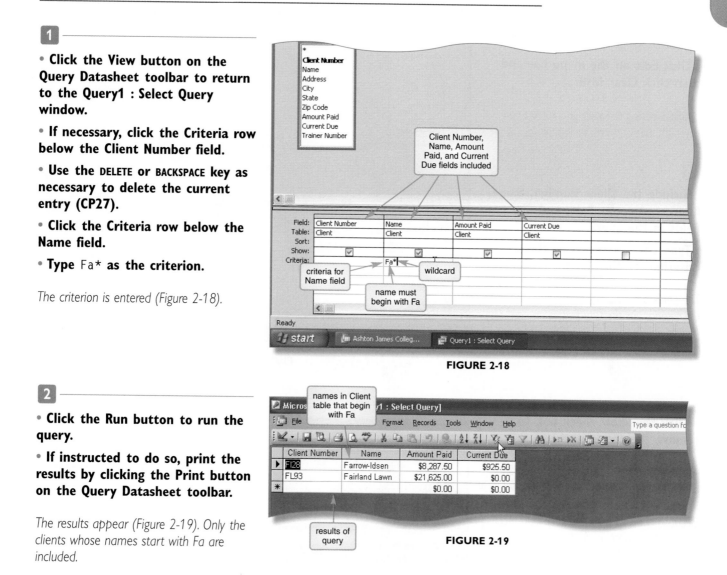

FIGURE 2-18

2

- **Click the Run button to run the query.**

- **If instructed to do so, print the results by clicking the Print button on the Query Datasheet toolbar.**

The results appear (Figure 2-19). Only the clients whose names start with Fa are included.

FIGURE 2-19

Criteria for a Field Not in the Result

In some cases, you may have criteria for a particular field that should not appear in the results of the query. For example, you may want to see the client number, name, address, and amount paid for all clients located in Lake Hammond. The criteria involve the City field, which is not one of the fields to be included in the results.

To enter a criterion for the City field, it must be included in the design grid. Normally, this also would mean it would appear in the results. To prevent this from happening, remove the check mark from its Show check box in the Show row of the grid. The steps on the next page illustrate the process by displaying the client number, name, and amount paid for clients located in Lake Hammond.

Q: Can you add records or edit records in Query Datasheet view?

A: Yes. If the data in the query result is based on one table, you can add and edit records just as you did when the table was displayed in Table Datasheet view.

To Use Criteria for a Field Not Included in the Results

1

• **Click the View button on the Query Datasheet toolbar to return to the Query1 : Select Query window.**

• **Click Edit on the menu bar and then click Clear Grid.**

Access clears the design grid so you can enter the next query.

2

• **Include the Client Number, Name, Address, Amount Paid, and City fields in the query.**

• **Type** Lake Hammond **as the criterion for the City field.**

The fields are included in the grid, and the criterion for the City field is entered (Figure 2-20).

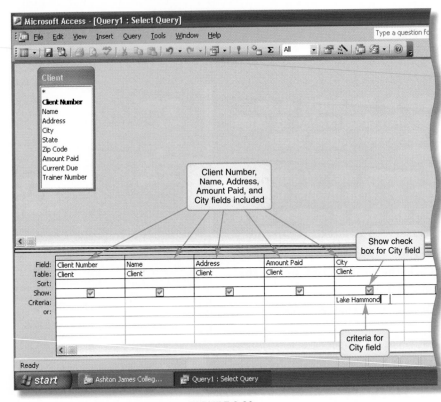

FIGURE 2-20

3

• **Click the Show check box to remove the check mark.**

The check mark is removed from the Show check box for the City field (Figure 2-21), indicating it will not show in the result. Because the City field is a text field, Access has added quotation marks before and after Lake Hammond automatically.

FIGURE 2-21

4

• **Click the Run button to run the query.**

• **If instructed to do so, print the results by clicking the Print button.**

The results appear (Figure 2-22). The City field does not appear. The only clients included are those located in Lake Hammond.

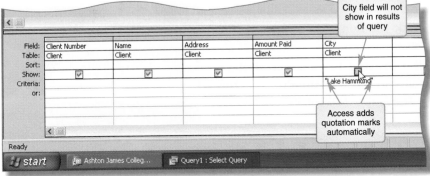

FIGURE 2-22

Creating a Parameter Query

Rather than giving a specific criterion when you first create the query, on occasion, you may want to be able to enter part of the criterion when you run the query and then have the appropriate results appear. For example, to include all the clients located in Tallmadge, you could enter Tallmadge as a criterion in the City field. From that point on, every time you ran the query, only the clients in Tallmadge would appear.

A better way is to allow the user to enter the city at the time the query is run. Thus a user could run the query, enter Tallmadge as the city and then see all the clients in Tallmadge. Later, the user could run the same query, but enter Lake Hammond as the city, and then see all the clients in Lake Hammond. To do this, you create a **parameter query**, which is a query that prompts for input whenever it is run. You enter a parameter, rather than a specific value as the criterion. You create one by enclosing a value in a criterion in square brackets. It is important that the value in the brackets does not match the name of any field. If you enter a field name in square brackets, Access assumes you want that particular field and will not prompt the user for input. For example, you could place [Enter City] as the criterion in the City field.

The following steps create a parameter query that will prompt the user to enter a city, and then display the client number, name, address, and amount paid for all clients located in that city.

Q & A

Q: What actions could you take to find clients located in Lake Hammond rather than Tallmadge?

A: Either create a new query or modify the existing query by replacing Tallmadge with Lake Hammond as the criterion.

More About

Parameter Queries

Parameter queries are especially useful in cases where the same query is run frequently with slight changes to one or more of the query's criteria. By using parameters rather than specific values, you can enter the values for the criterion as the query is run, rather than having to change the query design.

To Create and Run a Parameter Query

1

• **Click the View button on the Query Datasheet toolbar to return to the Query1 : Select Query window.**

• **Erase the current criterion in the City column, and then type** [Enter City] **as the new criterion.**

The criterion is entered (Figure 2-23).

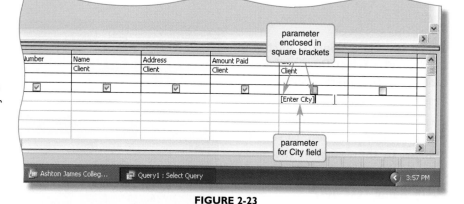

FIGURE 2-23

2

• **Click the Run button to run the query.**

Access displays the Enter Parameter Value dialog box (Figure 2-24). The value (Enter City) previously entered in brackets appears in the dialog box.

FIGURE 2-24

3

• **Type** Tallmadge **in the Enter City text box and then click the OK button.**

The results appear (Figure 2-25). Only clients whose city is Tallmadge are included. The city name is not displayed in the results.

FIGURE 2-25

Each time you run this query, you will be asked to enter a city. Only clients in the city you enter will be included in the results.

Saving a Query

In many cases, you will construct a query you will want to use again. By saving the query, you will eliminate the need to repeat all your entries. The following steps illustrate the process by saving the query you just have created and assigning it the name Client-City Query. You can save with either the query design or the query results appearing on the screen.

To Save a Query

1

• **Click the Close Window button for the Query1 : Select Query window containing the query results.**

• **Click the Yes button in the Microsoft Office Access dialog box when asked if you want to save the changes to the design of the query.**

• **Type** Client-City Query **in the Query Name text box.**

The Save As dialog box appears with the query name you typed (Figure 2-26).

2

• **Click the OK button to save the query.**

Access saves the query and closes the Query1 : Select Query window.

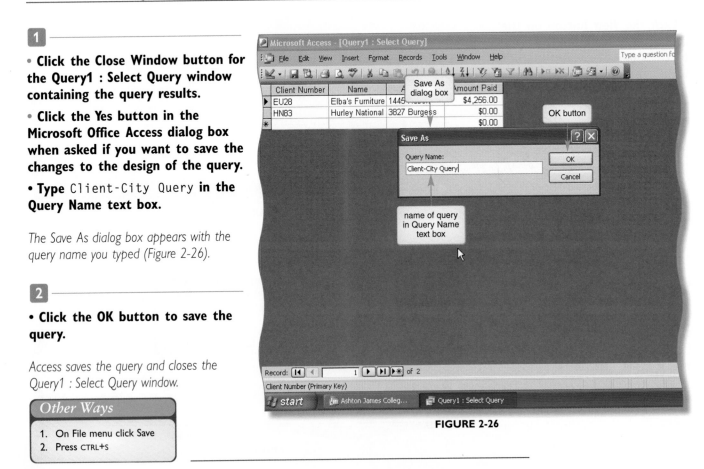

FIGURE 2-26

Other Ways

1. On File menu click Save
2. Press CTRL+S

Using a Saved Query

Once you have saved a query, you can use and manipulate it at any time in the future by opening it. When you right-click the query in the Database window, Access displays a shortcut menu containing commands that allow you to open, print, and change the design of the query. You also can print the results by clicking the Print button on the toolbar. If you want to print the query results without first opening the query, you would click Print on the shortcut menu.

The query is run against the current database. Thus, if changes have been made to the data since the last time you ran it, the results of the query may be different. The following steps use the query named Client-City Query.

More About

Saved Queries

Forms and reports can be based on either tables or saved queries. To create a report or form based on a query, click the Query tab, select the query, click the New Object button arrow, and then click the appropriate command (Report or Form). From that point on, the process is the same as for a table.

To Use a Saved Query

1

• **Click Queries on the Objects bar, and then right-click Client-City Query.**

The shortcut menu for Client-City Query appears (Figure 2-27).

2

• **Click Open on the shortcut menu, type** Tallmadge **in the Enter City text box, and then click the OK button.**

The results appear. They look like the results shown in Figure 2-25.

3

• **Click the Close Window button for the Client-City Query : Select Query window containing the query results.**

FIGURE 2-27

You can use the query at any time by following the above steps. Each time you do so, you will be prompted to enter a city. Only the clients in that city will be displayed in the results.

Using Numeric Data in Criteria

To enter a number in a criterion, type the number without any dollar signs or commas. The steps on the next page display all clients whose current due amount is $0.00.

To Use a Number in a Criterion

1

• **Click the Tables object on the Objects bar and ensure the Client table is selected.**

• **Click the New Object button arrow on the Database toolbar, click Query, and then click the OK button in the New Query dialog box.**

• **Drag the line separating the two panes to the approximate position shown in Figure 2-28, and drag the lower edge of the field box down far enough so all fields in the Client table appear.**

• **Include the Client Number, Name, Amount Paid, and Current Due fields in the query.**

• **Type 0 as the criterion for the Current Due field. You should not enter a dollar sign or decimal point in the criterion.**

The fields are selected and the criterion is entered (Figure 2-28).

FIGURE 2-28

2

• **Click the Run button to run the query.**

• **If instructed to print the results, click the Print button.**

The results appear (Figure 2-29). Only those clients that have a current due amount of $0.00 are included.

FIGURE 2-29

Using Comparison Operators

Unless you specify otherwise, Access assumes that the criteria you enter involve equality (exact matches). In the last query, for example, you were requesting those clients whose current due amount is equal to 0 (zero). If you want something other than an exact match, you must enter the appropriate **comparison operator**. The comparison operators are > (greater than), < (less than), >= (greater than or equal to), <= (less than or equal to), and NOT (not equal to).

The following steps use the > operator to find all clients whose amount paid is more than $20,000.00.

To Use a Comparison Operator in a Criterion

1

- **Click the View button on the Query Datasheet toolbar to return to the Query1 : Select Query window.**

- **Erase the 0 in the Current Due column.**

- **Type >20000 as the criterion for the Amount Paid field. Remember that you should not enter a dollar sign, a comma, or decimal point in the criterion.**

The fields are selected and the criterion is entered (Figure 2-30).

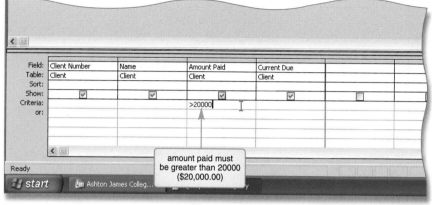

FIGURE 2-30

2

- **Click the Run button to run the query.**

- **If instructed to print the results, click the Print button.**

The results appear (Figure 2-31). Only those clients who have an amount paid greater than $20,000.00 are included.

FIGURE 2-31

Using Compound Criteria

Often you will have more than one criterion that the data for which you are searching must satisfy. This type of criterion is called a **compound criterion**. Two types of compound criteria exist.

In an **AND criterion**, each individual criterion must be true in order for the compound criterion to be true. For example, an AND criterion would allow you to find those clients that have an amount paid greater than $20,000.00 and whose trainer is trainer 48.

Conversely, an **OR criterion** is true provided either individual criterion is true. An OR criterion would allow you to find those clients that have an amount paid greater than $20,000.00 or whose trainer is trainer 48. In this case, any client whose amount paid is greater than $20,000.00 would be included in the answer whether or not the client's trainer is trainer 48. Likewise, any client whose trainer is trainer 48 would be included whether or not the client had an amount paid greater than $20,000.00.

More About

Compound Criteria

The BETWEEN operator allows you to search for a range of values in one field. For example, to find all clients whose amount paid amount is between $5,000 and $10,000, you would enter Between 5000 and 10000 in the Criteria row for the Amount Paid field. It also is possible to create compound criteria involving both OR and AND operators. For more information, visit the Access 2003 More About Web page (scsite.com/ac2003/more) and click Compound Criteria.

Using AND Criteria

To combine criteria with AND, place the criteria on the same line. The following steps use an AND criterion to find those clients whose amount paid is greater than $20,000.00 and whose trainer is trainer 48.

To Use a Compound Criterion Involving AND

1

- **Click the View button on the Query Datasheet toolbar to return to the Query1 : Select Query window.**
- **Include the Trainer Number field in the query.**
- **Type 48 as the criterion for the Trainer Number field.**

Criteria have been entered for the Amount Paid and Trainer Number fields (Figure 2-32).

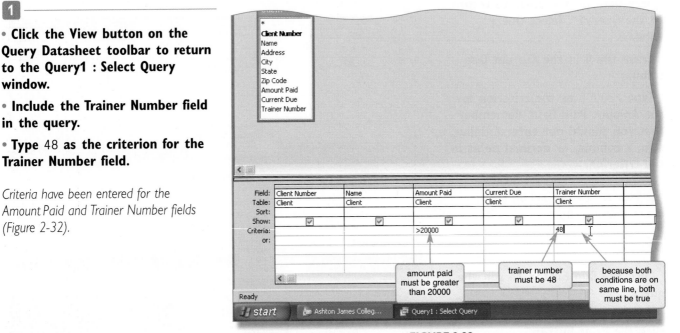

FIGURE 2-32

2

- **Click the Run button to run the query.**
- **If instructed to print the results, click the Print button.**

The results appear (Figure 2-33). Only the clients whose amount paid is greater than $20,000.00 and whose trainer number is 48 are included.

Client Number	Name	Amount Paid	Current Due	Trainer Number
CE16	Center Services	$26,512.00	$2,672.00	48
FL93	Fairland Lawn	$21,625.00	$0.00	48
*		$0.00	$0.00	

FIGURE 2-33

Using OR Criteria

To combine criteria with OR, the criteria must go on separate lines in the Criteria area of the grid. The following steps use an OR criterion to find those clients whose amount paid is greater than $20,000.00 or whose trainer is trainer 48 (or both).

To Use a Compound Criterion Involving OR

1

• **Click the View button on the Query Datasheet toolbar to return to the Query1 : Select Query window.**

2

• **If necessary, click the Criteria entry for the Trainer Number field and then use the BACKSPACE key or the DELETE key to erase the entry ("48").**

• **Click the or row (below the Criteria row) for the Trainer Number field and then type 48 as the entry.**

The criteria are entered for the Amount Paid and Trainer Number fields on different lines (Figure 2-34).

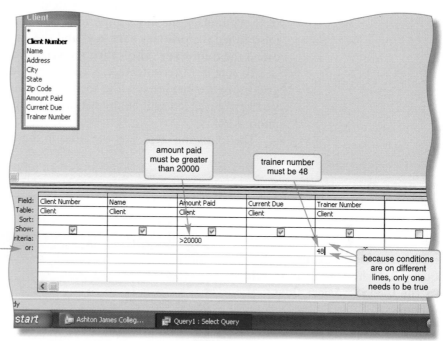

FIGURE 2-34

3

• **Click the Run button to run the query.**

• **If instructed to print the results, click the Print button.**

The results appear (Figure 2-35). Only those clients whose amount paid is greater than $20,000.00 or whose trainer number is 48 are included.

FIGURE 2-35

Sorting Data in a Query

In some queries, the order in which the records appear really does not matter. All you need be concerned about are the records that appear in the results. It does not matter which one is first or which one is last.

In other queries, however, the order can be very important. You may want to see the cities in which clients are located and would like them arranged alphabetically. Perhaps you want to see the clients listed by trainer number. Further, within all the clients of any given trainer, you might want them to be listed by amount paid.

To order the records in the answer to a query in a particular way, you **sort** the records. The field or fields on which the records are sorted is called the **sort key**. If you are sorting on more than one field (such as sorting by amount paid within trainer number), the more important field (Trainer Number) is called the **major key** (also called the **primary sort key**) and the less important field (Amount Paid) is called the **minor key** (also called the **secondary sort key**).

To sort in Microsoft Access, specify the sort order in the Sort row of the design grid below the field that is the sort key. If you specify more than one sort key, the sort key on the left will be the major sort key and the one on the right will be the minor key.

The following steps sort the cities in the Client table.

To Sort Data in a Query

1

• **Click the View button on the Query Datasheet toolbar to return to the Query1 : Select Query window.**

• **Click Edit on the menu bar and then click Clear Grid.**

2

• **Include the City field in the design grid.**

• **Click the Sort row below the City field, and then click the Sort row arrow that appears.**

The City field is included (Figure 2-36). A list of available sort orders appears.

3

• **Click Ascending.**

Ascending is selected as the order (Figure 2-37).

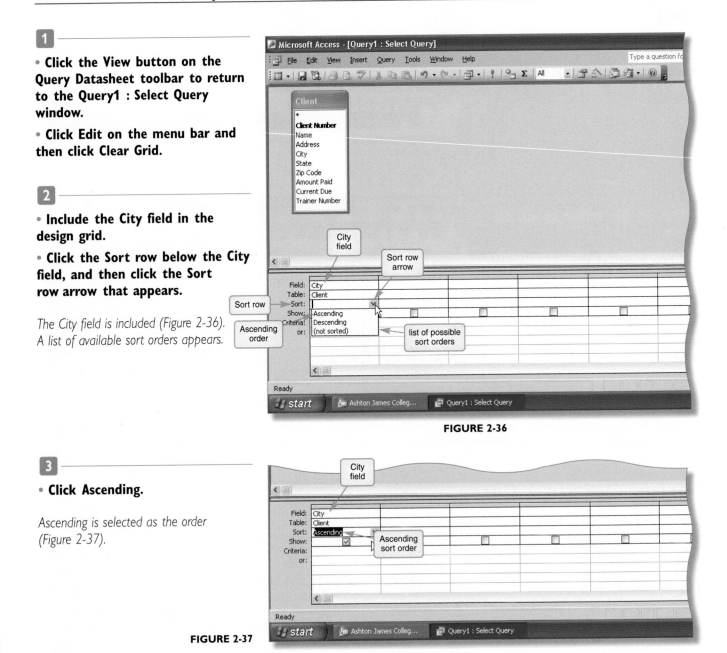

FIGURE 2-36

FIGURE 2-37

4

• **Click the Run button to run the query.**

• **If instructed to print the results, click the Print button.**

The results contain the cities from the Client table (Figure 2-38). The cities appear in alphabetical order. Duplicates, also called **identical rows**, *are included.*

FIGURE 2-38

Omitting Duplicates

When you sort data, duplicates normally are included. In Figure 2-38, for example, San Julio appeared twice, Lake Hammond appeared three times, and Tallmadge appeared twice. To sort to eliminate duplicates, use the Properties button on the Query Design toolbar or the Properties command on the shortcut menu to display the item's property sheet. A **property sheet** is a window containing the various properties of the object. To omit duplicates, you will use the property sheet to change the Unique Values property.

The following steps produce a sorted list of the cities in the Client table in which each city is listed only once.

To Omit Duplicates

1

• **Click the View button on the Query Datasheet toolbar to return to the Query1 : Select Query window.**

• **Click the second field in the design grid (the empty field following City). You must click the second field or you will not get the correct results and will have to repeat this step.**

• **Click the Properties button on the Query Design toolbar.**

Access displays the Query Properties sheet (Figure 2-39). (If your sheet looks different, you clicked the wrong place and will have to repeat the step.)

FIGURE 2-39

2

• **Click the Unique Values property box, and then click the arrow that appears to produce a list of available choices for Unique Values.**

• **Click Yes and then close the Query Properties sheet by clicking its Close button.**

• **Click the Run button to run the query.**

• **If instructed to print the results, click the Print button.**

The results appear (Figure 2-40). The cities are sorted alphabetically. Each city is included only once.

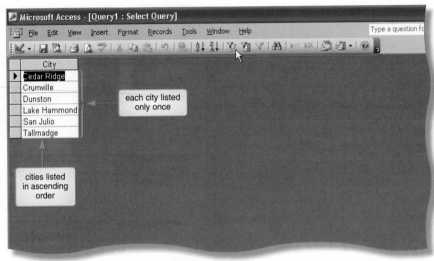

FIGURE 2-40

Other Ways

1. On View menu click Properties
2. Right-click second field in design grid, click Properties on shortcut menu
3. In Voice Command mode, say "Properties"

Sorting on Multiple Keys

The next example lists the number, name, trainer number, and amount paid for all clients. The data is to be sorted by amount paid (low to high) within trainer number, which means that the Trainer Number field is the major key and the Amount Paid field is the minor key.

The following steps accomplish this sorting by specifying the Trainer Number and Amount Paid fields as sort keys.

To Sort on Multiple Keys

1

• **Click the View button on the Query Datasheet toolbar to return to the Query1 : Select Query window.**

• **Click Edit on the menu bar and then click Clear Grid.**

2

• **Include the Client Number, Name, Trainer Number, and Amount Paid fields in the query in this order.**

• **Select Ascending as the sort order for both the Trainer Number field and the Amount Paid field (Figure 2-41).**

FIGURE 2-41

3

- **Click the Run button to run the query.**
- **If instructed to print the results, click the Print button.**

The results appear (Figure 2-42). The clients are sorted by trainer number. Within the collection of clients having the same trainer, the clients are sorted by amount paid.

within trainer numbers, clients sorted by amount paid

overall order is by trainer number

FIGURE 2-42

It is important to remember that the major sort key must appear to the left of the minor sort key in the design grid. If you attempted to sort by amount paid within trainer number, but placed the Amount Paid field to the left of the Trainer Number field, your results would be incorrect.

Creating a Top-Values Query

Rather than show all the results of a query, you may want to show only a specified number of records or a percentage of records. Creating a **top-values query** allows you to quantify the results. When you sort records, you can limit results to those records having the highest (descending sort) or lowest (ascending sort) values. To do so, first create a query that sorts the data in the desired order. Next, use the Top Values box on the Query Design toolbar to change the number of records to be included from All to the desired number. The following steps show the first four records that were included in the results of the previous query.

To Create a Top-Values Query

1

- **Click the View button on the Query Datasheet toolbar to return to the Query1 : Select Query window.**
- **Click the Top Values box on the Query Design toolbar, and then type 4 as the new value.**

The value in the Top Values box is changed from All to 4 (Figure 2-43).

FIGURE 2-43

Top Values box

query results will contain first 4 records

> **More About**
>
> **Joining Tables**
>
> One of the key features that distinguishes database management systems from file systems is the capability of joining tables, that is, of creating queries that draw data from two or more tables. Several types of joins are available. Both an inner join type and an outer join type are illustrated in this project. An inner join is the default join in Access. Access will select all records from two tables that have the same value in the fields that are joined. Outer joins are used to show all the records in one table as well as the common records, that is, the records that share the same value in the join field.

2

• **Click the Run button to run the query.**

• **If instructed to print the results, click the Print button.**

The results appear (Figure 2-44). Only the first four records are included.

3

• **Close the query by clicking the Close Window button for the Query1 : Select Query window.**

• **When asked if you want to save your changes, click the No button.**

The Query1 : Select Query window closes. The query is not saved.

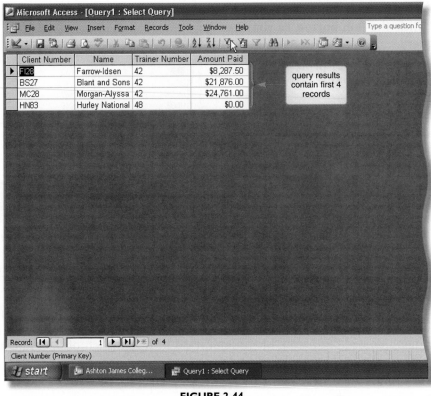

query results contain first 4 records

FIGURE 2-44

When you run a top-values query, it is important to change the value in the Top Values box back to All. If you do not change the Top Values value back to all, the previous value will remain in force. Consequently, you may very well not get all the records you should in the next query.

A good practice whenever you use a top-values query is to close the query as soon as you are done. That way, you will begin your next query from scratch, which guarantees that the value is set back to All.

Joining Tables

The Ashton James College database needs to satisfy a query that requires values from the Client table and the Trainer table. Specifically, the query needs to list the number and name of each client along with the number and name of the client's trainer. The client's name is in the Client table, whereas the trainer's name is in the Trainer table. Thus, this query cannot be satisfied using a single table. You need to **join** the tables; that is, to find records in the two tables that have identical values in matching fields (Figure 2-45). In this example, you need to find records in the Client table and the Trainer table that have the same value in the Trainer Number fields.

Give me the number and name of each client along with the number and name of each client's trainer.

Client table

CLIENT NUMBER	NAME	...	TRAINER NUMBER
BS27	Blant and Sons	...	42
CE16	Center Services	...	48
CP27	Calder Plastics	...	48
EU28	Elba's Furniture	...	53
FI28	Farrow-Idsen	...	42
FL93	Fairland Lawn	...	48
HN83	Hurley National	...	48
MC28	Morgan-Alyssa	...	42
PS82	PRIM Staffing	...	53
TE26	Telton-Edwards	...	48

Trainer table

TRAINER NUMBER	LAST NAME	FIRST NAME	...
42	Perry	Belinda	...
48	Stevens	Michael	...
53	Gonzalez	Manuel	...
67	Danville	Marty	...

Trainer table

CLIENT NUMBER	NAME	...	TRAINER NUMBER	LAST NAME	FIRST NAME	...
BS27	Blant and Sons	...	42	Perry	Belinda	...
CE16	Center Services	...	48	Stevens	Michael	...
CP27	Calder Plastics	...	48	Stevens	Michael	...
EU28	Elba's Furniture	...	53	Gonzalez	Manuel	...
FI28	Farrow-Idsen	...	42	Perry	Belinda	...
FL93	Fairland Lawn	...	48	Stevens	Michael	...
HN83	Hurley National	...	48	Stevens	Michael	...
MC28	Morgan-Alyssa	...	42	Perry	Belinda	...
PS82	PRIM Staffing	...	53	Gonzalez	Manuel	...
TE26	Telton-Edwards	...	48	Stevens	Michael	...

FIGURE 2-45

To join tables in Access, first you bring field lists for both tables to the upper pane of the Select Query window. Access will draw a line, called a **join line**, between matching fields in the two tables indicating that the tables are related. You then can select fields from either table. Access will join the tables automatically.

The first step is to select the Trainer table in the Database window and create a new query. Then, add the Client table to the query. A join line will appear connecting the Trainer Number fields in the two field lists. This join line indicates how the tables are related; that is, linked through these matching fields. (If you fail to give the matching fields the same name, Access will not insert the line. You can insert it manually, however, by clicking one of the two matching fields and dragging the mouse pointer to the other matching field.)

The steps on the next page create a new query, add the Client table and then select the appropriate fields.

Q: Assuming you want the Trainer Number field to be the major key and the Amount Paid field to be the minor key as in the previous steps, how could you display the Amount Paid field before the Trainer Number field?

A: Include the Trainer Number field, the Amount Paid field, and then the Trainer Number field a second time. Select Ascending as the sort order for the first Trainer Number field and for the Amount Paid field. Remove the check mark from the Show check box for the first Trainer Number field. Thus, the first Trainer Number field will be part of the sort key, but will not appear in the results. The second Trainer Number field will appear in the results after the Amount Paid field.

To Join Tables

1

- **With the Tables object selected and the Trainer table selected, click the New Object button arrow on the Database toolbar.**

- **Click Query, and then click the OK button.**

- **Drag the line separating the two panes to the approximate position shown in Figure 2-46, and then drag the lower edge of the field list box down far enough so all fields in the Trainer table appear.**

- **Click the Show Table button on the Query Design toolbar.**

Access displays the Show Table dialog box (Figure 2-46).

FIGURE 2-46

2

- **Be sure the Client table is selected, and then click the Add button.**

- **Close the Show Table dialog box by clicking the Close button.**

- **Expand the size of the field list so all the fields in the Client table appear.**

The field lists for both tables appear (Figure 2-47). A join line connects the two field lists.

FIGURE 2-47

3

• **Include the Trainer Number, Last Name, and First Name fields from the Trainer table as well as the Client Number and Name fields from the Client table.**

• **Select Ascending as the sort order for both the Trainer Number field and the Client Number field.**

The fields from both tables are selected (Figure 2-48).

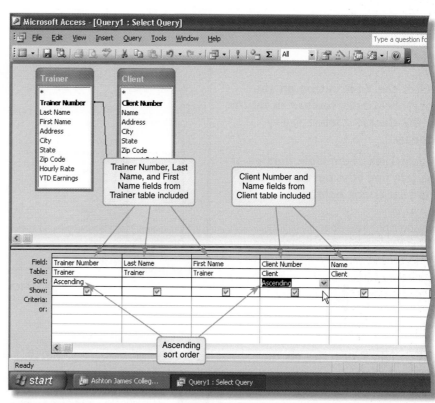

FIGURE 2-48

4

• **Click the Run button to run the query.**

• **If instructed to print the results, click the Print button.**

The results appear (Figure 2-49). They contain data from both the Trainer and Client tables. The records are sorted by trainer number and within trainer number by client number.

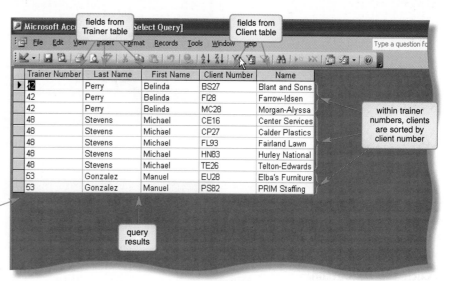

FIGURE 2-49

Changing Join Properties

Normally records that do not match will not appear in the results of a join query. A trainer such as Marty Danville, for whom no clients currently exist, for example, would not appear. To cause such a record to be displayed, you need to change the **join properties**, which are the properties that indicate which records appear in a join, of the query as the steps on the next page illustrate.

Other Ways

1. On Query menu click Show Table
2. Right-click any open area in upper pane, click Show Table on shortcut menu
3. In Voice Command mode, say "Show Table"

To Change Join Properties

1

• **Click the View button on the Query Datasheet toolbar to return to the Query1 : Select Query window.**

• **Right-click the middle portion of the join line (the portion of the line that is not bold).**

The shortcut menu appears (Figure 2-50). (If Join Properties does not appear on your shortcut menu, you did not point to the appropriate portion of the join line. You will need to right-click again.)

FIGURE 2-50

2

• **Click Join Properties on the shortcut menu.**

Access displays the Join Properties dialog box (Figure 2-51).

FIGURE 2-51

3

• **Click option button 2 to include all records from the Trainer table regardless of whether or not they match any clients.**

• **Click the OK button.**

• **Run the query by clicking the Run button.**

• **If instructed to print the results, click the Print button.**

The results appear (Figure 2-52).

FIGURE 2-52

With the change to the join properties, trainer 67 is included, even though the trainer does not have any clients.

Restricting Records in a Join

Sometimes you will want to join tables, but you will not want to include all possible records. In such cases, you will relate the tables and include fields just as you did before. You also will include criteria. For example, to include the same fields as in the previous query, but only those clients whose amount paid is more than $20,000.00, you will make the same entries as before, but also include >20000 as a criterion for the Amount Paid field.

The following steps modify the query from the previous example to restrict the records that will be included in the join.

Q: Why is trainer 67 (Marty Danville) not included in the results shown in Figure 2-54?

A: Trainer 67 currently does not have any clients and consequently does not match any rows in the Clients table.

To Restrict the Records in a Join

1

• **Click the View button on the Query Datasheet toolbar to return to the Query1 : Select Query window.**

• **Add the Amount Paid field to the query.**

• **Type >20000 as the criterion for the Amount Paid field and then click the Show check box for the Amount Paid field to remove the check mark.**

The Amount Paid field appears in the design grid (Figure 2-53). A criterion is entered for the Amount Paid field, and the Show check box is empty, indicating that the field will not appear in the results of the query.

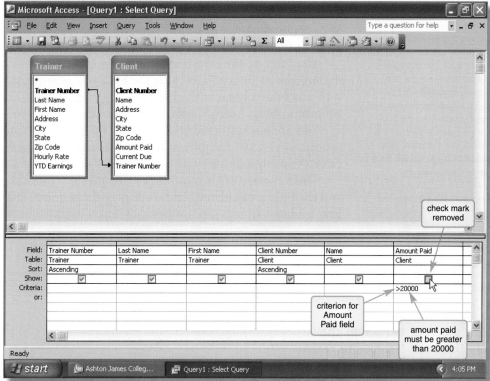

FIGURE 2-53

2

• **Click the Run button to run the query.**

• **If instructed to print the results, click the Print button.**

The results appear (Figure 2-54). Only those clients with an amount paid greater than $20,000.00 are displayed in the result. The Amount Paid field does not appear.

FIGURE 2-54

Calculations

Many types of calculations are available for use in queries. For example, you can add the values in two fields together, or you can calculate the sum or average of the values in one field.

Using Calculated Fields

More About

The Expression Builder

Access includes a tool to help you create complex expressions. If you click Build on the shortcut menu (see Figure 2-55), Access displays the Expression Builder dialog box. The dialog box includes an expression box, operator buttons, and expression elements. You use the expression box to build the expression. You can type parts of the expression directly and paste operator buttons and expression elements into the box. You also can use functions in expressions. For more information, visit the Access 2003 More About Web page (scsite.com/ac2003/more) and click Expression Builder and Functions.

Suppose that Ashton James College wants to know the number of hours worked by each trainer. This poses a problem because the Trainer table does not include a field for hours worked. You can calculate it, however, because the number of hours worked is equal to the YTD earnings divided by the hourly rate. A field that can be computed from other fields is called a **calculated field**.

To include calculated fields in queries, you enter a name for the calculated field, a colon, and then the expression in one of the columns in the Field row. Any fields included in the expression must be enclosed in square brackets ([ ]). For the number of hours worked, for example, you will type Hours Worked:[YTD Earnings]/[Hourly Rate] as the expression.

You can type the expression directly into the Field row. You will not be able to see the entire entry, however, because the Field row is not large enough. The preferred way is to select the column in the Field row and then use the Zoom command on its shortcut menu. When Access displays the Zoom dialog box, you can enter the expression.

You are not restricted to division in calculations. You can use addition (+), subtraction (-), or multiplication (*). You also can include parentheses in your calculations to indicate which calculations should be done first.

The following steps remove the Client table from the query (it is not needed), and then use a calculated field to display the number, last name, hourly rate, year-to-date earnings, and number of hours worked for all trainers.

To Use a Calculated Field in a Query

1

- **Click the View button on the Query Datasheet toolbar to return to the Query1 : Select Query window.**

- **Right-click any field in the Client table field list.**

- **Click Remove Table on the shortcut menu to remove the Client table from the Query1 : Select Query window.**

- **Click Edit on the menu bar and then click Clear Grid. Include the Trainer Number, Last Name, Hourly Rate, and YTD Earnings.**

- **Right-click the Field row in the first open column in the design grid.**

FIGURE 2-55

The shortcut menu appears (Figure 2-55).

2

- **Click Zoom on the shortcut menu.**
- **Type** Hours Worked:[YTD Earnings]/[Hourly Rate] **in the Zoom dialog box that appears.**

Access displays the Zoom dialog box (Figure 2-56). The expression you typed appears within the dialog box.

FIGURE 2-56

3

- **Click the OK button.**

A portion of the expression you entered appears in the fifth field in the design grid (Figure 2-57).

FIGURE 2-57

4

- **Click the Run button to run the query.**
- **If instructed to print the results, click the Print button.**

The results appear (Figure 2-58). Microsoft Access has calculated and displayed the number of hours worked for each trainer.

Trainer Number	Last Name	Hourly Rate	YTD Earnings	Hours Worked
42	Perry	$23.00	$27,620.00	1200.86956522
48	Stevens	$21.00	$23,567.50	1122.26190476
53	Gonzalez	$24.00	$29,885.00	1245.20833333
67	Danville	$20.00	$0.00	0

FIGURE 2-58

Other Ways

1. Press SHIFT+F2

Instead of clicking Zoom on the shortcut menu, you can click Build. Access displays the Expression Builder dialog box that provides assistance in creating the expression. If you know the expression you will need, however, usually it is easier to enter it using the Zoom command.

More About

Calculated Fields

Because it is easy to compute values in a query, it is not necessary to store calculated fields, also called computed fields, in a database. It is not necessary, for example, to store the total amount (the amount paid amount plus the current due amount), because it can be calculated whenever it is required.

Changing Format and Caption

You can change the way items appear in the results of a query by changing their format. You also can change the heading at the top of a column in the results by changing the caption. Just as when you omitted duplicates, you will make this change by using the field's property sheet. In the property sheet, you can change the desired property, such as the format, the number of decimal places, or the caption. The following steps change the format of Hours Worked to Fixed and the number of decimal places to 1, thus guaranteeing that the number on each row will contain exactly one decimal place. They also change the caption of the Hourly Rate field to Rate.

To Change a Format and a Caption

1

• **Click the View button on the Query Datasheet toolbar to return to the Query1 : Select Query window.**

• **If necessary, click the Hours Worked field in the design grid, and then click the Properties button on the Query Design toolbar.**

• **Click the Format box, click the Format box arrow, and then click Fixed.**

• **Click the Decimal Places box, and then type 1 as the number of decimal places.**

Access displays the Field Properties sheet (Figure 2-59). The format is changed to Fixed and the number of decimal places is set to 1.

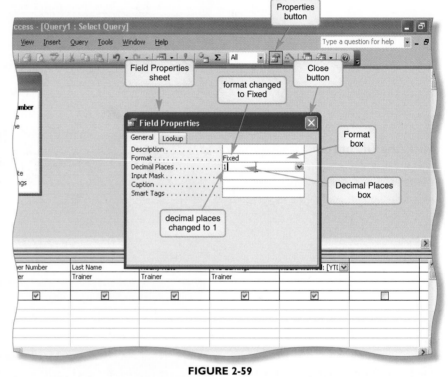

FIGURE 2-59

2

• **Close the Field Properties sheet by clicking its Close button.**

• **Click the Hourly Rate field in the design grid, and then click the Properties button on the Query Design toolbar.**

• **Click the Caption box, and then type Rate as the caption.**

Access displays the Field Properties sheet (Figure 2-60). The caption is changed to Rate.

FIGURE 2-60

3

- **Click the Run button to run the query.**
- **If instructed to print the results, click the Print button.**

The results appear (Figure 2-61). The Hourly Rate caption is changed to Rate. The numbers in the Hours Worked column all contain exactly one decimal place.

4

- **Click the Close Window button for the Query1 : Select Query window.**
- **When asked if you want to save your changes, click the No button.**

The Query1 : Select Query window closes. The query is not saved.

caption for Hourly Rate field changed to Rate

query results

Hours Worked values all have one decimal place

Trainer Number	Last Name	Rate	YTD Earnings	Hours Worked
42	Perry	$23.00	$27,620.00	1200.9
48	Stevens	$21.00	$23,567.50	1122.3
53	Gonzalez	$24.00	$29,885.00	1245.2
67	Danville	$20.00	$0.00	0.0

FIGURE 2-61

If you had saved the query, the changes you made to the properties would be saved along with the query.

Calculating Statistics

Microsoft Access supports the built-in statistics: COUNT, SUM, AVG (average), MAX (largest value), MIN (smallest value), STDEV (standard deviation), VAR (variance), FIRST, and LAST. These statistics are called aggregate functions. An **aggregate function** is a function that performs some mathematical function against a group of records. To use any of these aggregate functions in a query, you include it in the Total row in the design grid. The Total row routinely does not appear in the grid. To include it, click the Totals button on the Query Design toolbar.

The steps on the next page create a new query for the Client table and then calculate the average amount paid for all clients.

Other Ways

1. On View menu click Properties
2. Right-click field in design grid, click Properties on shortcut menu
3. In Voice Command mode, say "Properties"

More About

Calculating Statistics

Virtually all database management systems support the basic set of statistical calculations: sum, average, count, maximum, and minimum as part of their query feature. Some systems, including Access, add several more, such as standard deviation, variance, first, and last.

To Calculate Statistics

1

• **With the Tables object selected and the Client table selected, click the New Object button arrow on the Database toolbar.**

• **Click Query, and then click the OK button.**

• **Drag the line separating the two panes to the approximate position shown in Figure 2-62, and drag the lower edge of the field list box down far enough so all fields in the Client table appear.**

• **Click the Totals button on the Query Design toolbar, and then double-click the Amount Paid field.**

The Total row now is included in the design grid (Figure 2-62). The Amount Paid field is included, and the entry in the Total row is Group By.

FIGURE 2-62

2

• **Click the Total row in the Amount Paid column, and then click the Total row arrow that appears.**

The list of available options appears (Figure 2-63).

FIGURE 2-63

3

• **Click Avg.**

Avg is selected (Figure 2-64).

FIGURE 2-64

4

- **Click the Run button to run the query.**
- **If instructed to print the results, click the Print button.**

The result appears (Figure 2-65), showing the average amount paid for all clients.

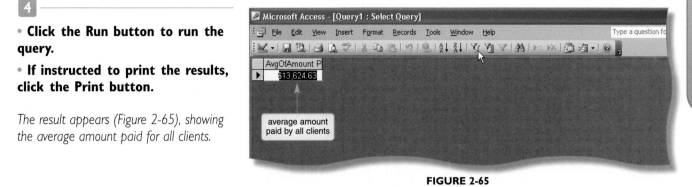

FIGURE 2-65

Using Criteria in Calculating Statistics

Sometimes calculating statistics for all the records in the table is appropriate. In other cases, however, you will need to calculate the statistics for only those records that satisfy certain criteria. To enter a criterion in a field, first you select Where as the entry in the Total row for the field and then enter the criterion in the Criteria row. The following steps use this technique to calculate the average amount paid for clients of trainer 48.

To Use Criteria in Calculating Statistics

1

- **Click the View button on the Query Datasheet toolbar to return to the Query1 : Select Query window.**

2

- **Include the Trainer Number field in the design grid.**
- **Produce the list of available options for the Total row entry just as you did when you selected Avg for the Amount Paid field.**
- **Use the vertical scroll bar to move through the options until the Where option appears.**

The list of available options appears (Figure 2-66). The Group By entry in the Trainer Number field may not be highlighted on your screen depending on where you clicked in the Total row.

FIGURE 2-66

3

• **Click Where.**

• **Type** 42 **as the criterion for the Trainer Number field.**

Where is selected as the entry in the Total row for the Trainer Number field and 42 is entered in the Criteria row (Figure 2-67).

FIGURE 2-67

4

• **Click the Run button to run the query.**

• **If instructed to print the results, click the Print button.**

The results appear (Figure 2-68), giving the average amount paid for clients of trainer 42.

FIGURE 2-68

More About

The Quick Reference

For a table that lists how to complete tasks covered in this book using the mouse, menu, shortcut menu, and keyboard, see the Quick Reference Summary at the back of this book, or visit the Access 2003 Quick Reference Web page (scsite.com/ac2003/qr).

Grouping

Another way statistics often are used is in combination with grouping; that is, statistics are calculated for groups of records. You may, for example, need to calculate the average amount paid for the clients of each trainer. You will want the average for the clients of trainer 42, the average for clients of trainer 48, and so on.

Grouping means creating groups of records that share some common characteristic. In grouping by Trainer Number, for example, the clients of trainer 42 would form one group, the clients of trainer 48 would be a second, and the clients of trainer 53 form a third group. The calculations then are made for each group. To indicate grouping in Access, select Group By as the entry in the Total row for the field to be used for grouping.

The following steps calculate the average amount paid for clients of each trainer.

To Use Grouping

1

- **Click the View button on the Query Datasheet toolbar to return to the Query1 : Select Query window.**

- **Click Edit on the menu bar and then click Clear Grid.**

- **Include the Trainer Number field.**

- **Include the Amount Paid field, and then click Avg as the calculation in the Total row.**

The Trainer Number and Amount Paid fields are included (Figure 2-69). Group By currently is the entry in the Total row for the Trainer Number field, which is correct; thus, it was not changed.

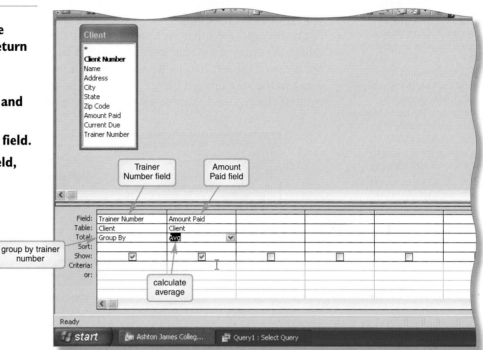

FIGURE 2-69

2

- **Click the Run button to run the query.**

- **If instructed to print the results, click the Print button.**

The results appear (Figure 2-70), showing each trainer's number along with the average amount paid for the clients of that trainer. Because the results are grouped by trainer number, a single row exists for each trainer summarizing all the clients of that trainer.

3

- **Close the query by clicking the Close Window button for the Query1 : Select Query window.**

- **When asked if you want to save your changes, click the No button.**

The Query1 : Select Query window closes. The query is not saved.

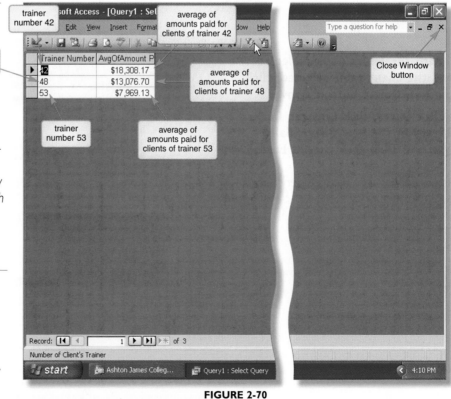

FIGURE 2-70

Microsoft Certification

The Microsoft Office Specialist Certification program provides an opportunity for you to obtain a valuable industry credential — proof that you have the Access 2003 skills required by employers. For more information, see Appendix E, or visit the Access 2003 Certification Web page (scsite.com/ac2003/cert).

More About

Crosstab Queries

Crosstab queries are useful for summarizing data. A **crosstab query** calculates a statistic (for example, sum, average, or count) for data that is grouped by two different types of information. One of the types will appear down the side of the resulting datasheet, and the other will appear across the top. Figure 2-71 shows a crosstab in which the total of amount paid is grouped by both city and trainer number with cities down the left-hand side and trainer numbers across the top. For example, the entry in the row labeled Cedar Ridge and in the column labeled 42 represents the total of the amount paid for all clients of trainer 42 who live in Cedar Ridge.

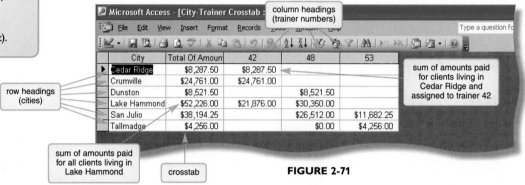

FIGURE 2-71

The following steps use the Crosstab Query wizard to create a crosstab query.

To Create a Crosstab Query

1

• **With the Tables object selected and the Client table selected, click the New Object button arrow.**

• **Click Query, click Crosstab Query Wizard in the New Query dialog box, and then click the OK button.**

Access displays the Crosstab Query Wizard dialog box (Figure 2-72).

FIGURE 2-72

2

• **With the Tables option button selected and the Client table selected, click the Next button.**

• **Click the City field, and then click the Add Field button.**

The Crosstab Query Wizard dialog box displays options for selecting field values as row headings (Figure 2-73). The City field is selected as the field whose values will provide the row headings.

FIGURE 2-73

3

• **Click the Next button, and then click the Trainer Number field.**

The Crosstab Query Wizard dialog box displays options for selecting field values as column headings (Figure 2-74). The Trainer Number field is selected as the field whose values will provide the column headings.

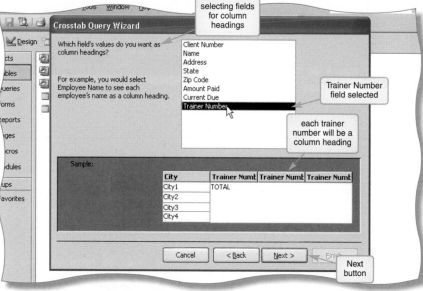

FIGURE 2-74

4

• **Click the Next button, click the Amount Paid field, and then click Sum.**

The Crosstab Query Wizard dialog box displays options for selecting fields for calculations for column and row intersections (Figure 2-75). The Amount Paid field is selected as the field whose value will be calculated for each row and column intersection. Because Sum is the selected function, the calculation will be the total amount paid.

FIGURE 2-75

5

• **Click the Next button, and then type** `City-Trainer Crosstab` **as the name of the query.**

The Crosstab Query Wizard dialog box displays options for naming and viewing the query and modifying the design (Figure 2-76). The name is entered.

6

• **Click the Finish button.**

• **If instructed to print the results, click the Print button.**

The results now can appear. They look like the results shown in Figure 2-71 on page AC 104.

7

• **Close the query by clicking its Close Window button.**

The query no longer appears.

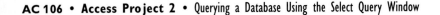

FIGURE 2-76

The query containing the crosstab now can be run just like any other query.

Closing a Database and Quitting Access

The following steps close the database and quit Access.

To Close a Database and Quit Access

1 Click the Close Window button for the **Ashton James College : Database** window.

2 Click the Close button for the **Microsoft Access** window.

Project Summary

In Project 2, you created and ran a variety of queries. You saw how to select fields in a query. You used text data and wildcards in criteria. You created a parameter query, which allowed users to enter a criterion when they run the query. You learned how to save a query for future use and how to use a query you have saved. You also used comparison operators in criteria involving numeric data. You combined criteria with both AND and OR. You saw how to sort the results of a query, how to join tables, how to restrict the records in a join, and how to change join properties. You created computed fields and calculated statistics. You changed formats and captions. You learned how to use grouping. Finally, you learned how to create a crosstab query.

If you have a SAM user profile, you may have access to hands-on instruction, practice, and assessment of the skills covered in this project. Log in to your SAM account and go to your assignments page to see what your instructor has assigned.

What You Should Know

Having completed this project, you should be able to perform the tasks below. The tasks are listed in the same order they were presented in this project. For a list of the buttons, menus, toolbars, and commands introduced in this project, see the Quick Reference Summary at the back of this book and refer to the Page Number column.

1. Open a Database   (AC 68)
2. Create a Query   (AC 68)
3. Include Fields in the Design Grid   (AC 71)
4. Run the Query   (AC 71)
5. Print the Results of a Query   (AC 72)
6. Return to the Select Query Window   (AC 72)
7. Close the Query   (AC 73)
8. Include All Fields in a Query   (AC 74)
9. Clear the Design Grid   (AC 75)
10. Use Text Data in a Criterion   (AC 76)
11. Use a Wildcard   (AC 77)
12. Use Criteria for a Field Not Included in the Results   (AC 78)
13. Create and Run a Parameter Query   (AC 79)
14. Save a Query   (AC 80)
15. Use a Saved Query   (AC 81)
16. Use a Number in a Criterion   (AC 82)
17. Use a Comparison Operator in a Criterion   (AC 83)
18. Use a Compound Criterion Involving AND   (AC 84)
19. Use a Compound Criterion Involving OR   (AC 85)
20. Sort Data in a Query   (AC 86)
21. Omit Duplicates   (AC 87)
22. Sort on Multiple Keys   (AC 88)
23. Create a Top-Values Query   (AC 89)
24. Join Tables   (AC 92)
25. Change Join Properties   (AC 94)
26. Restrict the Records in a Join   (AC 95)
27. Use a Calculated Field in a Query   (AC 96)
28. Change a Format and a Caption   (AC 98)
29. Calculate Statistics   (AC 100)
30. Use Criteria in Calculating Statistics   (AC 101)
31. Use Grouping   (AC 103)
32. Create a Crosstab Query   (AC 104)
33. Close a Database and Quit Access   (AC 106)

Learn It Online

Instructions: To complete the Learn It Online exercises, start your browser, click the Address bar, and then enter the Web address scsite.com/ac2003/learn. When the Access 2003 Learn It Online page is displayed, follow the instructions in the exercises below. Each exercise has instructions for printing your results, either for your own records or for submission to your instructor.

1 Project Reinforcement TF, MC, and SA

Below Access Project 2, click the Project Reinforcement link. Print the quiz by clicking Print on the File menu for each page. Answer each question.

Flash Cards

Below Access Project 2, click the Flash Cards link and read the instructions. Type 20 (or a number specified by your instructor) in the Number of playing cards text box, type your name in the Enter your Name text box, and then click the Flip Card button. When the flash card is displayed, read the question and then click the ANSWER box arrow to select an answer. Flip through Flash Cards. If your score is 15 (75%) correct or greater, click Print on the File menu to print your results. If your score is less than 15 (75%) correct, then redo this exercise by clicking the Replay button.

3 Practice Test

Below Access Project 2, click the Practice Test link. Answer each question, enter your first and last name at the bottom of the page, and then click the Grade Test button. When the graded practice test is displayed on your screen, click Print on the File menu to print a hard copy. Continue to take practice tests until you score 80% or better.

4 Who Wants To Be a Computer Genius?

Below Access Project 2, click the Computer Genius link. Read the instructions, enter your first and last name at the bottom of the page, and then click the PLAY button. When your score is displayed, click the PRINT RESULTS link to print a hard copy.

5 Wheel of Terms

Below Access Project 2, click the Wheel of Terms link. Read the instructions, and then enter your first and last name and your school name. Click the PLAY button. When your score is displayed, right-click the score and then click Print on the shortcut menu to print a hard copy.

6 Crossword Puzzle Challenge

Below Access Project 2, click the Crossword Puzzle Challenge link. Read the instructions, and then enter your first and last name. Click the SUBMIT button. Work the crossword puzzle. When you are finished, click the Submit button. When the crossword puzzle is redisplayed, click the Print Puzzle button to print a hard copy.

7 Tips and Tricks

Below Access Project 2, click the Tips and Tricks link. Click a topic that pertains to Project 2. Right-click the information and then click Print on the shortcut menu. Construct a brief example of what the information relates to in Access to confirm you understand how to use the tip or trick.

8 Newsgroups

Below Access Project 2, click the Newsgroups link. Click a topic that pertains to Project 2. Print three comments.

9 Expanding Your Horizons

Below Access Project 2, click the Expanding Your Horizons link. Click a topic that pertains to Project 2. Print the information. Construct a brief example of what the information relates to in Access to confirm you understand the contents of the article.

10 Search Sleuth

Below Access Project 2, click the Search Sleuth link. To search for a term that pertains to this project, select a term below the Project 2 title and then use the Google search engine at google.com (or any major search engine) to display and print two Web pages that present information on the term.

11 Access Online Training

Below Access Project 2, click the Access Online Training link. When your browser displays the Microsoft Office Online Web page, click the Access link. Click one of the Access courses that covers one or more of the objectives listed at the beginning of the project on page AC 66. Print the first page of the course before stepping through it.

12 Office Marketplace

Below Access Project 2, click the Office Marketplace link. When your browser displays the Microsoft Office Online Web page, click the Office Marketplace link. Click a topic that relates to Access. Print the first page.

Apply Your Knowledge

1 Querying the Begon Pest Control Database

Instructions: Start Access. Open the Begon Pest Control database that you modified in Apply Your Knowledge 1 in Project 1 on page AC 54. (If you did not complete this exercise, see your instructor for a copy of the modified database.) Perform the following tasks:

1. Create a query for the Customer table and add the Name and Address fields to the design grid.
2. Find only those records where the client has an address on Fletcher. Run the query and change the address for the client on 109 Fletcher to 190 Fletcher. Print the results. Return to Design view and clear the grid.
3. Add the Customer Number, Name, City, and Balance fields to the design grid. Sort the records in ascending order by City and descending by Balance. Run the query and print the results. Return to Design view.
4. Modify the query to allow the user to enter a different city each time the query is run. Run the query to find all customers who live in Kady. Print the query results. Save the query as Customer-City Query.
5. Open the Customer-City Query in Design view. Run the query to find all customers who live in Carlton but restrict retrieval to the top two records. Print the results. Close the query without saving it.
6. Create a new query for the Technician table and then join the Technician and Customer tables. Add the Technician Number, First Name and Last Name fields from the Technician table and the Customer Number, and Name fields from the Customer table. Sort the records in ascending order by Technician Number and Customer Number. All technicians should appear in the result even if they currently have no customers. Run the query and print the results.
7. Restrict the records retrieved in task 6 above to only those customers who have a balance greater than $350.00. Run the query and print the results. Close the query without saving it.
8. Create and print the crosstab shown in Figure 2-77. The crosstab groups total of customers' balances by city and technician number.

FIGURE 2-77

In the Lab

1 Querying the Birds2U Database

Problem: The management of Birds2U has determined a number of questions it wants the database management system to answer. You must obtain the answers to the questions posed by management.

Instructions: Use the database created in the In the Lab 1 of Project 1 on page AC 57 for this assignment or see your instructor for information on accessing the files required for this book. Perform the following tasks:

1. Open the Birds2U database and create a new query to display and print the Item Code, Description, On Hand, and Selling Price for all records in the Item table.
2. Display and print the Item Code, Description, Cost, and Supplier Code fields for all products where the Supplier Code is 13.

(continued)

In the Lab

1 Querying the Birds2U Database *(continued)*

3. Display and print the Item Code and Description fields for all items where the description includes the letters "bird."

4. Display and print the Item Code and Description fields for all items with a cost less than $15.00.

5. Display and print the Item Code and Description fields for all products that have a selling price greater than $50.00.

6. Display and print all fields for those items with a selling price greater than $30.00 and where the number on hand is at least 5.

7. Display and print all fields for those items that have a supplier code of 13 or a selling price less than $16.00.

8. Include the Item Code, Description, On Hand, and Selling Price in the design grid. Change the caption for the On Hand column to In Stock and sort the records in descending order by selling price. Run the query and print the results. Run the query again but this time limit retrieval to the top 3 records.

9. Join the Supplier table and the Item table. Display the Supplier Code and Name from the Supplier table and the Item Code, Description, On Hand, and Cost from the Item table. Sort the records in ascending order by Supplier Code and by Item Code. All suppliers should display in the result even if they currently supply no items. Run the query and print the results. Save the query as Suppliers and Items.

10. Restrict the records retrieved in task 9 above to only those products where number on hand is less than 5. Run the query and print the results. Close the query and do not save the changes.

11. Create a new query for the Item table and include the Item Code and Description fields in the design grid. Calculate the on-hand value (on hand * cost) for all records in the table. Run the query and print the results.

12. Display and print the average selling price of all items.

13. Display and print the average selling price of items grouped by supplier code.

2 Querying the Babbage Bookkeeping Database

Problem: Babbage Bookkeeping has determined a number of questions it wants the database management system to answer. You must obtain the answers to the questions posed by the bookkeeping service.

Instructions: Use the database created in the In the Lab 2 of Project 1 on page AC 59 for this assignment or see your instructor for information on accessing the files required for this book. Perform the following tasks:

1. Open the Babbage Bookkeeping database and create a new query for the Client table.

2. Display and print the Name and Balance fields for all clients where the bookkeeper number is 24.

3. Display and print the Client Number, Name, and Balance fields for all clients located in Empeer with a balance greater than $300.00.

4. Display and print the Client Number, Name, and Address fields for all clients with an address on Maum.

5. Display and print the cities in ascending order. Each city should appear only once.

6. Create a query that will allow the user to enter the city to search when the query is run. The query results should display the Client Number, Name, and Bookkeeper Number. Test the query by searching for those records where the client is located in Portage. Save the query as Client-City Query.

7. Include the Client Number, Name, and Balance fields in the design grid. Sort the records in descending order by the Balance field. Display and print the top half of the records.

In the Lab

8. Display and print the Client Number, Name, and Balance fields for all clients where the bookkeeper number is 24 or 34 and the balance is greater than $300.00. (***Hint:*** Use Microsoft Access Help to solve this problem.)

9. Display and print the First Name, Last Name, and Hourly Rate fields from the Bookkeeper table and the Client Number, Name, and Balance fields from the Client table. Sort the records in ascending order by bookkeeper's last name and client's name.

10. Create a new query for the Bookkeeper table and include the Bookkeeper Number, First Name, Last Name, and Hourly Rate in the design grid. Calculate the number of hours each bookkeeper has worked (YTD Earnings/ Hourly Rate). Display hours worked as an integer (0 decimal places). Run the query and print the results.

11. Display and print the following statistics: the total balance for all clients; the total balance for clients of bookkeeper 22; and the total balance for each bookkeeper.

12. Create the crosstab shown in Figure 2-78. The crosstab groups total of clients' balances by city and bookkeeper number. Save the crosstab as City-Bookkeeper Crosstab. Print the crosstab.

FIGURE 2-78

3 Querying the City Guide Database

Problem: The chamber of commerce has determined a number of questions it wants the database management system to answer. You must obtain the answers to the questions posed by the chamber.

Instructions: Use the database created in the In the Lab 3 of Project 1 on page AC 61 for this exercise or see your instructor for information on accessing the files required for this book. Print the answers to each question.

Instructions Part 1: Create a new query for the Advertiser table and include the Advertiser Number, Name, Balance, and Amount Paid fields in the design grid. Answer the following questions: (1) Which advertisers' names begin with C? (2) Which advertisers are located on Main? (3) Which advertisers have a current balance of $0.00? (4) Which advertisers have a balance greater than $150.00 and have an amount paid greater than $800.00? (5) Which five advertisers have the highest balances? (6) For each advertiser, what is the total of the current balance and the amount paid?

Instructions Part 2: Join the Ad Rep table and the Advertiser table. Include the Ad Rep Number, First Name, and Last Name from the Ad Rep table and the Advertiser Number, Name, and Balance from the Advertiser table in the design grid. Sort the records in ascending order by Ad Rep Number and Advertiser Number. Perform the following: (1) Calculate the pending commission (comm rate * balance) for each ad rep. The pending commission should display as currency. (2) Restrict retrieval to only those records where the pending commission is greater than $20.00.

Instructions Part 3: Calculate the following statistics: (1) What is the average balance for advertisers assigned to ad rep 26? (2) What is the total amount paid of all advertisers? (3) What is the total balance for each ad rep?

Cases and Places

The difficulty of these case studies varies:
■ are the least difficult and ■■ are more difficult. The last exercise is a group exercise.

1 ■ Use the College Dog Walkers database you created in Cases and Places 1 in Project 1 on page AC 63 for this assignment or see your instructor for information on accessing the files required for this book. Perform the following: (a) Display and print the number and name of all customers who live on Easton. (b) Display and print the number, name, telephone number, and balance for all customers who have a balance of at least $40.00. (c) Display and print the number, name, balance, walker first name, and walker last name for all customers. Sort the records in ascending order by walker last name. (d) Display and print the average balance of all customers. (e) Display and print the average balance of customers grouped by walker. (f) Display and print the total balance of all customers.

2 ■ Use the InPerson Fitness Company database you created in Cases and Places 2 in Project 1 on page AC 63 for this assignment or see your instructor for information on accessing the files required for this book. Perform the following: (a) Display and print the number, client name, and balance for all clients of a particular trainer. The owner should be able to enter a different trainer number each time the query is run. (b) Display and print the number, client name, and total of balance due and amount paid. (c) Display and print the number, client name, and balance of all clients whose amount paid is greater than $400.00. (d) Display and print the trainer number, trainer name, client number, client name, client address, and client telephone number for all clients. Sort the data ascending by trainer number and client number. (e) Display and print the total amount paid and total balance grouped by trainer.

3 ■■ Use the Regional Books database you created in Cases and Places 3 in Project 1 on page AC 63 for this assignment or see your instructor for information on accessing the files required for this book. Perform the following: (a) List the book code, title, and on-hand value (units on hand * price) of all books. (b) List the book code, title, and price of all paperback books. (c) List the book code, title, price, and publisher name for all books where there are less than 3 books on hand. (d) Display and print the book code, title, and author for all books. (e) Find the lowest priced book and the highest priced book.

4 ■■ Use the Campus Housing database you created in Cases and Places 4 in Project 1 on page AC 64 for this assignment or see your instructor for information on accessing the files required for this book. Display and print the following: (a) List all rental units that are located two miles or less from campus. (b) List all rental units that have parking and allow pets. (c) List all three-bedroom apartments that rent for less than $1,000.00 a month. (d) Find the average rent for two-bedroom apartments. (e) List the owners of all units that are efficiencies or rooms for rent. (f) List the different lease terms in ascending order. Each lease term should display only once.

5 ■■ **Working Together** Create an additional query for each of the four databases described in the Cases and Places. Each team must create a parameter query, a top values query, a crosstab query, and an aggregate query. Select the database to use to create each specific query type. Use all four databases, that is, one database per specific query type. Run each of the queries and print the results. Write a one-page paper that lists the queries the team created and explains why the team chose those queries.

Maintaining a Database Using the Design and Update Features of Access

PROJECT

CASE PERSPECTIVE

Dr. Gernaey and his colleagues at Ashton James College have received many benefits from the database they created and loaded, including the ability to ask questions concerning the data in the database. They now face the task of keeping the database up-to-date. As they take on new clients and trainers, they will need to add new records and make changes to existing records.

Access offers many features for maintaining a database that they want to utilize. For example, they must change the structure of the database to categorize the clients by type. They will do this by adding a Client Type field to the Client table. They discovered the Name field was too short to contain the name of one of the clients, so they will enlarge the size of the field. Along with these changes, they want to change the appearance of a datasheet when displaying data.

They would like the ability to make mass updates, that is, to update many records in a single operation. They want rules that make sure users can enter only valid data into the database, and they want to ensure that it is not possible for the database to contain a client who is not associated with a specific trainer. Finally, they want to improve the efficiency of certain types of processing, specifically sorting and retrieving data. Your task is to help the administration accomplish these goals.

As you read through this project, you will learn how to use the Access design and update features to maintain a database.

Client data

MICROSOFT
Office Access 2003

Maintaining a Database Using the Design and Update Features of Access

PROJECT

3

Introduction

Once a database has been created and loaded with data, it must be maintained. **Maintaining the database** means modifying the data to keep it up-to-date, such as adding new records, changing the data for existing records, and deleting records. Updating can include mass updates or mass deletions; that is, updates to, or deletions of, many records at the same time.

In addition to adding, changing, and deleting records, maintenance of a database can involve the need to **restructure the database** periodically; that is, to change the database structure. This can include adding new fields to a table, changing the characteristics of existing fields, and removing existing fields. It also can involve the creation of indexes, which are similar to indexes found in the back of books. Indexes are used to improve the efficiency of certain operations.

Figure 3-1 summarizes some of the various types of activities involved in maintaining a database.

- Add new records
- Change records
- Delete records
- Search for records
- Filter records
- Change field width
- Add a new field
- Change the appearance of a datasheet
- Use update and delete queries
- Use validation rules
- Create validation values
- Specify default values
- Specify relationships
- Use subdatasheets
- Sort records
- Create indexes to improve performance
- Backup a database
- Compact and repair a database

FIGURE 3-1

Project Three — Maintaining the Ashton James College Database

The steps in this project show how to make changes to the data in the Ashton James College database. They also illustrate how to search for records as well as filter records. The steps restructure the database, that is, make changes that meet the needs of the user, in this case, Ashton James College. This includes adding an additional field as well as increasing the width of one of the existing fields. Other changes modify the structure of the database in a way that prevents users from entering invalid data. Steps are presented to create indexes that reduce the time it takes for some operations, for example, those involving sorting the data.

Opening the Database

If you are stepping through this project on a computer and you want your screen to match the figures in this book, then you should change your computer's resolution to 800 × 600. For more information on how to change the resolution on your computer, see Appendix D. Before carrying out the steps in this project, first you must open the database. The steps on the next page start Access and open the database. The steps assume that the Ashton James College database is located on a disk in drive A. If your database is located anywhere else, you will need to adjust the appropriate steps.

To Open a Database

1 Click the Start button on the Windows taskbar, point to All Programs on the Start menu, point to Microsoft Office on the All Programs submenu, and then click Microsoft Office Access 2003 on the Microsoft Office submenu.

2 If the Access window is not maximized, double-click its title bar to maximize it.

3 If the Language bar appears, right-click it and then click Close the Language bar on the shortcut menu.

4 Click the Open button on the Database toolbar.

5 If necessary, click the Look in box arrow and then click 3½ Floppy (A:). Click Ashton James College, the database modified in Project 2. (If you did not complete the steps in Project 2, see your instructor for a copy of the database.)

6 Click the Open button in the Open dialog box. If the Security Warning dialog box appears, click the Open button.

The database opens and the Ashton James College : Database window appears.

Updating Records

Keeping the data in a database up-to-date requires updating records in three ways: adding new records, changing the data in existing records, and deleting existing records.

Adding Records

In Project 1, you added records to a database using Datasheet view; that is, as you were adding records, the records were appearing on the screen in the form of a datasheet, or table. When you need to add additional records, you can use the same techniques.

In Project 1, you used a form to view records. This is called Form view. You also can use **Form view** to update the data in a table. To add new records, change existing records, or delete records, you will use the same techniques you used in Datasheet view. The following steps add a record to the Client table with a form, for example. These steps use the Client form created in Project 1.

To Use a Form to Add Records

1

• **With the Ashton James College database open, click Forms on the Objects bar, and then right-click the Client form.**

The list of forms appears (Figure 3-2). The shortcut menu for the Client form also appears.

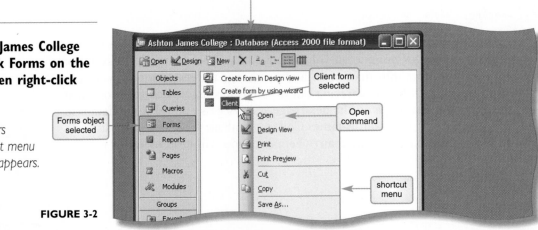

FIGURE 3-2

2

• **Click Open on the shortcut menu.**

The form for the Client table appears (Figure 3-3). Your toolbars may be arranged differently.

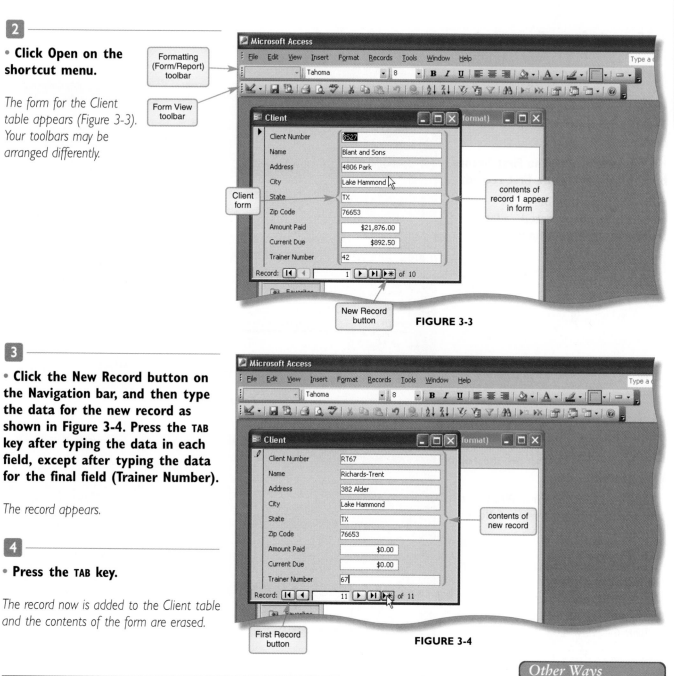

FIGURE 3-3

3

• **Click the New Record button on the Navigation bar, and then type the data for the new record as shown in Figure 3-4. Press the TAB key after typing the data in each field, except after typing the data for the final field (Trainer Number).**

The record appears.

4

• **Press the TAB key.**

The record now is added to the Client table and the contents of the form are erased.

FIGURE 3-4

Searching for a Record

In the database environment, **searching** means looking for records that satisfy some criteria. Looking for the client whose number is FL93 is an example of searching. The queries in Project 2 also were examples of searching. Access had to locate those records that satisfied the criteria.

A need for searching also exists when using Form view or Datasheet view. To update client FL93, for example, first you need to find the client.

You need a way to be able to go directly to a record just by giving the value in some field. This is the function of the Find button. Before clicking the Find button, select the field for the search.

The steps on the next page show how to search for the client whose number is FL93.

Other Ways

1. Click New Record button on Form View toolbar
2. On Insert menu click New Record
3. In Voice Command mode, say "Insert, New Record"

To Search for a Record

1

• **Make sure the Client table is open and the form for the Client table is displayed.**

• **If necessary, click the First Record button to display the first record.**

• **If the Client Number field currently is not selected, select it by clicking the field name.**

The first record appears on the form (Figure 3-5).

FIGURE 3-5

2

• **Click the Find button on the Form View toolbar.**

• **Type** FL93 **in the Find What text box and then click the Find Next button.**

Access displays the Find and Replace dialog box, locates the record for client FL93, and displays it in the Client form (Figure 3-6). The Find What text box contains the entry, FL93.

3

• **Click the Cancel button in the Find and Replace dialog box.**

FIGURE 3-6

Other Ways

1. On Edit menu click Find
2. Press CTRL+F
3. In Voice Command mode, say "Find"

In some cases, after locating a record that satisfies a criterion, you might need to find the next record that satisfies the same criterion. For example, if you just found the first client whose trainer number is 42, you then may want to find the second such client, then the third, and so on. To do so, repeat the same process. You will not need to retype the value each time, however.

Changing the Contents of a Record

After locating the record to be changed, select the field to be changed by clicking the field. You also can press the TAB key repeatedly. Then make the appropriate changes. (Clicking the field automatically produces an insertion point. If you use the TAB key, you will need to press F2 to produce an insertion point.)

Normally, Access is in **Insert mode**, so the characters typed will be inserted at the appropriate position. To change to **Overtype mode**, press the INSERT key. The letters, OVR, will appear near the bottom right edge of the status bar. To return to Insert mode, press the INSERT key. In Insert mode, if the data in the field completely fills the field, no additional characters can be inserted. In this case, you would need to increase the size of the field before inserting the characters. You will see how to do this later in the project.

The following steps use Form view to change the name of client FL93 to Fairland Lawns by inserting the letter s after Lawn. Sufficient room exists in the field to make this change.

To Update the Contents of a Field

1

• **Click in the Name field text box for client FL93 after the word Lawn, and then type s (the letter s) to change the name.**

The name is changed. The mouse pointer shape is an I-beam (Figure 3-7).

FIGURE 3-7

Once you move to another record or close this table, the change to the name will become permanent.

Switching Between Views

Sometimes, after working in Form view where you can see all fields, but only one record, it is helpful to see several records at a time. To do so, switch to Datasheet view. The steps on the next page switch from Form view to Datasheet view.

To Switch from Form View to Datasheet View

 1

• **Click the View button arrow on the Form View toolbar (see Figure 3-7 on the previous page).**

The View button list appears (Figure 3-8).

FIGURE 3-8

2

• **Click Datasheet View, and then maximize the window containing the datasheet by double-clicking its title bar.**

The datasheet appears (Figure 3-9). The position in the table is maintained. The current record selector points to client FL93, the client that appeared on the screen in Form view. The Name field, the field in which the insertion point appears, is selected. The new record for client RT67 is currently the last record in the table. When you close the table and open it later, client RT67 will be in its appropriate location.

FIGURE 3-9

If you want to return to Form view, use the same process. The only difference is that you click Form View rather than Datasheet View.

Filtering Records

You can use the Find button in either Datasheet view or Form view to locate a record quickly that satisfies some criterion (for example, the client number is FL93). All records appear, however, not just the record or records that satisfy the criterion. To have only the record or records that satisfy the criterion appear, use a **filter**. Three types of filters are available: Filter By Selection, Filter By Form, and Advanced Filter/Sort. You can use a filter in either Datasheet view or Form view.

Using Filter By Selection

The simplest type of filter is called **Filter By Selection**. To use Filter By Selection, you first must give Access an example of the data you want by selecting the data within the table. The following steps use Filter By Selection in Datasheet view to display only the records for clients in San Julio.

To Use Filter By Selection

1

• **Click the City field on the second record.**

The insertion point appears in the City field on the second record (Figure 3-10). The city on this record is San Julio.

Filter By Selection button

City field in which city is San Julio

Client Number	Name	Address	City	State	Zip Code	Amount Paid
BS27	Blant and Sons	4806 Park	Lake Hammond	TX	76653	$21,876.00
CE16	Center Services	725 Mitchell	San Julio	TX	78364	$26,512.00
CP27	Calder Plastics	7300 Cedar	Lake Hammond	TX	76653	$8,725.00
EU28	Elba's Furniture	1445 Hubert	Tallmadge	TX	77231	$4,256.00
FI28	Farrow-Idsen	829 Wooster	Cedar Ridge	TX	79342	$8,287.50
FL93	Fairland Lawns	143 Pangborn	Lake Hammond	TX	76653	$21,625.00
HN83	Hurley National	3827 Burgess	Tallmadge	TX	77231	$0.00
MC28	Morgan-Alyssa	923 Williams	Crumville	TX	76745	$24,761.00
PS82	PRIM Staffing	72 Crestview	San Julio	TX	78364	$11,682.25
TE26	Telton-Edwards	5672 Anderson	Dunston	TX	77893	$8,521.50
RT67	Richards-Trent	382 Alder	Lake Hammond	TX	76653	$0.00
*						$0.00

FIGURE 3-10

2

• **Click the Filter By Selection button on the Table Datasheet toolbar (see Figure 3-10).**

• **If instructed to do so, print the results by clicking the Print button on the Table Datasheet toolbar.**

Only the clients located in San Julio appear (Figure 3-11).

Remove Filter button

only records on which city is San Julio appear

Client Number	Name	Address	City	State	Zip Code	Amount Paid
CE16	Center Services	725 Mitchell	San Julio	TX	78364	$26,512.00
PS82	PRIM Staffing	72 Crestview	San Julio	TX	78364	$11,682.25
*						$0.00

FIGURE 3-11

To redisplay all the records, remove the filter as shown in the following step.

To Remove a Filter

1

• **Click the Remove Filter button on the Table Datasheet toolbar (see Figure 3-11 on the previous page).**

All records appear (Figure 3-12).

FIGURE 3-12

After you remove the filter, the button changes from the Remove Filter button to the Apply Filter button as the ScreenTip indicates.

Using Filter By Form

Filter By Selection is a quick and easy way to filter by the value in a single field. For more complex criteria, however, it is not appropriate. For example, you could not use Filter By Selection to restrict the records to those for which the city is Lake Hammond and the trainer number is 42. For this type of query, in which you want to specify multiple criteria, you can use **Filter By Form**. The following steps illustrate using this filtering method in Datasheet view.

To Use Filter By Form

1

• Click the **Filter By Form** button on the Table Datasheet toolbar (see Figure 3-12).

• Click the **City** field (San Julio may appear in the field), click the arrow that appears, and then click Lake Hammond.

• Click the right scroll arrow so the **Trainer Number** field is on the screen, click the **Trainer Number** field, click the down arrow that appears, and then click 42.

The form for filtering appears (Figure 3-13). Lake Hammond is selected as the city, and 42 is selected as the trainer number.

FIGURE 3-13

2

• Click the **Apply Filter** button on the Filter/Sort toolbar.

• If instructed to do so, print the results by clicking the **Print** button on the Table Datasheet toolbar.

The only record included is the record on which the city is Lake Hammond and the trainer number is 42 (Figure 3-14).

FIGURE 3-14

3

• Click the **Remove Filter** button on the Table Datasheet toolbar.

All records are shown.

Using Advanced Filter/Sort

In some cases, your criteria may be too complex even for Filter By Form. For example, you might want to include any client for which the city is Lake Hammond and the trainer is number 42. You also may want to include any client of trainer 48, no matter where the client is located. Further, you might want to have the results sorted by name. To filter records using complex criteria, you need to use **Advanced Filter/Sort** as illustrated in the steps on the next page.

Other Ways

1. On Records menu point to Filter, click Filter By Form on Filter submenu
2. In Voice Command mode, say "Filter By Form"

Microsoft Office
Access 2003

To Use Advanced Filter/Sort

1

• **Click Records on the menu bar, and then point to Filter.**

The Filter submenu appears (Figure 3-15).

FIGURE 3-15

2

• **Click Advanced Filter/Sort.**

Access displays the ClientFilter1 : Filter window (Figure 3-16). The screen looks just like the screens you used to create queries. The city and trainer number criteria from the previous filter appear. If you were creating a different filter, you could delete these.

FIGURE 3-16

3

• **Type** 48 **as the criterion in the second Criteria row (the or row) of the Trainer Number column, double-click the Name field to add the field to the filter, click the Sort row for the Name column, click the arrow that appears, and then click Ascending.**

The additional criteria for the Trainer Number field are entered (Figure 3-17). The data will be sorted on Name in ascending order.

FIGURE 3-17

4

- **Click the Apply Filter button on the Filter/Sort toolbar.**

- **If instructed to do so, print the results by clicking the Print button on the Table Datasheet toolbar.**

The filtered data appears (Figure 3-18). Only the clients who satisfy the criteria in the filter are included. The clients are ordered by name.

5

- **Click the Remove Filter button on the Table Datasheet toolbar.**

All records are shown.

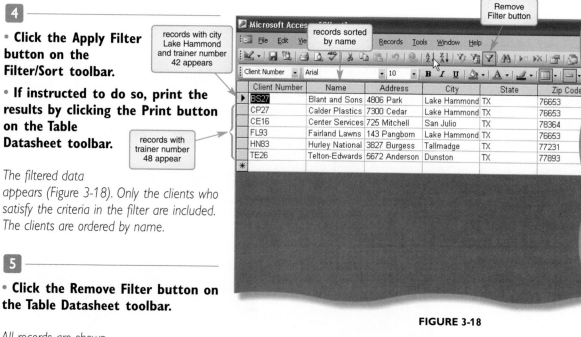

FIGURE 3-18

Deleting Records

When records no longer are needed, **delete the records** (remove them) from the table. For example, suppose client EU28 no longer is served by Ashton James College and its final payment is made. The record for that client should be deleted. The following steps delete client EU28.

To Delete a Record

1

- **With the datasheet for the Client table on the screen, click the record selector of the record in which the client number is EU28.**

The record is selected (Figure 3-19).

Q&A

Q: Can you filter records that have been retrieved as the result of a query?

A: Yes. You can use Filter By Selection, Filter By Form, and Advanced Filter/Sort in the Query Datasheet window just as you did in the Table Datasheet window. You also can use the command in Form view.

Client Number	Name	Address	City	State	Zip Code	Amount Paid
BS27	Blant and Sons	4806 Park	Lake Hammond	TX	76653	$21,876.00
CP27	Calder Plastics	7300 Cedar	Lake Hammond	TX	76653	$8,725.00
CE16	Center Services	725 Mitchell	San Julio	TX	78364	$26,512.00
EU28	Elba's Furniture	1445 Hubert	Tallmadge	TX	77231	$4,256.00
FL93	Fairland Lawns	143 Pangborn	Lake Hammond	TX	76653	$21,625.00
FI28	Farrow-Idsen	829 Wooster	Cedar Ridge	TX	79342	$8,287.50
HN83	Hurley National	3827 Burgess	Tallmadge	TX	77231	$0.00
MC28	Morland Alyssa	923 Williams	Crumville	TX	76745	$24,761.00
PS82	PRIM Staffing	72 Crestview	San Julio	TX	78364	$11,682.25
RT67	Richards-Trent	382 Alder	Lake Hammond	TX	76653	$0.00
TE26	Telton-Edwards	5672 Anderson	Dunston	TX	77893	$8,521.50
*						$0.00

FIGURE 3-19

2

• **Press the DELETE key to delete the record.**

Access displays the Microsoft Office Access dialog box (Figure 3-20). The message indicates that one record will be deleted.

3

• **Click the Yes button to complete the deletion.**

• **If instructed to do so, print the results by clicking the Print button on the Table Datasheet toolbar.**

• **Close the window containing the table by clicking its Close Window button.**

The record is deleted and the table no longer appears.

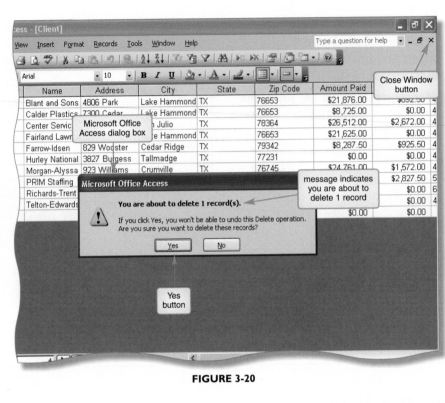

FIGURE 3-20

You can delete records using a form just as you delete records using a datasheet. To do so, first navigate to the record to be deleted. For example, you can use the Navigation buttons or you can locate the desired record using the Find button. The following steps illustrate how to delete a record in Form view after you have located the record to be deleted.

To Delete a Record in Form View

1. Click the Record Selector (the triangle in front of the record) to select the entire record.
2. Press the DELETE key.
3. When Access displays the dialog box asking if you want to delete the record, click the Yes button.

Changing the Structure

When you initially create a database, you define its **structure**; that is, you indicate the names, types, and sizes of all the fields. In many cases, the structure you first define will not continue to be appropriate as you use the database.

Characteristics of a given field may need to change. For example, a client name might be stored incorrectly in the database. In this example, the name Morgan-Alyssa actually should be Morgan-Alyssa Academy. The Name field is not large enough, however, to hold the correct name. To accommodate this change, you need to restructure the database by increasing the width of the Name field.

It may be that a field currently in the table no longer is necessary. If no one ever uses a particular field, it is not needed in the table. Because it is occupying space and serving no useful purpose, it should be removed from the table. You also would need to delete the field from any forms, reports, or queries that include it.

To make any of these changes, you first must open the table in Design view.

Changing the Size of a Field

The following steps change the size of the Name field from 20 to 25 to accommodate the change of name from Morgan-Alyssa to Morgan-Alyssa Academy.

To Change the Size of a Field

1

• **In the Database window, click Tables on the Objects bar, and then right-click Client.**

The shortcut menu for the Client table appears (Figure 3-21).

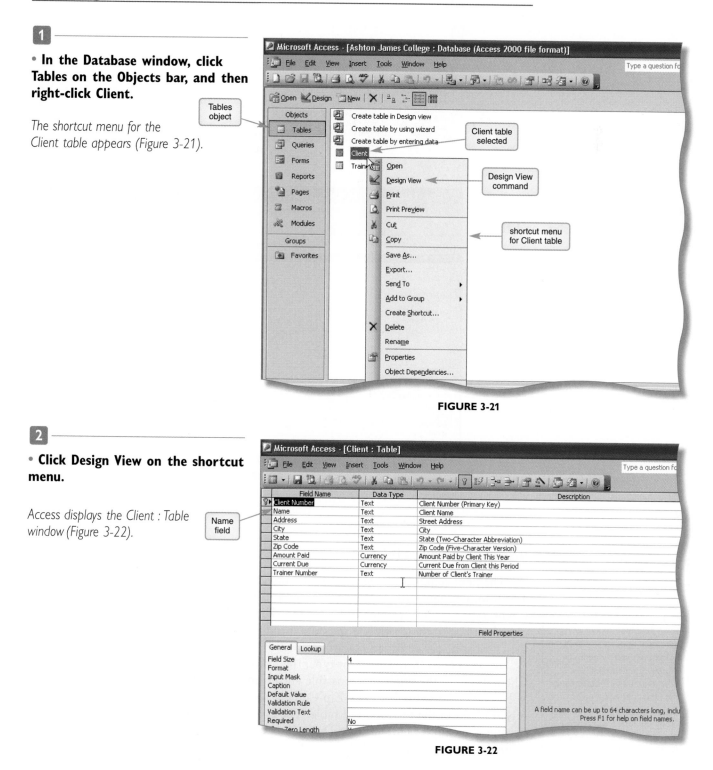

FIGURE 3-21

2

• **Click Design View on the shortcut menu.**

Access displays the Client : Table window (Figure 3-22).

FIGURE 3-22

3

- **Click the row selector for the Name field.**

The Name field is selected (Figure 3-23).

Microsoft Access - [Client : Table]

Name field selected

Field Name	Data Type	Description
Client Number	Text	Client Number (Primary Key)
Name	Text	Client Name
Address	Text	Street Address
City	Text	City
State	Text	State (Two-Character Abbreviation)
Zip Code	Text	Zip Code (Five-Character Version)
Amount Paid	Currency	Amount Paid by Client This Year
Current Due	Currency	Current Due from Client this Period
Trainer Number	Text	Number of Client's Trainer

Field Properties

General | Lookup

Field Size	20
Format	
Input Mask	
Caption	
Default Value	
Validation Rule	

current field size will be changed to 25

FIGURE 3-23

4

- **Press F6 to select the field size, type 25 as the new size, and then press F6 again.**

The field size is changed (Figure 3-24).

Microsoft Access - [Client : Table]

File Edit View Insert Tools Window Help

Field Name	Data Type	Description
Client Number	Text	Client Number (Primary Key)
Name	Text	Client Name
Address	Text	Street Address
City	Text	City
State	Text	State (Two-Character Abbreviation)
Zip Code	Text	Zip Code (Five-Character Version)
Amount Paid	Currency	Amount Paid by Client This Year
Current Due	Currency	Current Due from Client this Period
Trainer Number	Text	Number of Client's Trainer

Field Properties

General | Lookup

Field Size	25
Format	
Input Mask	
Caption	
Default Value	
Validation	

field size changed to 25

FIGURE 3-24

Adding a New Field

The next step is to categorize the clients of the Ashton James College database. To do so, you must add an additional field, Client Type. The possible values for Client Type are EDU (which indicates the client is an educational institution), MAN (which indicates the client is a manufacturing organization), or SER (which indicates the client is a service organization).

To be able to store the client type, the following steps add a new field, called Client Type, to the table. The possible entries in this field are EDU, MAN, and SER. The new field will follow Zip Code in the list of fields; that is, it will be the seventh field in the restructured table. The current seventh field (Amount Paid) will become the eighth field, Current Due will become the ninth field, and so on. The following steps add the field.

To Add a Field to a Table

1

- **Click the row selector for the Amount Paid field, and then press the INSERT key to insert a blank row.**

A blank row appears in the position for the new field (Figure 3-25).

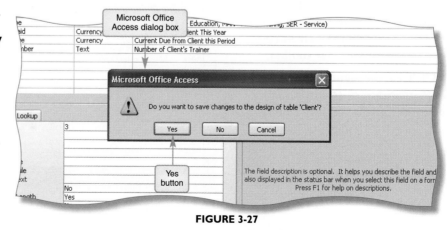

FIGURE 3-25

2

- **Click the Field Name column for the new field.**

- **Type** Client Type **as the field name and then press the TAB key. Select the Text data type by pressing the TAB key.**

- **Type** Client Type (EDU - Education, MAN - Manufacturing, SER - Service) **as the description.**

- **Press F6 to move to the Field Size text box, type** 3 **(the size of the Client Type field), and then press F6 again.**

The entries for the new field are complete (Figure 3-26).

FIGURE 3-26

3

- **Close the Client : Table window by clicking its Close Window button.**

The Microsoft Office Access dialog box is displayed (Figure 3-27).

4

Click the Yes button to save the changes.

The changes are saved.

FIGURE 3-27

Other Ways

1. Click Insert Rows button on Table Design toolbar
2. On Insert menu click Rows
3. In Voice Command mode, say "Insert Rows"

More About

Moving a Field in a Table Structure

If you add a field to a table and later realize the field is in the wrong location, you can move the field. To do so, click the row selector for the field twice, and then drag the field to the new location.

More About

Changing Data Types

It is possible to change the data type for a field that already contains data. Before you change a data type, however, you should consider what effect the change will have on other database objects, such as forms, queries, and reports. For example, you could convert a Text field to a Memo field or to a Hyperlink field. You also could convert a Number field to a Currency field or vice versa.

The Client Type field now is included in the table and available for use.

Deleting a Field

If a field in one of your tables no longer is needed; for example, it serves no useful purpose or it may have been included by mistake, you should delete the field. The following steps illustrate how to delete a field.

To Delete a Field

1. Open the table in Design view.
2. Click the row selector for the field to be deleted.
3. Press the DELETE key.
4. When Access displays the dialog box requesting confirmation that you want to delete the field, click the Yes button.

When you save your changes to the table structure, the field will be removed from the table.

Updating the Restructured Database

Changes to the structure are available immediately. The Name field is longer, although it does not appear that way on the screen, and the new Client Type field is included.

To make a change to a single field, such as changing the name from Morgan-Alyssa to Morgan-Alyssa Academy, click the field to be changed, and then make the necessary correction. If the record to be changed is not on the screen, use the Navigation buttons (Next Record, Previous Record) to move to it. If the field to be corrected simply is not visible on the screen, use the horizontal scroll bar along the bottom of the screen to shift all the fields until the correct one appears. Then make the change.

The following step changes the name of Morgan-Alyssa to Morgan-Alyssa Academy.

To Update the Contents of a Field

1

• **Be sure the Client table is selected in the Database window, and then click the Open button on the Database window toolbar.**

• **Click to the right of the final a in Morgan-Alyssa (client MC28), press the SPACEBAR, and then type** Academy **to change the name.**

The name is changed from Morgan-Alyssa to Morgan-Alyssa Academy (Figure 3-28). Only the final portion of the name currently appears.

Client Number	Name	Address	City	State	Zip Code	Client Type
BS27	Blant and Sons	4806 Park	Lake Hammond	TX	76653	
CE16	Center Services	ell	San Julio	TX	78364	
CP27	Calder Plastics		Lake Hammond	TX	76653	
FI28	Farrow-Idsen	829 Wooster	Cedar Ridge	TX	79342	
FL93	Fairland Lawns	143 Pangborn	Lake Hammond	TX	76653	
HN83	Hurley National	3827 Burgess	Tallmadge	TX	77231	
MC28	yssa Academy	923 Williams	Crumville	TX	76745	
PS82	PRIM Staffing	72 Crestview	San Julio	TX	78364	
RT67	Richards-Trent	382 Alder	Lake Hammond	TX	76653	
TE26	Telton-Edwards	5672 Anderson	Dunston	TX	77893	

FIGURE 3-28

Changing the Appearance of a Datasheet

You can change the appearance of a datasheet in a variety of ways. You can resize columns and rows. You can change the font, the font size, the font style, and the color. You also can change the color of the gridlines in the datasheet as well as the cell effects.

Resizing Columns

The Access default column sizes do not always allow all the data in the field to appear. You can correct this problem by **resizing** the column (changing its size) in the datasheet. In some instances, you actually may want to reduce the size of a column. The State field, for example, is short enough that it does not require all the space on the screen that is allotted to it.

Both types of changes are made the same way. Position the mouse pointer on the right boundary of the column's **field selector** (the line in the column heading immediately to the right of the name of the column to be resized). The mouse pointer will change to a two-headed arrow with a vertical bar. You then can drag the line to resize the column. In addition, you can double-click in the line, in which case Access will determine the **best fit** for the column.

The following steps illustrate the process for resizing the Name column to the size that best fits the data.

To Resize a Column

1

• **Point to the right boundary of the field selector for the Name field.**

The mouse pointer shape changes to a bar with a double-arrow, indicating that the column can be resized (Figure 3-29).

FIGURE 3-29

2

• **Double-click the right boundary of the field selector for the Name field.**

The Name column has been resized (Figure 3-30).

FIGURE 3-30

3

• **Use the same technique to resize the Client Number, Address, City, State, Zip Code, Client Type, and Amount Paid columns to best fit the data.**

The columns have been resized (Figure 3-31).

columns resized

Name	Address	City	State	Zip Code	Client Type	Amount Paid	↓Curren'
Blant and Sons	4806 Park	Lake Hammond	TX	76653		$21,876.00	$8
Center Services	725 Mitchell	San Julio	TX	78364		$26,512.00	$2,8
Calder Plastics	7300 Cedar	Lake Hammond	TX	76653		$8,725.00	
Farrow-Idsen	829 Wooster	Cedar Ridge	TX	79342		$8,287.50	$9
Fairland Lawns	143 Pangborn	Lake Hammond	TX	76653		$21,625.00	
Hurley National	3827 Burgess	Tallmadge	TX	77231		$0.00	
Morgan-Alyssa Academy	923 Williams	Crumville	TX	76745		$24,761.00	$1,5
PRIM Staffing	72 Crestview	San Julio	TX	78364		$11,682.25	$2,8
Richards-Trent	382 Alder	Lake Hammond	TX	76653		$0.00	
Telton-Edwards	5672 Anderson	Dunston	TX	77893		$8,521.50	

right scroll arrow

7 ▶ ▶| ▶* of 10

Ashton James Colleg...   Client : Table   9:00 AM

FIGURE 3-31

4

• **If necessary, click the right scroll arrow to display the Current Due and Trainer Number columns, and then resize the columns to best fit the data.**

All the columns have been resized (Figure 3-32).

remaining columns resized

City	State	Zip Code	Client Type	Amount Paid	Current Due	Trainer Number
Lake Hammond	TX	76653		$21,876.00	$892.50	42
San Julio	TX	78364		$26,512.00	$2,672.00	48
Lake Hammond	TX	76653		$8,725.00	$0.00	48
Cedar Ridge	TX	79342		$8,287.50	$925.50	42
Lake Hammond	TX	76653		$21,625.00	$0.00	48
Tallmadge	TX	77231		$0.00	$0.00	48
Crumville	TX	76745		$24,761.00	$1,572.00	42
San Julio	TX	78364		$11,682.25	$2,827.50	53
Lake Hammond	TX	76653		$0.00	$0.00	67
Dunston	TX	77893		$8,521.50	$0.00	48
				$0.00	$0.00	

Close Window button

FIGURE 3-32

5

• **Close the Client : Table window by clicking its Close Window button.**

The Microsoft Office Access dialog box is displayed (Figure 3-33). Changing a column width changes the layout, or design, of a table.

6

• **Click the Yes button.**

The next time the datasheet is displayed, the columns will have the new widths.

Microsoft Office Access dialog box

Microsoft Office Access

⚠ Do you want to save changes to the layout of table 'Client'?

Yes   No   Cancel

Yes button   No button

FIGURE 3-33

The change to the layout is saved.

Formatting a Datasheet

In addition to changing the column size, you can format a datasheet in other ways. You can change various aspects of the font, including the font itself, the font style, the size, and the color. You can change the cell effects to make the cells appear raised or sunken, and you can change the gridline color.

The changes to the datasheet will be reflected not only on the screen, but also when you print or preview the datasheet.

In this section, the following steps illustrate how to change the font in the datasheet and the format of the datasheet grid. You then will preview what the datasheet would look like when it is printed. At this point, you can print the datasheet if you so desire. Finally, you will close the datasheet without saving the changes. That way, the next time you view the datasheet, it will appear in its original format.

These steps show how to open the Trainer table in Datasheet view and then change the font.

To Change the Font in a Datasheet

1

- **With the Tables object selected and the Trainer table selected, click the Open button on the Database Window toolbar.**

- **Click Format on the menu bar.**

Access displays the Trainer table in Datasheet view (Figure 3-34). The Format menu appears.

FIGURE 3-34

2

- **Click Font, click Arial Rounded MT Bold in the Font list, and then click 9 in the Size list. (If you do not have Arial Rounded MT Bold available, click another similar font.)**

Access displays the Font dialog box (Figure 3-35). Arial Rounded MT Bold is selected as the font style and 9 is selected as the font size.

3

- **Click the OK button.**

The font is changed.

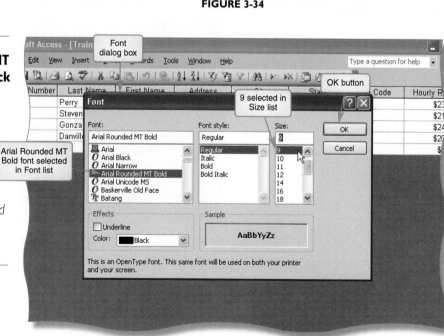

FIGURE 3-35

The following steps change the format of the grid.

To Change the Format of the Datasheet Grid

1

• **Click Format on the menu bar, and then click Datasheet.**

Access displays the Datasheet Formatting dialog box (Figure 3-36).

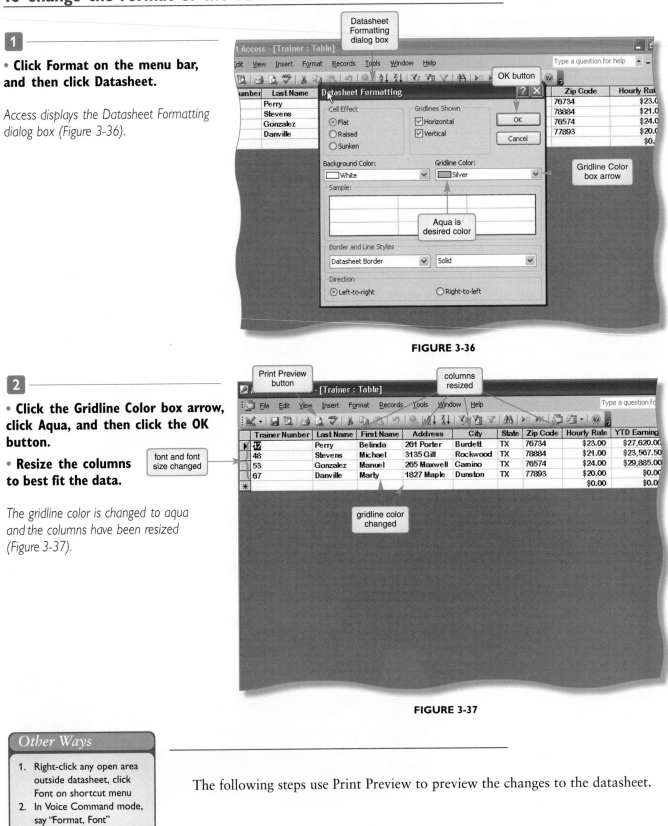

FIGURE 3-36

2

• **Click the Gridline Color box arrow, click Aqua, and then click the OK button.**

• **Resize the columns to best fit the data.**

The gridline color is changed to aqua and the columns have been resized (Figure 3-37).

FIGURE 3-37

The following steps use Print Preview to preview the changes to the datasheet.

To Use Print Preview

1

- Click the Print Preview button on the Table Datasheet toolbar.

- If instructed to do so, print the results by clicking the Print button on the Print Preview toolbar.

Access displays the pre-view window (Figure 3-38). The changes in the datasheet format are reflected in the preview.

2

- Click the Close button on the Print Preview toolbar.

The preview no longer appears.

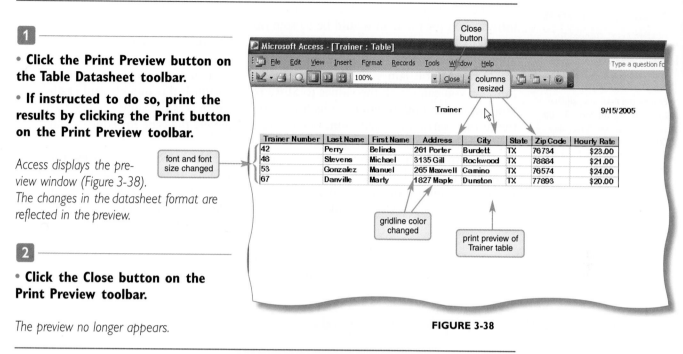

FIGURE 3-38

To print the datasheet, click the Print button on either the Table Datasheet toolbar or the Print Preview toolbar. The changes to the format are reflected in the printout.

The following steps show how to close the datasheet without saving the changes to the format.

To Close the Datasheet Without Saving the Format Changes

1 Click the Close Window button for the Trainer : Table window.

2 Click the No button in the Microsoft Office Access dialog box when asked if you want to save your changes.

Because the changes are not saved, the next time you open the Trainer table it will appear in the original format (see Figure 3-34 on page AC 133). If you had saved the changes, the changes would be reflected in its appearance.

Mass Changes

In some cases, rather than making individual changes, you will want to make mass changes. That is, you will want to add, change, or delete many records in a single operation. You can do this with queries. An update query allows you to make the same change to all records satisfying some criterion. If you omit the criterion, you will make the same changes to all records in the table. A delete query allows you to delete all the records satisfying some criterion. You can add the results of a query to an existing table by using an append query. You also can add the results to a new table by using a make-table query.

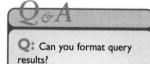

Q: Can you format query results?

A: Yes. You can format the results of a query in Query Datasheet view just as you can in Table Datasheet view. You can resize columns, change various aspects of the font, change cell effects, and change gridline colors.

More About

Action Queries

An action query is a query that makes changes to many records in just one operation. The four types of action queries are: delete, update, append, and make-table.

More About

Resizing Columns

After you have changed the size of a field, the forms you have created will not reflect your changes. If you used the AutoForm command, you can change the field sizes simply by recreating the form. To do so, right-click the form, click Delete on the shortcut menu, and then create the form as you did in Project 1.

Using an Update Query

The Client Type field is blank on every record. One approach to entering the information for the field would be to step through the entire table, assigning each record its appropriate value. If most of the clients have the same type, a simpler approach is available.

In the Ashton James College database, for example, most clients are type SER. Initially, you can set all the values to SER. To accomplish this quickly and easily, you can use an **update query**, which is a query that makes the same change to all the records satisfying a criterion. Later, you can change the type for educational institutions and manufacturing organizations.

The process for creating an update query begins the same as the process for creating the queries in Project 2. You select the table for the query and then use the Query Type button to change to an update query. In the design grid, an extra row, Update To, appears. Use this additional row to indicate the way the data will be updated. If a criterion is entered, then only those records that satisfy the criterion will be updated.

The following steps change the value in the Client Type field to SER for all the records. Because all records are to be updated, criteria are not required.

To Use an Update Query to Update All Records

1

• **With the Client table selected, click the New Object button arrow on the Database toolbar and then click Query. With Design View selected in the New Query dialog box, click the OK button.**

• **Be sure the Query1 : Select Query window is maximized.**

• **Resize the upper and lower panes of the window as well as the Client field list so all fields in the Client table field list appear (see Figure 2-6 on page AC 70 in Project 2).**

Click the Query Type button arrow on the Query Design toolbar.

The list of available query types appears (Figure 3-39).

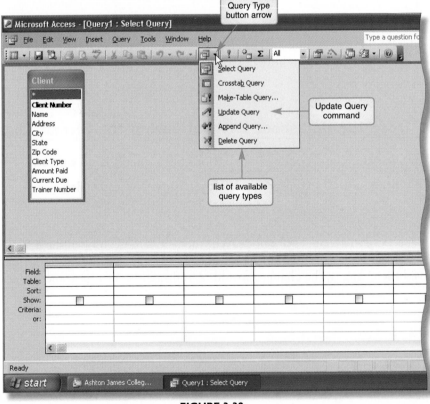

FIGURE 3-39

2

• **Click Update Query, double-click the Client Type field to select the field, click the Update To row in the first column of the design grid, and then type SER as the new value.**

The Client Type field is selected (Figure 3-40). In an update query, the Update To row appears in the design grid. The value to which the field is to be changed is entered as SER. Because no criteria are entered, the Client Type value on every row will be changed to SER.

FIGURE 3-40

3

• **Click the Run button on the Query Design toolbar.**

The Microsoft Office Access dialog box is displayed (Figure 3-41). The message indicates that 10 rows (records) will be updated by the query.

4

• **Click the Yes button.**

The changes are made.

FIGURE 3-41

Using a Delete Query

In some cases, you may need to delete several records at a time. If, for example, all clients in a particular Zip code are to be serviced by another firm, the clients with this Zip code can be deleted from the Ashton James College database. Instead of deleting these clients individually, which could be very time-consuming in a large database, you can delete them in one operation by using a **delete query**, which is a query that will delete all the records satisfying the criteria entered in the query.

You can preview the data to be deleted in a delete query before actually performing the deletion. To do so, click the View button arrow on the Query Design toolbar and then click Datasheet View after you create the query, but before you run it. The records to be deleted then would appear in Datasheet view. To delete the records, click the View button arrow on the Query Datasheet toolbar and then click Design View to return to Design view. Click the Run button on the Query Design toolbar, and then click the Yes button in the Microsoft Office Access dialog box when asked if you want to delete the records.

The steps on the next page use a delete query to delete any client whose Zip code is 77893 without first previewing the data to be deleted. (Only one such client currently exists in the database.)

Other Ways

1. On Query menu click Update Query
2. Right-click any open area in upper pane, point to Query Type on shortcut menu, click Update Query on Query Type submenu
3. In Voice Command mode, say "Query, Update Query"

Q&A

Q: Why should you preview the data before running a delete query?

A: If you inadvertently enter the wrong criterion and do not realize it before you click the Yes button, you will delete the incorrect set of records. Worse yet, you might not even realize that you have done so.

To Use a Delete Query to Delete a Group of Records

1

• **Click Edit on the menu bar and then click Clear Grid to clear the grid.**

• **Click the Query Type button arrow on the Query Design toolbar.**

The list of available query types appears (Figure 3-42).

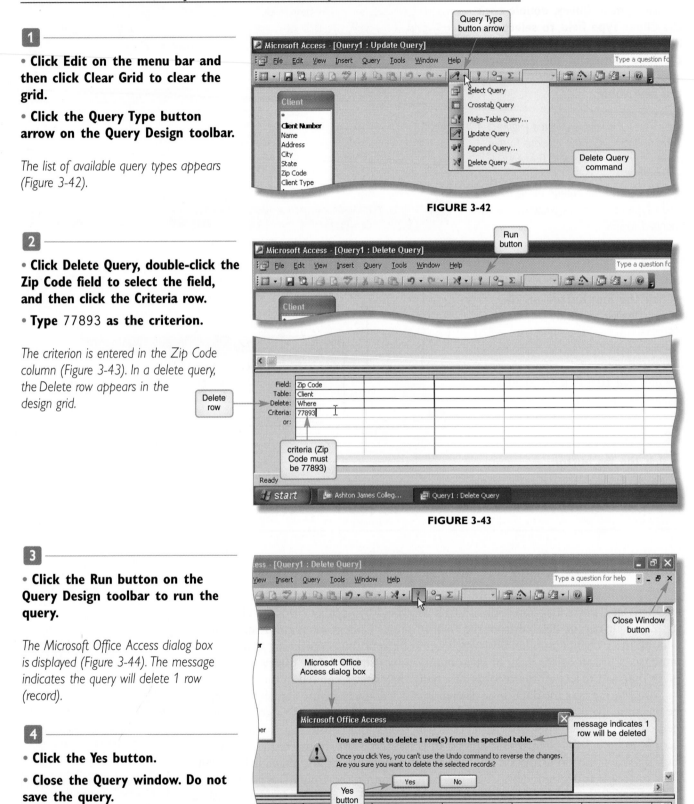

FIGURE 3-42

2

• **Click Delete Query, double-click the Zip Code field to select the field, and then click the Criteria row.**

• **Type** 77893 **as the criterion.**

The criterion is entered in the Zip Code column (Figure 3-43). In a delete query, the Delete row appears in the design grid.

FIGURE 3-43

3

• **Click the Run button on the Query Design toolbar to run the query.**

The Microsoft Office Access dialog box is displayed (Figure 3-44). The message indicates the query will delete 1 row (record).

4

• **Click the Yes button.**

• **Close the Query window. Do not save the query.**

The client with Zip code 77893 has been removed from the table.

FIGURE 3-44

Using Append and Make-Table Queries

An **append query** adds a group of records from one table to the end of another table. For example, suppose that Ashton James College acquires some new clients and a database containing a table with those clients. To avoid entering all this information manually, you can append it to the Client table in the Ashton James College database using the append query. The following steps illustrate how to create an append query.

To Create an Append Query

1. Create a select query for the table containing the records to append.
2. In the design grid, indicate the fields to include, and then enter any necessary criteria.
3. Run the query to be sure you have specified the correct data, and then return to the design grid.
4. Click the Query Type button arrow on the Query Design toolbar, and then click Append Query.
5. When Access displays the Append Query dialog box, specify the name of the table to receive the new records and its location. Run the query by clicking the OK button.
6. When Access indicates the number of records to be appended, click the OK button.

The records then are added to the indicated table.

In some cases, you might want to add the records to a new table, that is, a table that has not yet been created. If so, use a **make-table query** to add the records to a new table. Access will create this table as part of the process and add the records to it.

Other Ways

1. On Query menu click Delete Query
2. Right-click any open area in upper pane, point to Query Type on shortcut menu, click Delete Query on Query Type submenu
3. In Voice Command mode, say "Query, Delete Query"

Validation Rules

You now have created, loaded, queried, and updated a database. Nothing you have done so far, however, makes sure that users enter only valid data. To ensure the entry of valid data, you create **validation rules**; that is, rules that a user must follow when entering the data. As you will see, Access will prevent users from entering data that does not follow the rules. The steps also specify **validation text**, which is the message that will appear if a user violates the validation rule.

Validation rules can indicate a **required field**, a field in which the user actually must enter data. For example, by making the Name field a required field, a user actually must enter a name (that is, the field cannot be blank). Validation rules can make sure a user's entry lies within a certain **range of values**; for example that the values in the Amount Paid field are between $0.00 and $90,000.00. They can specify a **default value**; that is, a value that Access will display on the screen in a particular field before the user begins adding a record. To make data entry of client numbers more convenient, you also can have lowercase letters appear automatically as uppercase letters. Finally, validation rules can specify a collection of acceptable values; for example, that the only legitimate entries for the Client Type field are EDU, MAN, and SER.

Specifying a Required Field

To specify that a field is to be required, change the value for the Required property from No to Yes. The steps on the next page specify that the Name field is to be a required field.

To Specify a Required Field

1

• **With the Database window open, the Tables object selected, and the Client table selected, click the Design button on the Database Window toolbar.**

• **Select the Name field by clicking its row selector.**

Access displays the Client : Table window (Figure 3-45). The Name field is selected.

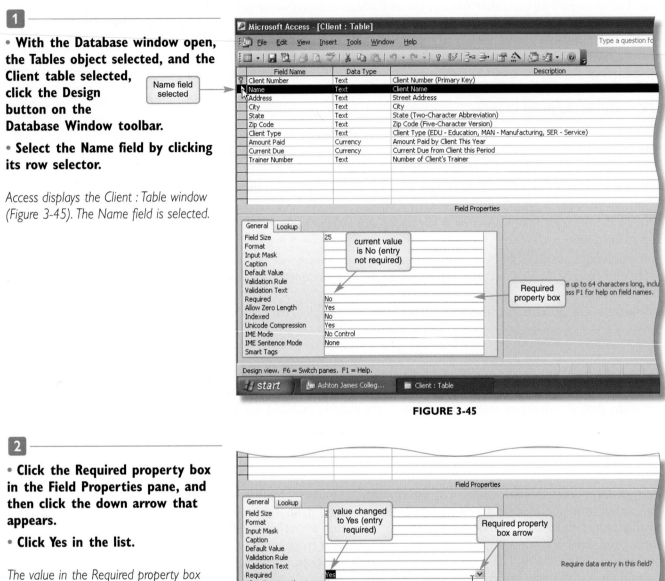

FIGURE 3-45

2

• **Click the Required property box in the Field Properties pane, and then click the down arrow that appears.**

• **Click Yes in the list.**

The value in the Required property box changes to Yes (Figure 3-46). It now is required that the user enter data into the Name field when adding a record.

FIGURE 3-46

Specifying a Range

The following step specifies that entries in the Amount Paid field must be between $0.00 and $90,000.00. To indicate this range, the criterion specifies that the amount paid amount must be both >= 0 (greater than or equal to 0) and <= 90000 (less than or equal to 90000).

To Specify a Range

1

• **Select the Amount Paid field by clicking its row selector. Click the Validation Rule property box to produce an insertion point, and then type** >=0 and <=90000 **as the rule.**

• **Click the Validation Text property box to produce an insertion point, and then type** Must be between $0.00 and $90,000.00 **as the text.**

The validation rule and text are entered (Figure 3-47). In the Validation Rule property box, Access automatically changed the lowercase letter, a, to uppercase in the word, and. In the Validation Text property box, you should type all the text, including the dollar signs, decimal points, and comma.

FIGURE 3-47

Users now will be prohibited from entering an amount paid amount that either is less than $0.00 or greater than $90,000.00 when they add records or change the value in the Amount Paid field.

Specifying a Default Value

To specify a default value, enter the value in the Default Value property box. The step on the next page specifies SER as the default value for the Client Type field. This simply means that if users do not enter a client type, the type will be SER.

To Specify a Default Value

1

• **Select the Client Type field. Click the Default Value property box, and then type** =SER **as the value.**

The Client Type field is selected. The default value is entered in the Default Value property box (Figure 3-48).

Client Type field selected

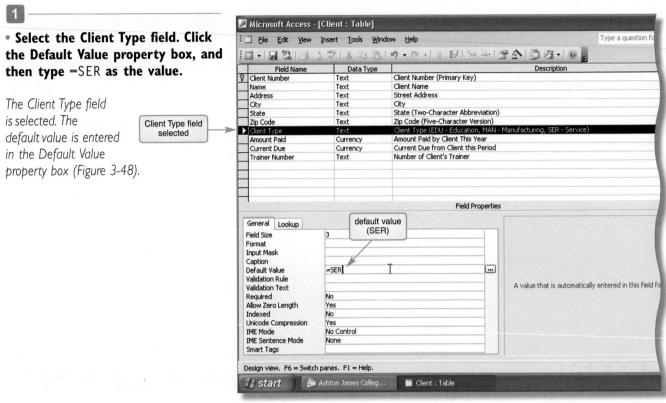

FIGURE 3-48

From this point on, if users do not make an entry in the Client Type field when adding records, Access will set the value equal to SER.

Specifying a Collection of Legal Values

The only **legal values** for the Client Type field are EDU, MAN, and SER. An appropriate validation rule for this field can direct Access to reject any entry other than these three possibilities. The following step specifies the legal values for the Client Type field.

To Specify a Collection of Legal Values

1

- **Make sure the Client Type field is selected.**

- **Click the Validation Rule property box and then type** =EDU or =MAN or =SER **as the validation rule.**

- **Click the Validation Text property box and then type** Must be EDU, MAN, or SER **as the validation text.**

The Client Type field is selected. The validation rule and text have been entered (Figure 3-49). In the Validation Rule property box, Access automatically inserted quotation marks around the EDU, MAN, and SER values and changed the lowercase letter, o, to uppercase in the word, or.

FIGURE 3-49

Users now will be allowed to enter only EDU, MAN, or SER in the Client Type field when they add records or make changes to this field.

Using a Format

To affect the way data appears in a field, you can use a **format**. To use a format with a Text field, you enter a special symbol, called a **format symbol**, in the field's Format property box. The Format property uses different settings for different data types. The following step specifies a format for the Client Number field in the Client table and illustrates the way you enter a format. The format symbol used in the example is >, which causes Access to display lowercase letters automatically as uppercase letters. The format symbol < causes Access to display uppercase letters automatically as lowercase letters.

To Specify a Format

1

• **Select the Client Number field. Click the Format property box and then type > (Figure 3-50).**

FIGURE 3-50

From this point on, any lowercase letters will appear automatically as uppercase when users add records or change the value in the Client Number field.

Saving Rules, Values, and Formats

The following steps save the validation rules, default values, and formats.

To Save the Validation Rules, Default Values, and Formats

1

• **Click the Close Window button for the Client : Table window to close the window (see Figure 3-50).**

The Microsoft Office Access dialog box is displayed, asking if you want to save your changes (Figure 3-51).

FIGURE 3-51

2

• **Click the Yes button to save the changes.**

The Microsoft Office Access dialog box is displayed (Figure 3-52). This message asks if you want the new rules applied to current records. If this were a database used to run a business or to solve some other critical need, you would click Yes. You would want to be sure that the data already in the database does not violate the rules.

3

• **Click the No button.**

The changes are saved. Existing data is not tested.

FIGURE 3-52

Updating a Table that Contains Validation Rules

When updating a table that contains validation rules, Access provides assistance in making sure the data entered is valid. It helps in making sure that data is formatted correctly. Access also will not accept invalid data. Entering a number that is out of the required range, for example, or entering a value that is not one of the possible choices, will produce an error message in the form of a dialog box. The database will not be updated until the error is corrected.

If the client number entered contains lowercase letters, such as st21 (Figure 3-53), Access will display the data automatically as ST21 (Figure 3-54).

client number contains lowercase letters

FIGURE 3-53

letters automatically appear as uppercase

FIGURE 3-54

FIGURE 3-55

FIGURE 3-56

FIGURE 3-57

If the client type is not valid, such as XYZ, Access will display the text message you specified (Figure 3-55) and not allow the data to enter the database.

If the amount paid value is not valid, such as 950000, which is too large, Access also displays the appropriate message (Figure 3-56) and refuses to accept the data.

If a required field contains no data, Access indicates this by displaying an error message as soon as you attempt to leave the record (Figure 3-57). The field must contain a valid entry before Access will move to a different record.

When entering data into a field with a validation rule, you may find that Access displays the error message and you are unable to make the necessary correction. It may be that you cannot remember the validation rule you created or it was created incorrectly. In such a case, you neither can leave the field nor close the table because you have entered data into a field that violates the validation rule.

If this happens, first try again to type an acceptable entry. If this does not work, repeatedly press the BACKSPACE key to erase the contents of the field and then try to leave the field. If you are unsuccessful using this procedure, press the ESC key until the record is removed from the screen. The record will not be added to the database.

Should the need arise to take this drastic action, you probably have a faulty validation rule. Use the techniques of the previous sections to correct the existing validation rules for the field.

Creating a Lookup Field

Currently, the data type for the Client Type field is text. Users must enter a type. The validation rules ensure that they can enter only a valid type, but they do not assist the users in making the entry. To assist them in the data-entry process, you can change the Client Type field to a lookup field. A **Lookup field** allows the user to select from a list of values.

To change a field to a lookup field that selects from a list of values, use the Lookup Wizard data type as shown in the following steps.

To Create a Lookup Field

1

• **If necessary, click the Tables object. Click Client and then click the Design button on the Database Window toolbar.**

• **Click the Data Type column for the Client Type field, and then click the arrow.**

The list of available data types appears (Figure 3-58).

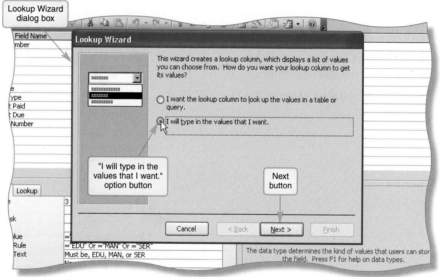

FIGURE 3-58

2

• **Click Lookup Wizard, and then click the "I will type in the values that I want" option button.**

Access displays the Lookup Wizard dialog box with options for creating a lookup column (Figure 3-59).

FIGURE 3-59

3

• **Click the Next button.**

The Lookup Wizard dialog box displays options for the number of columns and their values (Figure 3-60). In this screen, you enter the list of values.

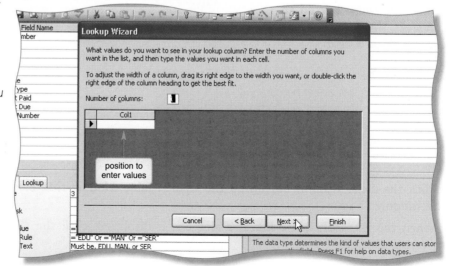

FIGURE 3-60

4

• **Click the first row of the table (below Col1), and then type** EDU **as the value in the first row.**

• **Press the DOWN ARROW key, and then type** MAN **as the value in the second row.**

• **Press the DOWN ARROW key, and then type** SER **as the value in the third row.**

The list of values for the lookup column is entered (Figure 3-61).

FIGURE 3-61

5

• **Click the Next button.**

• **Ensure Client Type is entered as the label for the lookup column.**

• **The label is entered (Figure 3-62).**

FIGURE 3-62

6

• **Click the Finish button to complete the definition of the Lookup Wizard field.**

Client Type is now a Lookup Wizard field, but the data type still is Text because the values entered in the wizard were entered as text (Figure 3-63).

FIGURE 3-63

7

• **Click the Close Window button on the Client : Table window title bar to close the window.**

• **When the Microsoft Office Access dialog box is displayed, click the Yes button to save your changes.**

The Client Type field is now a lookup field and the changes are saved.

Using a Lookup Field

Earlier, you changed all the entries in the Client Type field to SER. Thus, you have created a rule that will ensure that only legitimate values (EDU, MAN, or SER) can be entered in the field. You also made Client Type a Lookup field. You can make changes to a Lookup field by clicking the field to be changed, clicking the arrow that appears in the field, and then selecting the desired value from the list.

The following steps change the Client Type value on the second and sixth records to MAN and on the seventh and ninth records to SER.

More About

Lookup Fields

You also can create a lookup field that looks up the values in a table or query. To do so, click the "I want the lookup column to look up values in a table or query." option button (Figure 3-59 on AC 147) in the Lookup Wizard dialog box.

To Use a Lookup Field

1

• **Make sure the Client table is displayed in Datasheet view.**

• **Click to the right of the SER entry in the Client Type field on the second record.**

An insertion point and down arrow appear in the Client Type field on the second record (Figure 3-64).

FIGURE 3-64

2

• **Click the down arrow.**

The list of values for the Client Type field appears (Figure 3-65).

FIGURE 3-65

3

- Click MAN to change the value.

- In a similar fashion, change the SER on the sixth record to MAN, on the seventh record to EDU, and on the ninth record to EDU (Figure 3-66).

- If instructed to do so, print the results by clicking the Print button on the Table Datasheet.

4

- Close the Client : Table window by clicking its Close Window button.

The Client Type field changes now are complete.

Name	Address	City	State	Zip Code	Client Type	Amount Paid	Current
Blant and Sons	4806 Park	Lake Hammond	TX	76653	SER		92
Center Services	725 Mitchell	San Julio	TX	78364	MAN		72
Calder Plastics	7300 Cedar	Lake Hammond	TX	76653	SER	$8,725.00	$0
Farrow-Idsen	829 Wooster	Cedar Ridge	TX	79342	SER	$8,287.50	$925
Fairland Lawns	143 Pangborn	Lake Hammond	TX	76653	SER	$21,625.00	$0
Hurley National	3827 Burgess	Tallmadge	TX	77231	MAN		$0
Morgan-Alyssa Academy	923 Williams	Crumville	TX	76745	EDU	$2	$1,572
PRIM Staffing	72 Crestview	San Julio	TX	78364	SER	$1	$2,827
Richards-Trent	382 Alder	Lake Hammond	TX	76653	EDU	$0.00	$0
					SER	$0.00	$0

Close Window button

values changed

FIGURE 3-66

Referential Integrity

The property that ensures that the value in a foreign key must match that of another table's primary key is called **referential integrity**. A **foreign key** is a field in one table whose values are required to match the *primary key* of another table. In the Client table, the Trainer Number field is a foreign key that must match the primary key of the Trainer table; that is, the trainer number for any client must be a trainer currently in the Trainer table. A client whose trainer number is 92, for example, should not be stored because no such trainer exists.

Specifying Referential Integrity

In Access, to specify referential integrity, you must define a relationship between the tables by using the Relationships command. Access then prohibits any updates to the database that would violate the referential integrity.

The type of relationship between two tables specified by the Relationships command is referred to as a **one-to-many relationship**. This means that *one* record in the first table is related to (matches) *many* records in the second table, but each record in the second table is related to only *one* record in the first. In the Ashton James College database, for example, a one-to-many relationship exists between the Trainer table and the Client table. *One* trainer is associated with *many* clients, but each client is associated with only a single trainer. In general, the table containing the foreign key will be the *many* part of the relationship.

When specifying referential integrity, two ways exist to handle deletions. In the relationship between clients and trainers, for example, deletion of a trainer for whom clients exist, such as trainer number 42, would violate referential integrity. Any clients for trainer number 42 no longer would relate to any trainer in the database. The normal way to avoid this problem is to prohibit such a deletion. The other option is to **cascade the delete**, that is, have Access allow the deletion but then automatically delete any clients related to the deleted trainer.

Two ways also exist to handle the update of the primary key of the Trainer table. In the relationship between trainers and clients, for example, changing the trainer number for trainer 42 to 62 in the Trainer table would cause a problem. Clients are in the Client table on which the trainer number is 42. These clients no longer would relate to any trainer. Again, the normal way of avoiding the problem is to prohibit this type of update. The other option is to **cascade the update**; that is, have Access allow the update but then automatically make the corresponding change for any client whose trainer number was 42. It now will be 62.

The following steps use the Relationships command to specify referential integrity by specifying a relationship between the Trainer and Client tables. The steps also ensure that update will cascade, but that delete will not.

More About

Relationships: Printing Relationships

You can obtain a printed copy of your relationships after you have created them. To do so, first click the Relationships button to display the relationships. Next click File on the menu bar and then click Print Relationships. When Access displays the Print Preview window, click the Print button on the Print Preview toolbar

To Specify Referential Integrity

1

• **With the Database window displaying, click the Relationships button on the Database toolbar.**

Access displays the Show Table dialog box (Figure 3-67).

FIGURE 3-67

2

• **Click the Trainer table and then click the Add button. Click the Client table, click the Add button again, and then click the Close button in the Show Table dialog box.**

• **Resize the field lists that appear so all fields are visible.**

Field lists for the Trainer and Client tables appear (Figure 3-68). The lists have been resized so all fields are visible.

FIGURE 3-68

3

• **Drag the Trainer Number field in the Trainer table field list to the Trainer Number field in the Client table field list.**

Access displays the Edit Relationships dialog box (Figure 3-69). The correct fields (the Trainer Number fields) have been identified as the matching fields.

FIGURE 3-69

4

• **Click Enforce Referential Integrity to select it, and then click Cascade Update Related Fields to select it.**

The Enforce Referential Integrity and Cascade Update Related Fields check boxes are selected (Figure 3-70).

FIGURE 3-70

5

• **Click the Create button.**

*Access creates the relationship and displays it visually with the **relationship line** joining the two Trainer Number fields (Figure 3-71). The number 1 at the top of the relationship line close to the Trainer Number field in the Trainer table indicates that the Trainer table is the one part of the relationship. The infinity symbol at the other end of the relationship line indicates that the Client table is the many part of the relationship.*

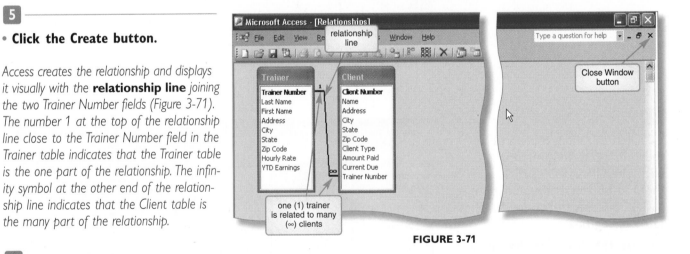

FIGURE 3-71

6

• **Close the Relationships window by clicking its Close Window button.**

• **Click the Yes button in the Microsoft Office Access dialog box to save the relationship you created.**

Other Ways

1. On Tools menu click Relationships
2. Right-click Database window, click Relationships on shortcut menu

Referential integrity now exists between the Trainer and Client tables. Access now will reject any number in the Trainer Number field in the Client table that does not match a trainer number in the Trainer table. Attempting to add a client whose

Trainer Number field does not match would result in the error message shown in Figure 3-72.

A deletion of a trainer for whom related clients exist also would be rejected. Attempting to delete trainer 53 from the Trainer table, for example, would result in the message shown in Figure 3-73.

Access would, however, allow the change of a trainer number in the Trainer table. Then it automatically makes the corresponding change to the trainer number for all the trainer's clients. For example, if you changed the trainer number of trainer 42 to 62, the same 62 would appear in the trainer number field for clients.

Using Subdatasheets

Now that the Trainer table is related to the Client table, it is possible to view the clients of a given trainer when you are viewing the datasheet for the Trainer table. The clients for the trainer will appear below the trainer in a **subdatasheet**. The fact that such a subdatasheet is available is indicated by a plus sign that appears in front of the rows in the Trainer table. The following steps display the subdatasheet for trainer 48.

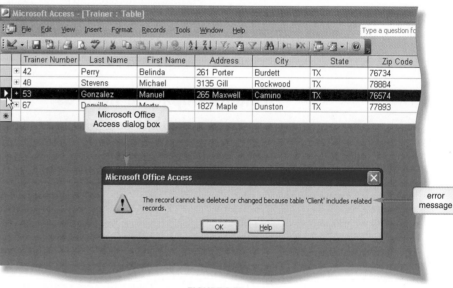

FIGURE 3-72

FIGURE 3-73

To Use a Subdatasheet

1

• **With the Database window on the screen, the Tables object selected, and the Trainer table selected, click the Open button on the Database Window toolbar.**

The datasheet for the Trainer table appears (Figure 3-74).

FIGURE 3-74

2

- **Click the plus sign in front of the row for trainer 48.**

The subdatasheet appears (Figure 3-75). It contains only those clients that are assigned to trainer 48.

3

- **Click the minus sign to remove the subdatasheet, and then close the datasheet for the Trainer table by clicking its Close Window button.**

The datasheet no longer appears.

FIGURE 3-75

Q&A

Q: Can I delete a trainer from the Trainer table?

A: If a trainer currently has clients in the Client table, Access will not allow you to delete the trainer. For example, trainer 48 currently has clients in the Client table. If you deleted trainer 48, these clients' trainer numbers would no longer match anyone in the Trainer table.

More About

Referential Integrity

Referential integrity is an essential property for databases, but providing support for it proved to be one of the more difficult tasks facing the developers of relational database management systems. For more information about referential integrity, visit the Access 2003 More About Web page (scsite.com/ac2003/ more) and click Referential Integrity.

Finding Duplicate Records

One reason to include a primary key for a table is to eliminate duplicate records. A possibility still exists, however, that duplicate records can get into your database. Perhaps, a client's name was misspelled and the data entry person assumed it was a new client. The **Find Duplicates Query Wizard** allows you to find duplicate records. The following steps illustrate how to use the Find Duplicates Query Wizard to find duplicate records.

To Find Duplicate Records

1. Select the table that you want to query.
2. Click the New Object button arrow, and then click Query.
3. When Access displays the New Query dialog box, click the Find Duplicates Query Wizard and then click the OK button.
4. Follow the directions in the Find Duplicates Query Wizard dialog boxes.

Finding Unmatched Records

Occasionally, you may want to find records in one table that have no matching records in another table. For example, suppose the clients of Ashton James College placed requests for training materials. You may want to know which clients have no requests. The **Find Unmatched Query Wizard** allows you to find unmatched records. The following steps illustrate how to find unmatched records using the Find Unmatched Query Wizard.

To Find Unmatched Records

1. Click the New Object button arrow, and then click Query.
2. When Access displays the New Query dialog box, click Find Unmatched Query Wizard and then click the OK button.
3. Follow the directions in the Find Unmatched Query Wizard dialog boxes.

Ordering Records

Normally, Access sequences the records in the Client table by client number whenever listing them because the Client Number field is the primary key. You can change this order, if desired.

Using the Sort Ascending Button to Order Records

To change the order in which records appear, use the Sort Ascending or Sort Descending buttons. Either button reorders the records based on the field in which the insertion point is located.

The following steps order the records by city using the Sort Ascending button.

To Use the Sort Ascending Button to Order Records

1

• **With the Database window on the screen, the Tables object selected, and the Client table selected, click the Open button on the Database Window toolbar.**

• **Click the City field on the first record (any other record would do as well).**

An insertion point appears in the City field (Figure 3-76).

FIGURE 3-76

2

• **Click the Sort Ascending button on the Table Datasheet toolbar.**

• **If instructed to do so, print the table by clicking the Print button on the Table Datasheet toolbar.**

The rows now are ordered by city (Figure 3-77).

FIGURE 3-77

If you wanted to sort the data in reverse order, you would use the Sort Descending button instead of the Sort Ascending button.

Other Ways

1. On Records menu point to Sort, click Sort Ascending on Sort submenu
2. In Voice Command mode, say "Sort Ascending"

Ordering Records on Multiple Fields

Just as you are able to sort the answer to a query on multiple fields, you also can sort the data that appears in a datasheet on multiple fields. To do so, the major and minor keys must be next to each other in the datasheet with the major key on the left. (If this is not the case, you can drag the columns into the correct position. Instead of dragging, however, usually it will be easier to use a query that has the data sorted in the desired order.)

The following steps order records that have the major and minor keys in the correct position on the combination of the Client Type and Amount Paid fields. To select the fields, use the field selector, which is the small bar at the top of the column that you click to select an entire field in a datasheet.

To Use the Sort Ascending Button to Order Records on Multiple Fields

1

• **Click the field selector at the top of the Client Type column to select the entire column (see Figure 3-77 on the previous page).**

• **Hold down the SHIFT key and then click the field selector for the Amount Paid column.**

The Client Type and Amount Paid columns both are selected (Figure 3-78).

Sort Ascending button

both Client Type and Amount Paid columns selected

Name	Address	City	State	Zip Code	Client Type	Amount Paid	Current
Farrow-Idsen	829 Wooster	Cedar Ridge	TX	79342	SER	$8,287.50	$925
Morgan-Alyssa Academy	923 Williams	Crumville	TX	76745	EDU	$24,761.00	$1,572
Richards-Trent	382 Alder	Lake Hammond	TX	76653	EDU	$0.00	$0
Fairland Lawns	143 Pangborn	Lake Hammond	TX	76653	SER	$21,625.00	$0
Calder Plastics	7300 Cedar	Lake Hammond	TX	76653	SER	$8,725.00	$0
Blant and Sons	4806 Park	Lake Hammond	TX	76653	SER	$21,876.00	$892
PRIM Staffing	72 Crestview	San Julio	TX	78364	SER	$11,682.25	$2,827
Center Services	725 Mitchell	San Julio	TX	78364	MAN	$26,512.00	$2,672
Hurley National	3827 Burgess	Tallmadge	TX	77231	MAN	$0.00	$0
					SER	$0.00	$0

FIGURE 3-78

2

• **Click the Sort Ascending button.**

• **If instructed to do so, print the table by clicking the Print button on the Table Datasheet toolbar.**

The rows are ordered by client type (Figure 3-79). Within each group of clients of the same type, the rows are ordered by the amount paid amount.

records sorted by client type

cess - [Client : Table]

View Insert Format Records Tools Window Help   Type a question for help

Name	Address	City	State	Zip Code	Client Type	Amount Paid	Current
Richards-Trent	382 Alder	Lake Hammond	TX	76653	EDU	$0.00	$0
Morgan-Alyssa Academy	923 Williams	Crumville	TX	76745	EDU	$24,761.00	$1,572
Hurley National	3827 Burgess	Tallmadge	TX	77231	MAN	$0.00	$0
Center Services	725 Mitchell	San Julio	TX	78364	MAN	$26,512.00	$2,672
Farrow-Idsen	829 Wooster	Cedar Ridge	TX	79342	SER	$8,287.50	$925
Calder Plastics	7300 Cedar		X	76653	SER	$8,725.00	$0
PRIM Staffing	72 Crestview			78364	SER	$11,682.25	$2,827
Fairland Lawns	143 Pangborn		X	76653	SER	$21,625.00	$0
Blant and Sons	4806 Park		X	76653	SER	$21,876.00	$892
					SER	$0.00	$0

Sort Ascending

final SER is default value for next client to be added

within clients of a given type, records are sorted further by amount paid

3

• **Close the Client : Table window by clicking its Close Window button.**

• **Click the No button in the Microsoft Office Access dialog box to abandon the changes.**

The next time the table is open, the records will appear in their original order.

FIGURE 3-79

Creating and Using Indexes

You already are familiar with the concept of an index. The index in the back of a book contains important words or phrases together with a list of pages on which the given words or phrases can be found. An **index** for a table is similar. Figure 3-80, for example, shows the Client table along with an index built on client names. In this case, the items of interest are names instead of keywords or phrases as is the case in the back of this book. The field or fields on which the index is built is called the **index key**. Thus, in Figure 3-80, the Name field is the index key. (The structure of an index actually is a little more complicated than the one shown in the figure and is beyond the scope of this book. The concept is the same, however, and the structure shown in the figure illustrates the important concepts.)

Index on Name

NAME	RECORD NUMBER
Blant and Sons	1
Calder Plastics	3
Center Services	2
Fairland Lawns	5
Farrow-Idsen	4
Hurley National	6
Morgan-Alyssa Academy	7
PRIM Staffing	8
Richards-Trent	9

Client Table

RECORD NUMBER	CLIENT NUMBER	NAME	ADDRESS	CITY	STATE	ZIP CODE	...
1	BS27	Blant and Sons	4806 Park	Lake Hammond	TX	76653	...
2	CE16	Center Services	725 Mitchell	San Julio	TX	78364	...
3	CP27	Calder Plastics	7300 Cedar	Lake Hammond	TX	76653	...
4	FI28	Farrow-Idsen	829 Wooster	Cedar Ridge	TX	79342	...
5	FL93	Fairland Lawns	143 Pangborn	Lake Hammond	TX	76653	...
6	HN83	Hurley National	3827 Burgess	Tallmadge	TX	77231	...
7	MC28	Morgan-Alyssa Academy	923 Williams	Crumville	TX	76745	...
8	PS82	PRIM Staffing	72 Crestview	San Julio	TX	78364	...
9	RT67	Richards-Trent	382 Alder	Lake Hammond	TX	76653	...

FIGURE 3-80

Each name occurs in the index along with the number of the record on which the corresponding client is located. Further, the names appear in the index in alphabetical order. If Access were to use this index to find the record on which the name is Farrow-Idsen, for example, it could scan the names in the index rapidly to find Farrow-Idsen. Once it did, it would determine the corresponding record number (4) and then go immediately to record 4 in the Client table, thus finding this client more quickly than if it had to look through the entire Client table one record at a time. Indexes make the process of retrieving records very fast and efficient. (With relatively small tables, the increased efficiency associated with indexes will not be as apparent as in larger tables. In practice, it is common to encounter tables with thousands, tens of thousands, or even hundreds of thousands of records. In such cases, the increase in efficiency is dramatic. In fact, without indexes, many operations in such databases simply would not be practical. They would take too long to complete.)

Because no two clients happen to have the same name, the Record Number column contains only single values. This may not always be the case. Consider the index on the Zip Code field shown in Figure 3-81 on the next page. In this index, the Record Number column contains several values, namely all the records on which the corresponding Zip code appears. The first row, for example, indicates that Zip code 76653 is found on records 1, 3, 5, and 9; the fourth row indicates that Zip code 78364 is found on records 2 and 8. If Access were to use this index to find all clients in Zip code 78364, it could scan the Zip codes in the index rapidly to find

More About

Indexes

The most common structure for high-performance indexes is called a B-tree. It is a highly efficient structure that supports very rapid access to records in the database as well as a rapid alternative to sorting records. Virtually all systems use some version of the B-tree structure. For more information about B-tree indexes, visit the Access 2003 More About Web page (scsite.com/ac2003/more) and click B-tree.

78364. Once it did, it would determine the corresponding record numbers (2 and 8) and then go immediately to these records. It would not have to examine any other records in the Client table.

Index on Zip Code			Client Table							
ZIP CODE	**RECORD NUMBER**		**RECORD NUMBER**	**CLIENT NUMBER**	**NAME**	**ADDRESS**	**CITY**	**STATE**	**ZIP CODE**	**...**
76653	1, 3, 5, 9		1	BS27	Blant and Sons	4806 Park	Lake Hammond	TX	76653	...
76745	7		2	CE16	Center Services	725 Mitchell	San Julio	TX	78364	...
77231	6		3	CP27	Calder Plastics	7300 Cedar	Lake Hammond	TX	76653	...
78364	2, 8		4	FI28	Farrow-Idsen	829 Wooster	Cedar Ridge	TX	79342	...
79342	4		5	FL93	Fairland Lawns	143 Pangborn	Lake Hammond	TX	76653	...
			6	HN83	Hurley National	3827 Burgess	Tallmadge	TX	77231	...
			7	MC28	Morgan-Alyssa Academy	923 Williams	Crumville	TX	76745	...
			8	PS82	PRIM Staffing	72 Crestview	San Julio	TX	78364	...
			9	RT67	Richards-Trent	382 Alder	Lake Hammond	TX	76653	...

FIGURE 3-81

Another benefit of indexes is that they provide an efficient way to order records. That is, if the records are to appear in a certain order, Access can use an index instead of physically having to rearrange the records in the database. Physically rearranging the records in a different order can be a very time-consuming process.

To use the index to order records, use record numbers in the index; that is, simply follow down the Record Number column, listing the corresponding clients. In this index, you would first list the client on record 1 (Blant and Sons), then the client on record 3 (Calder Plastics), then the client on record 2 (Center Services), and so on. The clients would be listed alphabetically by name without actually sorting the table.

To gain the benefits from an index, you first must create one. Access automatically creates an index on the primary key as well as some other special fields. If, as is the case with both the Client and Trainer tables, a table contains a field called Zip Code, for example, Access will create an index for it automatically. You must create any other indexes you feel you need, indicating the field or fields on which the index is to be built.

Although the index key usually will be a single field, it can be a combination of fields. For example, you might want to sort records by amount paid within client type. In other words, the records are ordered by a combination of fields: Client Type and Amount Paid. An index can be used for this purpose by using a combination of fields for the index key. In this case, you must assign a name to the index. It is a good idea to assign a name that represents the combination of fields. For example, an index whose key is the combination of the Client Type and Amount Paid fields might be called TypePaid.

How Does Access Use an Index?

Access creates an index whenever you request that it do so. It takes care of all the work in setting up and maintaining the index. In addition, Access will use the index automatically.

If you request that data be sorted in a particular order and Access determines that an index is available that it can use to make the process efficient, it will do so. If no index is available, it still will sort the data in the order you requested; it will just take longer.

Similarly, if you request that Access locate a particular record that has a certain value in a particular field, Access will use an index if an appropriate one exists. If not, it will have to examine each record until it finds the one you want.

In both cases, the added efficiency provided by an index will not be apparent readily in tables that have only a few records. As you add more records to your tables, however, the difference can be dramatic. Even with only 50 to 100 records, you will notice a difference. You can imagine how dramatic the difference would be in a table with 50,000 records.

When Should You Create an Index?

An index improves efficiency for sorting and finding records. On the other hand, indexes occupy space on your disk. They also require Access to do extra work. Access must keep all the indexes that have been created up-to-date. Thus, both advantages and disadvantages exist to using indexes. Consequently, the decision as to which indexes to create is an important one. The following guidelines should help you in this process.

Create an index on a field (or combination of fields) if one or more of the following conditions are present:

1. The field is the primary key of the table (Access will create this index automatically).
2. The field is the foreign key in a relationship you have created.
3. You frequently will need your data to be sorted on the field.
4. You frequently will need to locate a record based on a value in this field.

Because Access handles 1 automatically, you need only to concern yourself about 2, 3, and 4. If you think you will need to see client data arranged in order of amount paid amounts, for example, you should create an index on the Amount Paid field. If you think you will need to see the data arranged by amount paid within trainer number, you should create an index on the combination of the Trainer Number field and the Amount Paid field. Similarly, if you think you will need to find a client given the client's name, you should create an index on the Name field.

Creating Single-Field Indexes

A **single-field index** is an index whose key is a single field. In this case, the index key is to be the Name field. In creating an index, you need to indicate whether to allow duplicates in the index key; that is, two records that have the same value. For example, in the index for the Name field, if duplicates are not allowed, Access would not allow the addition of a client whose name is the same as the name of a client already in the database. In the index for the Name field, duplicates will be allowed. The steps on the next page create a single-field index.

More About

Changing Table Properties

You can change the properties of a table by opening the table in Design view and then clicking the Properties button on the Table Design toolbar. Access will display the property sheet for the table. To display the records in a table in an order other than primary key order (the default sort order), use the Order By property. For example, to display the Client table automatically in Name order, click the Order By property box, type `Client.Name` in the property box, close the property sheet, and save the change to the table design. When you open the Client table in Datasheet view, the records will be sorted in Name order.

To Create a Single-Field Index

1

• **With the Database window on the screen, the Tables object selected, and the Client table selected, click the Design button on the Database Window toolbar.**

• **Be sure the Client : Table window is maximized.**

• **Click the row selector to select the Name field.**

• **Click the Indexed property box in the Field Properties pane.**

• **Click the down arrow that appears.**

The Indexed list appears (Figure 3-82). The items in the list are No (no index), Yes (Duplicates OK) (create an index and allow duplicates), and Yes (No Duplicates) (create an index but reject (do not allow) duplicates).

FIGURE 3-82

2

• **Click the Yes (Duplicates OK) item in the list.**

The index on the Name field now will be created and is ready for use as soon as you save your work.

Creating Multiple-Field Indexes

Creating **multiple-field indexes**, that is, indexes whose key is a combination of fields, involves a different process from creating single-field indexes. To create multiple-field indexes, you will use the Indexes button, enter a name for the index, and then enter the combination of fields that make up the index key. The following steps create a multiple-field index with the name TypePaid. The key will be the combination of the Client Type field and the Amount Paid field.

To Create a Multiple-Field Index

1

• **Click the Indexes button on the Table Design toolbar (see Figure 3-82).**

• **Click the blank row (the row following Name) in the Index Name column in the Indexes: Client dialog box.**

• **Type** TypePaid **as the index name, and then press the TAB key.**

Access displays the Indexes: Client dialog box. It shows the indexes that already have been created and allows you to create additional indexes (Figure 3-83). The index name has been entered as TypePaid. An insertion point appears in the Field Name column. The index on the Client Number field is the primary index and was created automatically by Access. The index on the Name field is the one just created. Access created other indexes (for example, the Zip Code and Amount Paid fields) automatically. In this dialog box, you can create additional indexes.

FIGURE 3-83

2

• **Click the down arrow in the Field Name column to produce a list of fields in the Client table. Select Client Type.**

• **Press the TAB key three times to move to the Field Name column on the following row.**

• **Select the Amount Paid field in the same manner as the Client Type field.**

Client Type and Amount Paid are selected as the two fields for the TypePaid index (Figure 3-84). The absence of an index name on the row containing the Amount Paid field indicates that it is part of the previous index, TypePaid.

FIGURE 3-84

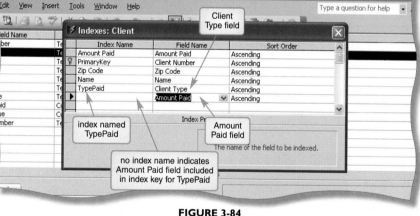

3

• **Close the Indexes: Client dialog box by clicking its Close button, and then close the Client : Table window by clicking its Close Window button.**

• **Click the Yes button in the Microsoft Office Access dialog box to save your changes.**

The indexes are created and Access displays the Database window.

Other Ways

1. On View menu click Indexes
2. In Voice Command mode, say "Indexes"

The indexes are created. Access will use them automatically whenever possible to improve efficiency of ordering or finding records. Access also will maintain them automatically. That is, whenever the data in the Client table is changed, Access will make appropriate changes in the indexes automatically.

Closing the Database and Quitting Access

The following steps close the database and quit Access.

To Close a Database and Quit Access

1 **Click the Close Window button for the Ashton James College : Database window.**

2 **Click the Close button for the Microsoft Access window.**

The database and Access close.

Special Database Operations

The special operations involved in maintaining a database are backup, recovery, compacting a database, and repairing a database.

Backup and Recovery

It is possible to damage or destroy a database. Users can enter data that is incorrect; programs that are updating the database can end abnormally during an update; a hardware problem can occur; and so on. After any such event has occurred, the database may contain invalid data. It even may be totally destroyed.

Obviously, you cannot allow a situation in which data has been damaged or destroyed to go uncorrected. You must somehow return the database to a correct state. This process is called **recovery**; that is, you say that you **recover** the database.

The simplest approach to recovery involves periodically making a copy of the database (called a **backup copy** or a **save copy**). This is referred to as **backing up** the database. If a problem occurs, you correct the problem by copying this backup copy over the actual database, often referred to as the **live database**.

To backup the database that is currently open, you use the Back Up Database command on the File menu. In the process, Access suggests a name that is a combination of the database name and the current date. For example, if you back up the Ashton James College database on April 20, 2005, Access will suggest the name Ashton James College_2005-04-20. You can change this name if you desire, although it is a good idea to use this name. By doing so, it will be easy to distinguish between all the backup copies you have made to determine which is the most recent. In addition, if you discover that a critical problem occurred on April 18, 2005, you may want to go back to the most recent backup before April 18. If, for example, the database was not backed up on April 17 but was backed up on April 16, you would use Ashton James College_2005-04-16.

More About

The Quick Reference

For a table that lists how to complete tasks covered in this book using the mouse, menu, shortcut menu, and keyboard, see the Quick Reference Summary at the back of this book, or visit the Access 2003 Quick Reference Web page (scsite.com/ac2003/qr).

More About

Microsoft Certification

The Microsoft Office Specialist Certification program provides an opportunity for you to obtain a valuable industry credential — proof that you have the Access 2003 skills required by employers. For more information, see Appendix E, or visit the Access 2003 Certification Web page (scsite.com/ac2003/cert).

The following steps back up a database to a file on a hard disk or high-capacity removable disk. You should check with your instructor before completing these steps.

To Backup a Database

1. Open the database to be backed up.
2. Click File on the menu bar, and then click Back Up Database.
3. Selected the desired location in the Save in box. If you do not want the name Access has suggested, enter the desired name in the File name text box.
4. Click the Save button.

Access creates a backup copy with the desired name in the desired location. Should you ever need to recover the database using this backup copy, you can simply copy it over the live version.

Compacting and Repairing a Database

As you add more data to a database, it naturally grows larger. Pictures will increase the size significantly. When you delete objects (for example, records, tables, forms, or pictures), the space previously occupied by the object does not become available for additional objects. Instead, the additional objects are given new space, that is, space that was not already allocated. If you decide to change a picture, for example, the new picture will not occupy the same space as the previous picture, but instead it will be given space of its own.

To remove this wasted space from the database, you must **compact** the database. Compacting the database makes an additional copy of the database, one that contains the same data, but does not contain the wasted space that the original does. The original database will still exist in its unaltered form.

A typical three-step process for compacting a database is as follows:

1. Compact the original database (for example, Ashton James College) and give the compacted database a different name (for example, Ashton James College Compacted).
2. Assuming that the compacting operation completed successfully, delete the original database (Ashton James College).
3. Also assuming that the compacting operation completed successfully, rename the compacted database (Ashton James College Compacted) with the name of the original database (Ashton James College).

Of course, if a problem occurs in the compacting operation, you should continue to use the original database; that is, do not complete Steps 2 and 3.

The operation can be carried out on a floppy disk, provided sufficient space is available. If the database to be compacted occupies more than half the floppy disk, however, Access may not have enough room to create the compacted database. In such a case, you should first copy the database to a hard disk or network drive. (You can use whatever Windows technique you prefer for copying files to do so.) You then can complete the process on the hard disk or network drive.

In addition to compacting the database, the same operation is used to **repair** the database in case of problems. If Microsoft Access reports a problem with the database or if some aspect of the database seems to be behaving in an unpredictable fashion, you should run the Compact and Repair operation to attempt to correct the problem. If Access is unable to repair the database, you will need to revert to your most recent backup copy.

More About

Compacting and Repairing a Database

You can require Access to compact a database automatically whenever the database is closed. To do so, click Tools on the menu bar and then click Options. When Access displays the Options dialog box, click the General tab. Click the Compact on Close check box.

More About

Backup and Recovery

Before making changes to the database, such as the changes made in this project, it is a good idea to make a copy of the database. Then, if a problem occurs that damages either the data in the database or the structure of the database, you can recover the database by copying the backup copy over it.

Q: Is it possible to compact an open database?

A: Yes, to do so, click Tools on the menu bar, point to Database Utilities, and then click Compact and Repair Database on the Database Utilities submenu.

The following steps compact a database and repair any problems after you have copied the database to a hard disk. If you have not copied the database to a hard disk, check with your instructor before completing these steps.

To Compact and Repair a Database

1. Be sure the database is closed. Click Tools on the menu bar, point to Database Utilities, and then click Compact and Repair Database on the Database Utilities submenu.
2. In the Database to Compact From dialog box, select the database to be compacted and then click the Compact button.
3. In the Compact Database Into dialog box, enter a new name for the compacted database and then click the Save button in the Database to Compact From dialog box.
4. Assuming the operation is completed successfully, delete the original database and rename the compacted database as the original name.

The database now is the compacted form of the original.

Project Summary

In Project 3, you learned how to maintain a database. You saw how to use Form view to add records to a table. You learned how to locate and filter records. You saw how to change the contents of records in a table and how to delete records from a table. You restructured a table, both by changing field characteristics and by adding a new field. You saw how to make a variety of changes to the appearance of a datasheet. You learned how to make changes to groups of records and delete a group of records. You created a variety of validation rules that specified a required field, a range, a default value, legal values, and a format. You examined the issues involved in updating a table with validation rules. You also saw how to specify referential integrity. You learned how to view related data by using subdatasheets. You learned how to order records. You saw how to improve performance by creating single-field and multiple-field indexes.

What You Should Know

Having completed this project, you should be able to perform the tasks below. The tasks are listed in the same order they were presented in this project. For a list of the buttons, menus, toolbars, and commands introduced in this project, see the Quick Reference Summary at the back of this book and refer to the Page Number column.

1. Open a Database   (AC 115)
2. Use a Form to Add Records   (AC 116)
3. Search for a Record   (AC 118)
4. Update the Contents of a Field   (AC 119)
5. Switch from Form View to Datasheet View (AC 120)
6. Use Filter By Selection   (AC 121)
7. Remove a Filter   (AC 122)
8. Use Filter By Form   (AC 123)
9. Use Advanced Filter/Sort   (AC 124)
10. Delete a Record   (AC 125)
11. Delete a Record in Form View   (AC 126)
12. Change the Size of a Field   (AC 127)
13. Add a Field to a Table   (AC 129)
14. Delete a Field   (AC 130)
15. Update the Contents of a Field   (AC 130)
16. Resize a Column   (AC 131)
17. Change the Font in a Datasheet   (AC 133)
18. Change the Format of the Datasheet Grid (AC 134)
19. Use Print Preview   (AC 135)
20. Close the Datasheet Without Saving the Format Changes   (AC 135)
21. Use an Update Query to Update All Records (AC 136)
22. Use a Delete Query to Delete a Group of Records (AC 138)
23. Create an Append Query   (AC 139)
24. Specify a Required Field   (AC 140)
25. Specify a Range   (AC 141)
26. Specify a Default Value   (AC 142)
27. Specify a Collection of Legal Values   (AC 143)
28. Specify a Format   (AC 144)
29. Save the Validation Rules, Default Values, and Formats   (AC 144)
30. Create a Lookup Field   (AC 147)
31. Use a Lookup Field   (AC 149)
32. Specify Referential Integrity   (AC 151)
33. Use a Subdatasheet   (AC 153)
34. Find Duplicate Records   (AC 154)
35. Find Unmatched Records   (AC 154)
36. Use the Sort Ascending Button to Order Records (AC 155)
37. Use the Sort Ascending Button to Order Records on Multiple Fields   (AC 156)
38. Create a Single-Field Index   (AC 160)
39. Create a Multiple-Field Index   (AC 161)
40. Close a Database and Quit Access   (AC 162)
41. Backup a Database   (AC 163)
42. Compact and Repair a Database   (AC 164)

Learn It Online

Instructions: To complete the Learn It Online exercises, start your browser, click the Address bar, and then enter the Web address scsite.com/ac2003/learn. When the Access 2003 Learn It Online page is displayed, follow the instructions in the exercises below. Each exercise has instructions for printing your results, either for your own records or for submission to your instructor.

1 Project Reinforcement TF, MC, and SA

Below Access Project 3, click the Project Reinforcement link. Print the quiz by clicking Print on the File menu for each page. Answer each question.

2 Flash Cards

Below Access Project 3, click the Flash Cards link and read the instructions. Type 20 (or a number specified by your instructor) in the Number of playing cards text box, type your name in the Enter your Name text box, and then click the Flip Card button. When the flash card is displayed, read the question and then click the ANSWER box arrow to select an answer. Flip through Flash Cards. If your score is 15 (75%) correct or greater, click Print on the File menu to print your results. If your score is less than 15 (75%) correct, then redo this exercise by clicking the Replay button.

3 Practice Test

Below Access Project 3, click the Practice Test link. Answer each question, enter your first and last name at the bottom of the page, and then click the Grade Test button. When the graded practice test is displayed on your screen, click Print on the File menu to print a hard copy. Continue to take practice tests until you score 80% or better.

4 Who Wants To Be a Computer Genius?

Below Access Project 3, click the Computer Genius link. Read the instructions, enter your first and last name at the bottom of the page, and then click the PLAY button. When your score is displayed, click the PRINT RESULTS link to print a hard copy.

5 Wheel of Terms

Below Access Project 3, click the Wheel of Terms link. Read the instructions, and then enter your first and last name and your school name. Click the PLAY button. When your score is displayed, right-click the score and then click Print on the shortcut menu to print a hard copy.

6 Crossword Puzzle Challenge

Below Access Project 3, click the Crossword Puzzle Challenge link. Read the instructions, and then enter your first and last name. Click the SUBMIT button. Work the crossword puzzle. When you are finished, click the Submit button. When the crossword puzzle is redisplayed, click the Print Puzzle button to print a hard copy.

7 Tips and Tricks

Below Access Project 3, click the Tips and Tricks link. Click a topic that pertains to Project 3. Right-click the information and then click Print on the shortcut menu. Construct a brief example of what the information relates to in Access to confirm you understand how to use the tip or trick.

8 Newsgroups

Below Access Project 3, click the Newsgroups link. Click a topic that pertains to Project 3. Print three comments.

9 Expanding Your Horizons

Below Access Project 3, click the Expanding Your Horizons link. Click a topic that pertains to Project 3. Print the information. Construct a brief example of what the information relates to in Access to confirm you understand the contents of the article.

10 Search Sleuth

Below Access Project 3, click the Search Sleuth link. To search for a term that pertains to this project, select a term below the Project 3 title and then use the Google search engine at google.com (or any major search engine) to display and print two Web pages that present information on the term.

11 Access Online Training

Below Access Project 3, click the Access Online Training link. When your browser displays the Microsoft Office Online Web page, click the Access link. Click one of the Access courses that covers one or more of the objectives listed at the beginning of the project on page AC 114. Print the first page of the course before stepping through it.

12 Office Marketplace

Below Access Project 3, click the Office Marketplace link. When your browser displays the Microsoft Office Online Web page, click the Office Marketplace link. Click a topic that relates to Access. Print the first page.

1 Maintaining the Begon Pest Control Database

Instructions: Start Access. Open the Begon Pest Control database that you modified in Apply Your Knowledge 1 in Project 2 on page AC 109. (If you did not complete this exercise, see your instructor for a copy of the modified database.) Perform the following tasks:

1. Open the Customer table in Design view as shown in Figure 3-85.

FIGURE 3-85

2. Increase the size of the Name field to 25.
3. Format the Customer Number and State fields so any lowercase letters appear in uppercase.
4. Make the Name field a required field.
5. Specify that balance amounts must be less than or equal to $2,000.00. Include validation text.
6. Create an index that allows duplicates for the Name field.
7. Save the changes to the structure.
8. Open the Customer table in Datasheet view.
9. Change the name of customer SE05 to Servete Manufacturing and the address of customer MC10 to 109 Fletcher.
10. Resize the Name column so the complete name for customer SE05 appears. Resize the remaining columns to the best fit.
11. Close the table and click the Yes button to save the changes to the layout of the table.
12. Print the table. If necessary, change the margins so the table prints on one page in landscape orientation.
13. Open the Customer table and use Filter By Selection to find the record for client CM90. Delete the record.
14. Remove the filter and then print the table.
15. Sort the data in descending order by balance.
16. Print the table in landscape orientation. Close the table. If you are asked to save changes to the design of the table, click the No button.
17. Establish referential integrity between the Technician table (the one table) and the Customer table (the many table). Cascade the update but do not cascade the delete. Print the Relationships window by making sure the Relationships window is open, clicking File on the menu bar, and then clicking Print Relationships. When Access displays the Print Preview window, click the Print button on the Print Preview toolbar. Do not save the report.
18. Backup the database.

In the Lab

1 Maintaining the Birds2U Database

Problem: The management of Birds2U recently acquired some items from a store that is going out of business. You now need to append these new items to the current item table. Because the business has expanded, you also need to change the database structure and add some validation rules to the database.

FIGURE 3-86

Instructions: Use both the Birds2U database created in the In the Lab 1 of Project 1 on page AC 56 and the More Birds database for this assignment. Perform the following tasks:

1. Open the More Birds database from the Data Disk.
2. Create a new query for the Item table and double-click the asterisk in the field list to add all fields to the query.
3. Change the query type to an Append Query. When Access displays the Append dialog box, make the entries shown in Figure 3-86 and then click the OK button. If your Birds2U database is not located on the floppy disk in drive A, you will need to enter the appropriate information in the File name text box.
4. Click the Run button on the Query Design toolbar to run the append query. Click the Yes button in the Microsoft Office Access dialog box that displays the message that you are about to append 4 rows.
5. Close the append query without saving it, and then close the More Birds database. Open the Birds2U database, and then open the Item table in Datasheet view. The table should contain 14 records.
6. The items added from the More Birds database do not have a supplier assigned to them. Assign items BS10, FS11, and LM05 to supplier 17. Assign item BO22 to supplier 21.
7. Resize the columns to best fit the data and print the Item table. Save the changes to the layout.
8. Using a query, delete all records in the Item table where the description starts with the letter S. (*Hint:* Use Help to solve this problem.) Close the query without saving it. Print the Item table.
9. Open the Supplier table in Design view and add a new field to the end of the table. Name the field, Fax Number. This new field has the same data type and length as Telephone Number. Enter the same comment as Telephone Number but replace Telephone with Fax. Save the change to the table design.
10. Add the following data to the Fax Number field.
11. Resize all columns in the Supplier table to the best fit.
12. Print the table on one page in landscape orientation. Save the change to the layout.
13. Specify referential integrity between the Supplier table (the one table) and the Item table (the many table). Cascade the update but not the delete. Print the Relationships window.
14. Compact the database.

05	602-555-6574
13	512-555-8967
17	707-555-9991
21	610-555-3344

2 Maintaining the Babbage Bookkeeping Database

Problem: Babbage Bookkeeping is expanding rapidly and needs to make some database changes to handle the expansion. The company needs to know more about its clients, such as the type of business and it needs to ensure that data that is entered in the database is valid. It also needs to add some new clients to the database.

Instructions: Use the Babbage Bookkeeping database created in the In the Lab 2 of Project 1 on page AC 59 or see your instructor for information about accessing the files required for this book. Perform the following tasks:

1. Open the Babbage Bookkeeping database and then open the Client table in Design view.
2. Add the field, Client Type, to the Client table. The field should appear after the Zip Code field. Define the field as text with a width of 3. This field will contain data on the type of client. The client types are MAN (Manufacturing), RET (Retail), and SER (Service). Save these changes to the structure.
3. Using a query, change all the entries in the Client Type column to RET. This will be the type of most clients. Do not save the query.
4. Open the Client table and resize all columns to best fit the data. Print the table in landscape orientation. Save the changes to the layout of the table.
5. Create the following validation rules for the Client table and save the changes to the table. List the steps involved on your own paper.
   a. Increase the size of the Name field to 25 and make the Name field a required field.
   b. Specify the legal values MAN, RET, and SER for the Client Type field. Include validation text.
   c. Assign a default value of RET to the Client Type field.
   d. Ensure that any letters entered in the Client Number field appear as uppercase.
   e. Specify that balance must be less than or equal to $1,500.00. Include validation text.
   f. Make the Client Type field a Lookup field.
6. Make the following changes to the Client table. You can use either the Find button or Filter By Selection to locate the records to change:
   a. Change the client type for clients G56, J77, and T45 to SER.
   b. Change the client type for clients B26 and S56 to MAN.
   c. Change the name of client S56 to SeeSaw Industries.
7. Add the following clients to the Client table:

| C21 | Crompton Meat Market | 72 Main | Empeer | 58216 | RET | $0.00 | 24 |
| L50 | Lou's Salon | 124 Fulton | Grant City | 58121 | SER | $125.00 | 34 |

8. Resize the Name column to best fit the new data, and save the changes to the layout of the table.
9. Open the Client table and use Filter By Form to find all records where the client has a balance of $0.00 and has the Client Type of SER. Delete these records.
10. Remove the filter, change the font to Courier New and the font size to 9. Change the gridline color to blue. Print the table in landscape orientation. Close the Client table and do not save any changes.
11. Specify referential integrity between the Bookkeeper table (the one table) and the Client table (the many table). Cascade the update but not the delete. Print the Relationships window. Do not save the report.
12. Compact the database and then backup the database.

3 Maintaining the City Guide Database

Problem: The chamber of commerce has determined that some changes must be made to the database structure. Another field must be added. Because several individuals update the data, the chamber also would like to add some validation rules to the database. Finally, some additions and deletions are required to the database.

Instructions: Use the database created in the In the Lab 3 of Project 1 on page AC 61 for this exercise or see your instructor for information about accessing the files required for this book.

Instructions Part 1: Several changes must be made to the database structure. For example, the chamber would like to categorize the businesses that advertise in the guide. It has determined that the businesses should be categorized as Retail, Dining, or Service establishments and suggest you use the advertiser types RET, DIN, and SER, respectively. Further, the chamber has identified advertisers A228, C135, G346, M321, and W456 as retail businesses. Advertisers C048, D217, P124, and S111 are service establishments and advertiser B103 is a restaurant. The chamber wants to ensure that only those types are entered and it wants to provide some type of lookup to help the individuals that do the data entry. It also wants to ensure that an entry always appears in the Name field and that any letters entered in the Advertiser Number field appear in uppercase. Because it often sorts the data by advertiser name, it wants to make the sorting process more efficient. Make the changes to the database structure and then print the Advertiser table. Place the Advertiser Type field after the Telephone Number field. To ensure that the table prints on one page, adjust the column widths to best fit the data and print the table in landscape orientation.

Instructions Part 2: The chamber has acquired three new advertisers. These advertisers are:

A245	AAA Diner	23 Berton	19363	555-0998	DIN	$50.00	$0.00	26
F410	Fran's Nails	145 Lincoln	19362	555-4218	SER	$75.00	$0.00	32
M111	Main Street Grille	20 Main	19364	555-4455	DIN	$0.00	$0.00	29

Also, the owner of Chloe's Salon has sold the business and the new owner now wants to advertise under the name, Clara for Hair. Another advertiser, Gold's Clothes, has gone out of business. Use the Advertiser form you created in Project 1 to make these changes. To show the chamber that you have made the appropriate changes, adjust column widths, and print the Advertiser table. Be sure the table prints on one page.

Instructions Part 3: Because the ad reps work on commission, the chamber wants to make sure that advertisers are not assigned to an ad rep that is not in the database. It also wants the ability to change an ad rep number in the Ad Rep table and have the change applied to the Advertiser table. Create the appropriate relationship that would satisfy the chamber's needs and print the relationship. Then, change the ad rep number for ad rep 26 to 21. Print the Advertiser table. Be sure the table prints on one page.

Cases and Places

The difficulty of these case studies varies: ■ are the least difficult and ■■ are more difficult. The last exercise is a group exercise.

1 ■ Use the College Dog Walkers database you created in Case Study 1 of Project 1 on page AC 63 for this assignment or see your instructor for information about accessing the files required for this book. Perform each of the following tasks and then print the results:

(a) Melissa Menteer recently married. Her new name is Melissa MacFarlandson.

(b) Frank Bishop adopted a stray dog and now has two dogs that are walked. Frank's per walk amount has been increased to $12.00. Frank's new balance is $30.00.

(c) The minimum per walk amount is now $8.00. The new minimum per walk amount should be the default for all new customers. No per walk amount should be less than $8.00 or more than $24.00.

(d) Specify referential integrity. Cascade the update but not the delete.

(e) Compact and then backup the database.

2 ■ Use the InPerson Fitness Company database you created in Case Study 2 of Project 1 on page AC 63 for this assignment or see your instructor for information about accessing the files required for this book. Perform each of these tasks and then print the results:

(a) Create an index on the Amount Paid and Balance fields in the Client table. Sort the records in the table in descending order by amount paid and balance.

(b) Add a Telephone Number field to the Trainer table. The field should appear after the First Name field. The field should have the same length and the same comment as the Telephone Number field in the Client table. The telephone number for trainer 203 is 555-0101. For trainer 205 and 207, the telephone numbers are 555-1243 and 555-2662, respectively.

(c) Resize the columns in both tables to best fit the data.

(d) Change the cell effect for the Trainer table to Sunken and change the gridline color to red.

(e) Specify referential integrity. Cascade the update but not the delete.

(f) Compact and then backup the database.

3 ■■ Use the Regional Books database you created in Case Study 3 of Project 1 on page AC 63 for this assignment or see your instructor for information about accessing the files required for this book:

(a) The bookstore has added a used book section. Add a field to the database to indicate whether a book is used or new. All books currently in the database are new books.

(b) All books must have a title and the units on hand should never be less than 0.

(c) The default sort order for the Books table should be by title rather than book code (*Hint*: See More About Changing Table Properties on page AC 159 to solve this problem.)

(d) The title for the book 5890 actually is Great Regional Recipes and Food.

(e) Add the used book, County Politics to the database and use 9867 as the book code. County Politics was written by Estelle Dearling and published by VanNestor. The book is a hardback and sells for $7.95. There is only one copy of the book.

(f) The owner sold the last copy of Quirky Architecture, and the book is now out of print.

(g) Determine whether any records are in one table that do not have related records in another table.

(h) Analyze the database and determine if you have a one-to-many relationship between any tables. If so, specify referential integrity between the tables. Cascade the update but not the delete.

Cases and Places

4 ◼◼ Use the Campus Housing database you created in Case Study 4 of Project 1 on page AC 64 for this assignment or see your instructor for information about accessing the files required for this book:

(a) Determine which units are located less than 2 miles from campus and have parking or which units allow pets. Sort the records by distance.

(b) All units must have at least one bathroom.

(c) The only valid lease terms are 3, 6, 9, and 12 months. Most units have a lease term of 9 months.

(d) Many users sort the data in ascending order by bedroom and bathroom. The users are complaining about the length of time it takes to sort the records.

(e) The unit that is located .25 miles from campus no longer is for rent.

(f) Alan Kindall has increased the rent on all his units by $25.00.

(g) Determine whether your database contains any duplicate records.

(h) Analyze the database and determine if you have a one-to-many relationship between any tables. If so, specify referential integrity. Cascade the update but not the delete.

5 ◼◼ **Working Together** With a make-table query, a user can create a new table from one or more tables in the database. The table can be stored in the same database or a new database. As a team, use the Access Help system to learn more about make-table queries. Then, choose one of the Cases and Places databases and create a make-table query. The query must use two tables to create one new table and must store the table in a new database that your team must create. For example, for the Birds2U database, the owner could create a table named Supplier Call List that would include the item code, description, and cost of each item as well as the supplier name and telephone number. Write a one-page paper that (1) explains the purpose for which the new table is intended and (2) suggests at least two additional uses for make-table queries.

Open the Contact Management database that you created in Project 1. As a team, review the data types for each of the fields that are in the database. Do any of these data types need to be changed? For example, is there a Text field that is storing notes about the company? Change the data types as necessary and write a one-page paper that explains your reasons for changing (or not changing) the data types in the Contact Management database.

Make a copy of the College Dog Walkers database and name it University Dog Walkers. Research the purpose of the Find Unmatched Query Wizard and the Find Duplicates Query Wizard. Create queries using each of these wizards. Did the queries perform as expected? Open each query in Design view and modify it, for example, add another field to the query. What happened to the query results? Write a one-page paper that explains the purpose of each query wizard and describes your experiences with creating and modifying the queries.

MICROSOFT
Office Access 2003

Sharing Data among Applications

CASE PERSPECTIVE

Harton-Janes Clinic specializes in physical therapy. Employees have been using Microsoft Excel to automate a variety of tasks for several years. When deciding to maintain patient data, the administrators decided to maintain the data as an Excel worksheet. Employees recently completed Microsoft Office training at Ashton James College (AJC) and now have decided they need to maintain the data in an Access database. They need an easy way to copy the data to Access.

AJC has determined that it needs to export (copy) some of the data in its database to other formats. Some users need the data in Excel, others want it placed in a Microsoft Word document, and still others want the ability to send a report via e-mail.

AJC would like to export the Client and Trainer tables in such a way that they can be imported easily to a database of a related organization, AJ Consulting, which handles various accounting functions for AJC. The users have learned that the easiest way to do this is to use XML (Extensible Markup Language).

As you read through this Integration Feature, you will learn how to use Access to convert data in the manner desired by Harton-Janes Clinic and Ashton James College.

Objectives

You will have mastered the material in this Integration Feature when you can:

- Import or link an Excel worksheet
- Export data to Excel and Word
- Create report snapshots
- Export and import XML data

Introduction

It is not uncommon for people to use an application for some specific purpose, only to find later that another application may be better suited. For example, an organization such as Harton-Janes Clinic initially might keep data in an Excel worksheet, only to discover later that the data would be better maintained in an Access database. The following are some common reasons for using a database instead of a worksheet:

1. The worksheet contains a great deal of redundant data. As discussed in Project 1 on pages AC 50 and AC 51, databases can be designed to eliminate redundant data.
2. The worksheet would need to be larger than Excel can handle. Excel has a limit of 16,384 rows. In Access, no such limit exists.
3. The data to be maintained consists of multiple interrelated items. For example, the Ashton James College database maintains data on two items, clients and trainers, and these items are interrelated. A client has a single trainer and each trainer is responsible for several clients. The Ashton James College database is a very simple one. Databases easily can contain thirty or more interrelated items.

4. You want to use the extremely powerful query and report capabilities of Microsoft Access.

Regardless of the reasons for making the change from a worksheet to a database, it is important to be able to make the change easily. In the not-too-distant past, converting data from one tool to another often could be a very difficult, time-consuming task. Fortunately, an easy way of converting data from Excel to Access is available.

Figures 1a and 1b illustrate the conversion process. The type of worksheet that can be converted is one in which the data is stored as a **list**, that is, a labeled series of rows in which each row contains the same type of data. For example, in the worksheet in Figure 1a, the first row contains the labels, which are entries indicating the type of data found in the column. The entry in the first column, for example, is Patient Number, indicating that all the other values in the column are patient numbers. The entry in the second column is Last Name, indicating that all the other values in the column are last names. Other than the first row, which contains the labels, all the rows contain precisely the same type of data shown in the Access database in Figure 1b: a patient number in the first column, a last name in the second column, a first name in the third column, and so on.

(a) Microsoft Office Excel Worksheet

(b) Microsoft Office Access Database

FIGURE 1

As the figures illustrate, the worksheet, shown in Figure 1a, is copied to a database table, shown in Figure 1b. The columns in the worksheet become the fields. The column headings in the first row of the worksheet become the field names. The rows of the worksheet, other than the first row, which contains the labels, become the records in the table. In the process, each field will be assigned the data type that seems the most reasonable, given the data currently in the worksheet.

Conversely, you can copy data from an Access database so that another application (for example, Excel) can use the data. Several different ways exist to

Access Integration Feature

export data. The two most common are to use the Export command on the File menu, which you will use to export a query to an Excel worksheet (Figure 2a), and to use drag-and-drop, which you will use to export a query to a Word document (Figure 2b).

At times you may want to send a report to a user via e-mail. It would be prohibitive to send the whole database to the other user, just so the user could print or view the report. In addition, doing so would require the other user to have Microsoft Access installed. A better way is to create a snapshot of the report. A **snapshot** is a special file that contains the report exactly as it appears when printed (Figure 2c). The other user then can use the Snapshot Viewer, which is a Microsoft Office tool, to view or print the report.

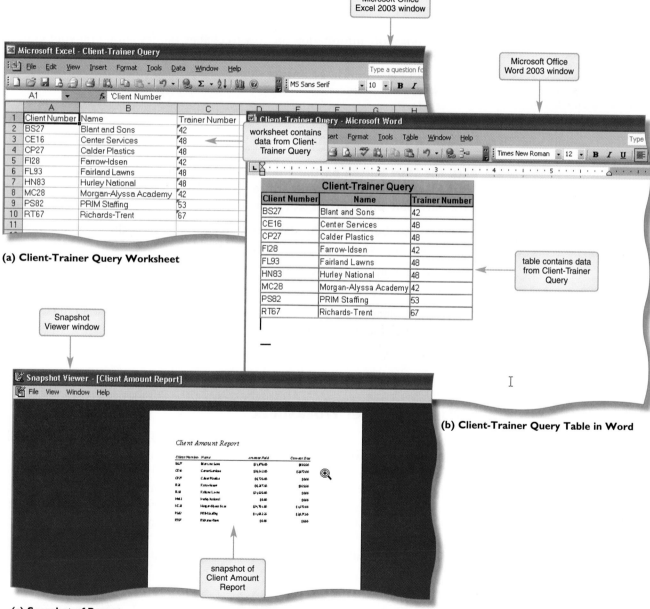

(a) Client-Trainer Query Worksheet

(b) Client-Trainer Query Table in Word

(c) Snapshot of Report

FIGURE 2

You also can export and import data using XML, which is a format for exchanging data between dissimilar applications. The XML format allows you to export and import both data and structure of multiple related tables in a single operation.

Convert Data from Other Applications to Access

The process of converting data to an Access database, referred to as **importing**, uses an Import wizard. Specifically, if the data is copied from an Excel worksheet, the process will use the **Import Spreadsheet Wizard**. The wizard takes you through some basic steps, asking a few simple questions. After you have answered the questions, the wizard will perform the conversion, creating an appropriate table in the database and filling it with the data from the worksheet.

Creating an Access Database

If you are stepping through this project on a computer and you want your screen to match the figures in this book, then you should change your computer's resolution to 800 × 600. For more information on how to change the resolution on your computer, see Appendix D. Before converting the data, you need to create the database that will contain the data. The following steps show how to create the Harton-Janes Clinic database.

To Create a New Database

1. **Click the Start button on the Windows taskbar, click All Programs on the Start menu, point to Microsoft Office on the All Programs submenu, and then click Microsoft Office Access 2003 on the Microsoft Office submenu.**

2. **Click the New button on the Database toolbar, and then click Blank database in the New area of the New File task pane.**

3. **Click the Save in box arrow in the File New Database dialog box and then click 3½ Floppy (A:).**

4. **Erase the current entry in the File name text box, type** Harton-Janes Clinic **as the file name, and then click the Create button.**

Access creates the database. It is open and ready for use.

Importing an Excel Worksheet

To convert the data, use the Import Spreadsheet Wizard. In the process, you will indicate that the first row contains the column headings. These column headings then will become the field names in the Access table. In addition, you will indicate the primary key for the table. As part of the process, you can, if you desire, choose not to include all the fields from the worksheet in the resulting table. You should be aware that some of the steps might take a significant amount of time for Access to execute.

The following steps illustrate the process of importing an Excel worksheet.

To Import an Excel Worksheet

1

- **With the Harton-Janes Clinic database open, right-click in the open area of the Database window.**

The shortcut menu appears (Figure 3).

FIGURE 3

2

- **Click Import.**
- **When Access displays the Import dialog box, click the Files of type box arrow and then click Microsoft Excel.**
- **If necessary, select 3½ Floppy (A:) in the Look in list.**
- **Make sure the Patient workbook is selected, and then click the Import button.**
- **When Access displays the Import Spreadsheet Wizard dialog box, if necessary, click Show Worksheets and then click the Next button.**
- **Be sure the Patient worksheet is selected, and then click the Next button.**

Access displays the Import Spreadsheet Wizard dialog box requesting you to indicate whether the first row contains column headings (Figure 4).

FIGURE 4

3

• **If necessary, click First Row Contains Column Headings to select it.**

• **Click the Next button.**

The Import Spreadsheet Wizard dialog box displays options for storing data in a new table or in an existing table (Figure 5).

FIGURE 5

4

• **If necessary, click In a New Table to select it and then click the Next button.**

• **Because the Field Options need not be specified, click the Next button.**

The Import Spreadsheet Wizard dialog box displays options for defining a primary key for the new Access table (Figure 6). Options allow Access to add a special field to serve as the primary key, allow the user to choose an existing field to serve as the primary key, or allow the user to indicate no primary key. Most of the time, one of the existing fields will serve as the primary key. In this work-sheet, for example, the Patient Number serves as the primary key.

FIGURE 6

5

• **Click Choose my own primary key.**

• **Because the Patient Number field, which is the correct field, is already selected as the primary key, click the Next button. (If some other field were to be the primary key, you could click the down arrow and select the other field from the list of available fields.)**

• **Be sure Patient appears in the Import to Table text box.**

• **Click the Finish button.**

The worksheet is converted into an Access table named Patient. When the process is completed, Access displays the Import Spreadsheet Wizard dialog box (Figure 7).

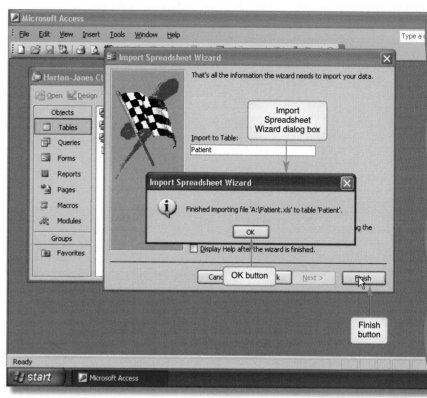

FIGURE 7

6

• **Click the OK button.**

Access has created the table (Figure 8). The table name appears in the Database window.

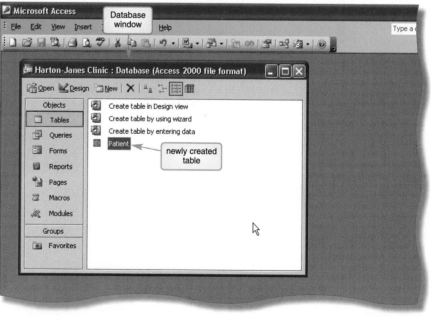

FIGURE 8

> ### Other Ways
>
> 1. On File menu click Get External Data, click Import
> 2. In Voice Command mode, say "File, Get External Data, Import"

Using the Access Table

After the Access version of the table has been created, you can treat it as you would any other table. You can open the table in Datasheet view (Figure 1b on page AC 174). You can make changes to the data. You can create queries that use the data in the table.

By clicking Design View on the table's shortcut menu, you can view the table's structure and make any necessary changes to the structure. The changes may include changing field sizes and types (for those that may not be correct), creating indexes, specifying the primary key, or adding additional fields. If you have imported multiple tables that are to be related, you will need to relate the tables. To accomplish any of these tasks, use the same steps you used in Project 3. In the Patient table shown in Figure 1b, for example, the columns have been resized to best fit the data.

Linking versus Importing

When an external table or worksheet is imported, or converted, into an Access database, a copy of the data is placed as a table in the database. The original data still exists, just as it did before, but no further connection exists between it and the data in the database. Changes to the original data do not affect the data in the database. Likewise, changes in the database do not affect the original data.

It also is possible to **link** data stored in a variety of formats to Access databases by selecting Link instead of Import on the shortcut menu. (The available formats include several other database management systems as well as a variety of nondatabase formats, including Excel worksheets.) With linking, the connection is maintained.

When an Excel worksheet is linked, for example, the worksheet is not stored in the database. Instead Access simply establishes a connection to the worksheet so you can view or edit the data in either Access or Excel. Any change made in either one will be immediately visible in the other. For example, if you would change an address in Access and then view the worksheet in Excel, you would see the new address. If you add a new row in Excel and then view the table in Access, the row would appear as a new record.

To identify that a table is linked to other data, Access places an arrow in front of the table (Figure 9). In addition, the Excel icon in front of the name identifies the fact that the data is linked to an Excel worksheet.

After you link tables between a worksheet and a database or between two databases, you can modify many of the linked table's features. For example, you can rename the linked table, set view properties, and set links between tables in queries. If you move, rename, or modify linked tables, you can use the **Linked Table Manager** to update the links. To do so, use the Tools menu, click Database Utilities, and then click Linked Table Manager. The Linked Table Manager dialog box that appears includes instructions on how to update the links.

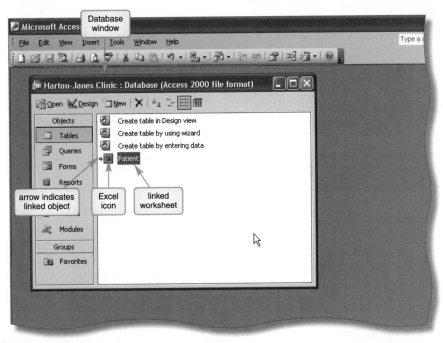

FIGURE 9

Closing the Database

The following step shows how to close the database by closing its Database window.

To Close a Database

1 Click the Close button for the Harton-Janes Clinic : Database window.

Copy Data from Access to Other Applications

Exporting is the process of copying database objects to another database, to a worksheet, or to some other format so another application (for example, Excel) can use the data. Several ways exist for exporting data. The two most common are to use the Export command, which you will use to export a query to Excel, and to use drag-and-drop, which you will use to export a query to a Word document. You also will use the Export command to export a report as a snapshot.

Opening the Database

Before exporting the Ashton James College data, you first must open the database. The following steps show how to open a database.

To Open a Database

1 Click the Open button on the Database toolbar.

2 If necessary, click the Look in box arrow and then click 3½ Floppy (A:). Click Ashton James College, the database modified in Project 3. (If you did not complete the steps in Project 3, see your instructor for a copy of the database.)

3 Click the Open button in the Open dialog box. If a Security Warning dialog box appears, click the Open button.

Access opens the Ashton James College database in the Database window.

Using the Export Command to Export Data to Excel

One way to export data to Excel, as well as to a variety of other formats, is to select the database object to be exported and then select the Export command on the shortcut menu. After you have selected the command, indicate the file type (for example, Microsoft Excel 97-2003) and then click the Save button. For some of the formats, including Excel, you can select Save formatted, in which case the export process will attempt to preserve as much of the Access formatting of the data as possible. You also can select Autostart in which case, the application receiving the data will start automatically once the data is exported. The resulting data then will appear in the application.

The steps on the next page show how to use the Export command to export the Client-Trainer Query to Excel.

Q: How could you export records from a table?

A: The process of exporting records from a table is identical to that of exporting records from a query. Simply select the Tables object and then the table containing the records to be exported before selecting the Export command. All records and fields from the table then will be exported.

To Use the Export Command to Export Data to Excel

1

• **Click Queries on the Objects bar, and then right-click Client-Trainer Query.**

The shortcut menu appears (Figure 10).

2

• **Click Export.**

• **If necessary, click the Save in box arrow and then click 3½ Floppy (A:).**

• **Click the Save as type box arrow, and then click Microsoft Excel 97-2003 in the Save as type list.**

• **Be sure the file name is Client-Trainer Query, and then click the Export button.**

The worksheet is created.

FIGURE 10

Other Ways

1. On File menu click Export
2. In Voice Command mode, say "File, Export"

To view the worksheet, you could open it in Excel. You then could make any changes to it. For example, you could resize the columns to best fit the data by double-clicking the right edge of the column heading. Figure 2a on page AC 175 shows the worksheet displayed in Excel with the columns resized.

Q & A

Q: Can you use drag-and-drop to export data to Excel?

A: Yes. You can use drag-and-drop to export data to Excel just as you can to export data to Word. Be sure that Excel is running instead of Word. Drag the table or query from the Database window in Access to the Excel worksheet. The records will be converted to rows in the worksheet and the fields will be converted to columns.

Using Drag-and-Drop to Export Data to Word

When using the Export command, Microsoft Word is not one of the available file types. You would need to select one of the file types that can be imported into Word, export from Access to the selected file type, and then import the file that is created into Word. A simpler way to export to Word is to use the drag-and-drop method. In this method, both Access and Word must be open simultaneously. You then drag the object to be imported from Access to the Word document. The following steps show how to export the Client-Trainer Query to Word using the drag-and-drop method.

To Use Drag-and-Drop to Export Data to Word

1

• **Click the Start button on the Windows taskbar, point to All Programs on the Start menu, point to Microsoft Office on the All Programs submenu, and then click Microsoft Office Word 2003 on the Microsoft Office submenu.**

• **Close the Getting Started task pane.**

• **Click the Microsoft Access button on the taskbar to return to Microsoft Access.**

• **Click the Restore Down button or resize the Access window so the Access window does not occupy the full screen.**

• **Be sure the Queries object is selected.**

• **Drag the Client-Trainer Query icon to the upper-left corner of the Word document. Do not release the mouse button.**

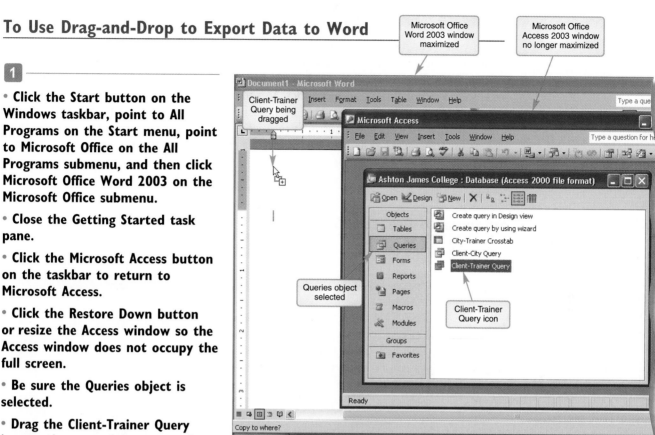

FIGURE 11

Microsoft Office Word is displayed in a maximized window (Figure 11). Microsoft Office Access is displayed in a resized, smaller window. The Queries object is selected and the Client-Trainer Query is selected. The mouse pointer indicates that the Client-Trainer Query is being dragged to Word.

2

• **Release the mouse button and then click the Save button on the Standard toolbar in Microsoft Word.**

• **Type** Client-Trainer Query **in the File name text box, and then click the Save button in the Save As dialog box.**

• **Click in the Word window to deselect the table.**

The data from the query is inserted in the Word document. The title of the query appears in bold at the top of the document. The data is inserted as a Word table. The document is saved. It looks like the one shown in Figure 2b on page AC 175.

3

• **Quit Word by clicking its Close button.**

• **Maximize the Microsoft Office Access window by double-clicking its title bar.**

Microsoft Word no longer appears. The file is saved and available for use.

Using the Export Command to Create a Snapshot

If you want to send a report to someone via e-mail, the simplest way is to create a snapshot of the report. The **snapshot** is stored in a separate file with an extension of snp. This file contains all the details of the report, including fonts, effects (for example, bold or italic), and graphics. In other words, the contents of the snapshot file look precisely like the report. The snapshot file can be viewed by anyone having the Snapshot Viewer; Microsoft Office Access 2003 is *not* required. You can use the **Snapshot Viewer** to e-mail the snapshot; the recipient can use the Snapshot Viewer to view or print the snapshot.

The following steps illustrate how to create a snapshot.

To Use the Export Command to Create a Snapshot

1

• **If the Microsoft Access Database window is not maximized, maximize the window by double-clicking its title bar.**

• **Click the Reports object, right-click the Client Amount Report, and then click Print Preview on the shortcut menu.**

• **Right-click the preview of the report.**

Access displays the Client Amount Report window with a preview of the report (Figure 12). The shortcut menu appears.

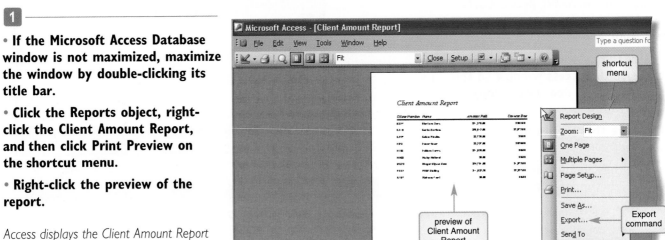

FIGURE 12

2

• **Click Export.**

• **If necessary, click the Save in box arrow and then click 3½ Floppy (A:).**

• **Click the Save as type box arrow, select Snapshot Format, be sure the Autostart check box is checked, and then click the Export button.**

• **If a Microsoft Office Access dialog box is displayed asking if you want to install Snapshot Viewer, click the No button and see your instructor.**

The snapshot of the report is created. It looks similar to the one in Figure 2c on page AC 175.

3

• **Click the Close button for the Snapshot Viewer - [Client Amount Report] window.**

• **Click the Close button on the Print Preview toolbar.**

The Snapshot Viewer and Print Preview windows close. Access displays the Database window.

You can e-mail the snapshot to other users. The other users can use the Snapshot Viewer to view the report online or to print the report.

XML

Just as Hypertext Markup Language (HTML) is the standard language for creating and displaying Web pages, **Extensible Markup Language** (**XML**) is the standard language for describing and delivering data on the Web. XML is a data interchange format that allows you to exchange data between dissimilar systems or applications. With XML, you can describe both the data and the structure (**schema**) of the data. You can export tables, queries, forms, or reports.

When exporting XML data, you can choose to export multiple related tables in a single operation to a single XML file. If you later import this XML data to another database, you will import all the tables in a single operation. Thus, the new database would contain each of the tables. All the fields would have all the correct data types and sizes. The primary keys would be correct, and the tables would be related exactly as they were in the original database.

Exporting XML Data

To export XML data, you use the same Export command you used to export to other formats. You then select XML as the Save as type. You indicate whether to just save the data or to save both the data and the schema (that is, the structure). If you have made changes to the appearance of the data, such as changing the font, and want these changes saved as well, you save what is termed the **presentation**. The data is saved in a file with the XML extension, the schema is saved in a file with the XSD extension, and the presentation is saved in a file with the XSL extension. The default choice, which usually is appropriate, is to save both the data and schema, but not the presentation. If multiple tables are related, such as the Client and Trainer tables in the Ashton James College data, you can export both tables to a single file.

The following steps export both the Client and Trainer tables to a single XML file called Client. The steps save the data and the schema, but do not save the presentation.

To Export XML Data

1

• **Click the Tables object, and then right-click Client.**

The shortcut menu for the Client table appears (Figure 13).

FIGURE 13

2

• **Click Export on the shortcut menu.**

• **Click the Save as type box arrow, scroll down, and then click XML in the list.**

• **If necessary, select 3½ Floppy (A:) in the Save in list.**

Access displays the Export Table 'Client' As dialog box (Figure 14). The file name is Client and the Save as type is XML.

FIGURE 14

3

• **Click the Export button.**

Access displays the Export XML dialog box (Figure 15). The current selections call for the data and schema to be exported. The presentation will not be exported.

FIGURE 15

4

• **Click the More Options button.**

Access displays the Export XML dialog box (Figure 16). The Data tab is selected.

FIGURE 16

5

• **Click the expand indicator (the plus sign) to the left of [Lookup Data], and then click the Trainer check box to select the Trainer table.**

Both the Client table and the Trainer table are selected (Figure 17). The export location is A:\Client.xml.

6

• **Click the OK button.**

• **Click the Close button for the Microsoft Access [Ashton James College : Database (Access 2000 file format)] window.**

FIGURE 17

The data and structure for both the Client table and the Trainer table are exported to the file named Client. The file also contains the relationship between the two tables. The Ashton James College database is closed.

Creating an Access Database

Before importing the data, you need to create the database that will contain the data. The following steps create the AJ Consulting database.

To Create a New Database

1 Click the New button on the Database toolbar, and then click Blank database in the New area of the New File task pane.

2 If necessary, click the Save in box arrow in the File New Database dialog box and then click 3½ Floppy (A:).

3 Type AJ Consulting in the File name text box and then click the Create button.

Access creates the database. It is open and ready for use.

Importing XML Data

To import XML data, use the Import command and select XML as the type. You then select the XML file that contains the data to be imported. The steps on the next page import the Client and Trainer tables stored in the XML file called Client.

To Import XML Data

1

• **Right-click in the Database window.**

The shortcut menu for the Database window appears (Figure 18).

FIGURE 18

2

• **Click Import on the shortcut menu.**

• **Click the Files of type box arrow, scroll down, and then click XML in the list.**

• **If necessary, select 3½ Floppy (A:) in the Look in list.**

• **Click the Client file. (Do not click the xsd version. If you do, you will import both tables, but none of the data. That is, the tables will be empty.)**

Access displays the Import dialog box (Figure 19). The Client file is selected. XML is the file type.

FIGURE 19

3

• **Click the Import button.**

Access displays the Import XML dialog box (Figure 20). Both the Client and Trainer tables will be imported. Clicking the expand indicator to the left of either table will display a list of fields in the table.

FIGURE 20

4

• **Click the OK button.**

The data is imported and the Microsoft Office Access dialog box is displayed (Figure 21).

5

• **Click the OK button.**

FIGURE 21

Both tables have been imported as part of this single Import operation. In addition to having the same data, the fields in both tables have precisely the same data types and sizes as in the original database. Also, the same fields have been designated primary keys.

Closing the Database and Quitting Access

The following steps close the database and quit Access.

To Close a Database and Quit Access

1 Click the Close Window button for the AJ Consulting : Database window.

2 Click the Close button for the Microsoft Access window.

Integration Feature Summary

The Integration Feature covered the process of integrating an Excel worksheet into an Access database. To convert a worksheet to an Access table, you learned to use the Import Spreadsheet Wizard. Working with the wizard, you identified the first row of the worksheet as the row containing the column headings and you indicated the primary key. The wizard then created the table for you and placed it in a new database. You also saw how you could link data instead of importing it.

You learned to use the Export command and used it to export data to an Excel worksheet. You also learned to use the drag-and-drop feature and used it to export data to a Word document. The project illustrated how to use the Export command to create a snapshot of a report. You learned how to export XML data. You exported both structure and data for multiple related tables in a single operation. Finally, you learned how to import the XML data to a separate database and discovered that a single import operation imported both tables and their structures.

> *SAM* If you have a SAM user profile, you may have access to hands-on instruction, practice, and assessment of the skills covered in this project. Log in to your SAM account and go to your assignments page to see what your instructor has assigned.

What You Should Know

Having completed this project, you should be able to perform the tasks below. The tasks are listed in the same order they were presented in this project. For a list of the buttons, menus, toolbars, and commands introduced in this project, see the Quick Reference Summary at the back of this book and refer to the Page Number column.

1. Create a New Database   (AC 176)
2. Import an Excel Worksheet   (AC 177)
3. Close a Database   (AC 181)
4. Open a Database   (AC 181)
5. Use the Export Command to Export Data to Excel   (AC 182)
6. Use Drag-and-Drop to Export Data to Word (AC 183)
7. Use the Export Command to Create a Snapshot (AC 184)
8. Export XML Data   (AC 185)
9. Create a New Database   (AC 187)
10. Import XML Data   (AC 188)
11. Close a Database and Quit Access   (AC 190)

In the Lab

1 Importing Data to an Access Database

Problem: CAC Logo Company has been using Excel for a number of tasks. The company sells logo-imprinted novelty items and clothing to organizations. CAC uses several worksheets to keep track of inventory, and customers. CAC realizes that the customer data would be better handled if maintained in an Access database. The company wants to maintain the items inventory in Excel worksheets but also would like to be able to use the query and report features of Access.

Instructions: For this assignment, you will need two files: Customer.xls and Logo Items.xls. These files are on the Data Disk. See the inside back cover of this book for instructions for downloading the Data Disk or see your instructor for information about accessing the files required for this book. Perform the following tasks:

1. Start Access and create a new database in which to store all the objects for CAC Logo Company. Call the database CAC Logo Company.

2. Import the Customer worksheet shown in Figure 22 into Access. The worksheet is in the Customer workbook on the Data Disk.

3. Use Customer as the name of the Access table and Customer Number as the primary key.

4. Open the Customer table in Datasheet view and resize the columns to best fit the data. Print the table.

5. Link the Logo Items worksheet shown in Figure 23 to the database. The worksheet is in the Logo Items workbook on the Data Disk.

6. Open the linked Logo Items table in Datasheet view and resize the columns to best fit the data. Print the table.

7. Rename the linked Logo Items table as Items. Then, use the Linked Table Manager to update the link between the Excel worksheet and the Access table. (If the Linked Table Manager wizard is not installed on your computer, see your instructor before continuing.)

FIGURE 22

FIGURE 23

(continued)

Importing Data to an Access Database *(continued)*

8. Print the Items table.
9. Link the Trainer table in the AJ Consulting database to the CAC Logo database. Trainers of AJ Consulting may become potential sales reps for CAC Logo.
10. Rename the Trainer table as Potential Sales Reps. Then, use the Linked Table Manager to update the link between the two tables.
11. Print the Potential Sales Rep table.

2 Exporting Data to Other Applications

Problem: Begon Pest Control wants to be able to export some of the data in the Access database to other applications. The company wants to export the City-Technician Crosstab query for further processing in Excel. It also wants to use the Customer-Technician query in a Word document as well as e-mail the Customer Amount Report to the company's accounting firm. The company has decided to branch out and offer pest control services that will focus on outside pest control, that is, pest control for lawns and gardens. It wants to export the Customer and Technician tables as a single XML file and then import it to a new database.

Instructions: Start Access. Open the Begon Pest Control database that you modified in Apply Your Knowledge 1 in Project 3 on page AC 167. (If you did not complete this exercise, see your instructor for a copy of the modified database.) Perform the following tasks:

1. Export the City-Technician Crosstab query to Excel as shown in Figure 24.
2. Resize the columns to best fit the data as shown in Figure 24.
3. Print the Excel worksheet.
4. Use drag-and-drop to place the Customer-Technician query in a Word document.
5. Print the Word document.
6. Preview the Customer Amount Report and then export the report as a snapshot.
7. Open the report in the Snapshot Viewer and print it. (If a Microsoft Office Access dialog box is displayed asking if you want to install Snapshot Viewer, click the No button and see your instructor.)
8. Export both the Customer and Technician tables in XML format. Be sure that both tables are exported to the same file.
9. Create a new database called Begon Garden Services.
10. Import the Customer file containing both the Customer and Technician tables to the Begon Garden Services database.
11. Change the name of customer CJ45 to C Joseph Diner.
12. Change the first name of technician 220 to Christy.
13. Print the Customer and Technician tables.

	B	C	D	E	F	G	H	I	J	K
1	Total Of Balance	203	210	214						
2	$763.00	$398.00		$365.00						
3	$300.00		$300.00	$0.00						
4	$1,302.00	$335.00	$967.00							
5										

FIGURE 24

Appendix A

Microsoft Office Access Help System

Using the Access Help System

This appendix shows you how to use the Access Help system. At anytime while you are using Access, you can interact with its Help system and display information on any Access topic. It is a complete reference manual at your fingertips.

As shown in Figure A-1, five methods for accessing the Access Help system are available:

1. Microsoft Access Help button on the Database toolbar
2. Microsoft Access Help command on the Help menu
3. Function key F1 on the keyboard
4. Type a question for help box on the menu bar
5. Office Assistant

FIGURE A-1

(a) Microsoft Access Help Task Pane

(b) Search Results Task Pane

(c) Microsoft Access Help Window

All five methods result in the Access Help system displaying a task pane on the right side of the Access window. The first three methods cause the **Microsoft Office Access Help task pane** to appear (Figure A-1a on the previous page). This task pane includes a Search text box in which you can enter a word or phrase on which you want help. Once you enter the word or phrase, the Access Help system displays the Search Results task pane (Figure A-1b on the previous page). With the Search Results task pane displayed, you can select specific Help topics.

As shown in Figure A-1, methods 4 and 5 bypass the Microsoft Access Help task pane and immediately display the **Search Results task pane** (Figure A-1b) with a list of links that pertain to the selected topic. Thus, the result of any of the five methods for accessing the Access Help system is the Search Results task pane. Once the Access Help system displays this task pane, you can choose links that relate to the word or phrase on which you searched. In Figure A-1, for example, data types was the searched topic, and the link chosen, About changing a field's data type (MDB), resulted in the Access Help system displaying the Microsoft Office Access Help window with information about changing a field's data type (Figure A-1c on the previous page).

Navigating the Access Help System

The quickest way to enter the Access Help system is through the Type a question for help box on the right side of the menu bar at the top of the screen. Here you can type words, such as report or print. You also can type phrases, such as create a report or how do I create a report. The Access Help system responds by displaying the Search Results task pane with a list of links.

Here are two tips regarding the words or phrases you enter to initiate a search: (1) check the spelling of the word or phrase; and (2) keep your search very specific, with fewer than seven words, to return the most accurate results.

Assume for the following example that you want to print the design of a database object, and you do not know how to do it. The likely keyword is print, because you know that printing the design of a database object is a form of printing. The following steps show how to use the Type a question for help box to obtain useful information by entering the keyword print. The steps also show you how to navigate the Access Help system. In the example, the Ashton James College database is open. You do not need to have a database open to use the Help system.

To Obtain Help Using the Type a Question for Help Box

1

• **Click the Type a question for help box on the right side of the menu bar, type** print **and then press the ENTER key.**

The Access Help system displays the Search Results task pane on the right side of the window. The Search Results task pane includes 30 resulting links (Figure A-2). If you do not find what you are looking for, you can modify or refine the search in the Search area at the bottom of the Search Results task pane. The results returned in your Search Results task pane may be different.

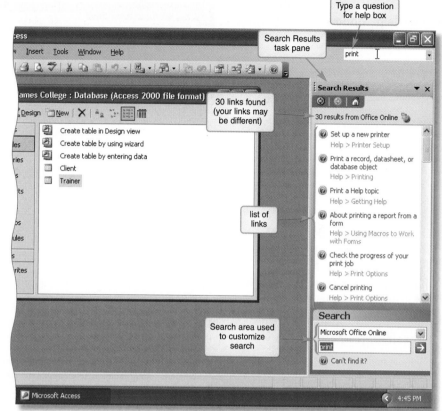

FIGURE A-2

2

• **Scroll down to the bottom of the list of links in the Search Results task pane and then click the Print the design of a database or a database object (MDB) link.**

• **When the Access Help system displays the Microsoft Office Access Help window, click its Auto Tile button in the upper-right corner of the window.**

The Access Help system displays the Microsoft Office Access Help window with the desired information about printing the design of a database or a database object (Figure A-3). With the Microsoft Office Access Help window and Microsoft Office Access window tiled, you can read the information in one window and complete the task in the other window.

FIGURE A-3

3

• **Double-click the Microsoft Office Access Help window title bar.**

The Microsoft Office Access Help window is maximized so it fills the entire screen (Figure A-4). If you are connected to the Internet, you can give Microsoft your opinion as to whether the information was helpful by clicking the Yes or No button at the bottom of the page.

4

• **Click the Restore Down button on the right side of the Microsoft Office Access Help window title bar to return to the tiled state shown in Figure A-3.**

• **Click the Close button on the Microsoft Office Access Help window title bar.**

The Microsoft Office Access Help window closes and the database is active.

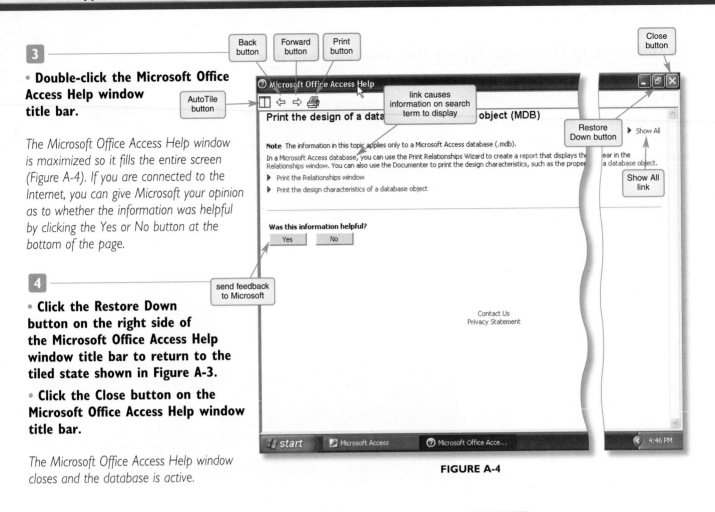

FIGURE A-4

Use the four buttons in the upper-left corner of the Microsoft Office Access Help window (Figure A-4) to tile or untile, navigate through the Help system, or print the contents of the window. As you click links in the Search Results task pane, the Access Help system displays new pages of information. The Access Help system remembers the links you visited and allows you to redisplay the pages visited during a session by clicking the Back and Forward buttons (Figures A-3 on the previous page and A-4).

If none of the links presents the information you want, you can refine the search by entering another word or phrase in the Search text box in the Search Results task pane (Figure A-3). If you have access to the Web, then the scope is global for the initial search. **Global** means all the categories listed in the Search box of the Search area in Figure A-5 are searched. For example, you can restrict the scope to **Offline Help**, which results in a search of related links only on your hard disk.

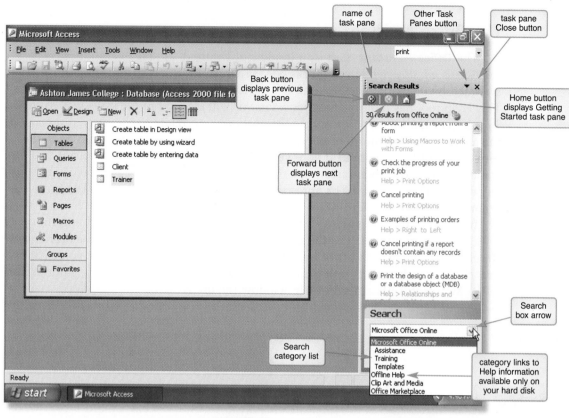

FIGURE A-5

Figure A-5 shows several additional features of the Search Results task pane with which you should be familiar. The buttons immediately below the name of the task pane allow you to navigate between task panes. The Other Task Panes button and the Close button on the Search Results task pane title bar let you change task panes and close the active task pane.

As you enter questions and terms in the Type a question for help box, the Access Help system adds them to its list. Thus, if you click the Type a question for help box arrow, a list of previously used words and phrases are displayed (Figure A-6).

FIGURE A-6

The Office Assistant

The **Office Assistant** is an icon (middle of Figure A-7) that Access displays in the Access window while you work. For the Office Assistant to appear, it must be activated by invoking the Show the Office Assistant command on the Help menu. This Help tool has multiple functions. First, it will respond in the same way as the Type a question for help box with a list of topics that relate to the entry you make in the text box at the bottom of the Office Assistant balloon. The entry can be in the form of a word or phrase as if you were talking to a person. For example, if you want to learn more about creating a report, in the balloon text box, you can type any of the following words or phrases: report, create a report, how do I create a report, or anything similar.

In the example in Figure A-7, the phrase, create a report, is entered into the Office Assistant balloon. The Office Assistant responds by displaying the Search Results task pane with a list of links from which you can choose. Once you click a link in the Search Results task pane, the Access Help system displays the information in the Microsoft Office Access Help window (Figure A-7).

FIGURE A-7

Second, the Office Assistant monitors your work and accumulates tips during a session on how you might increase your productivity and efficiency. The accumulation of tips must be enabled. You enable the accumulation of tips by right-clicking the Office Assistant, clicking Options on the shortcut menu, and then selecting the types of tips you want accumulated. You can view the tips at anytime. The accumulated tips appear when you activate the Office Assistant balloon. Also, if at anytime you see a lightbulb above the Office Assistant, click it to display the most recent tip. If the Office Assistant is hidden, then the lightbulb shows on the Microsoft Office Access Help button on the Database toolbar.

You hide the Office Assistant by invoking the Hide the Office Assistant command on the Help menu or by right-clicking the Office Assistant and then clicking Hide on the shortcut menu. The Hide the Office Assistant command shows on the Help menu only when the Office Assistant is active in the Access window. If the Office Assistant begins showing up on your screen without you instructing it to show, then right-click the Office Assistant, click Options on the shortcut menu, click the Use the Office Assistant check box to remove the check mark, and then click the OK button.

Third, if the Office Assistant is active in the Access window, then Access displays all program and system messages in the Office Assistant balloon.

You may or may not want the Office Assistant to appear on the screen at all times. As indicated earlier, you can hide it and then show it later through the Help menu. For more information about the Office Assistant, type `office assistant` in the Type a question for help box and then click the links in the Search Results task pane.

Help Buttons in Dialog Boxes and Subsystem Windows

As you invoke commands that display dialog boxes or other windows, such as the Print Preview window, you will see buttons and links that offer helpful information. Figures A-8a and A-8b (on the next page) shows the types of Help buttons and links you will see as you work with Access.

FIGURE A-8a

FIGURE A-8b

Other Help Commands on the Help Menu

Thus far, this appendix has discussed the first two commands on the Help menu:
(1) the Microsoft Office Access Help command (Figure A-1 on page APP 1) and
(2) the Show the Office Assistant command (Figure A-7 on page APP 6). Several
additional commands are available on the Help menu as shown in Figure A-9.
Table A-1 summarizes these commands.

FIGURE A-9

Table A-1   Summary of Other Help Commands on the Help Menu

COMMAND ON HELP MENU	FUNCTION
Microsoft Office Online	Activates your browser, which displays the Microsoft Office Online Home page. The Microsoft Office Online Home page contains links that can improve your Office productivity.
Access Developer Resources	Activates your browser, which displays information and links specific to developing applications using Microsoft Office Access.
Contact Us	Activates your browser, which displays Microsoft contact information and a list of useful links.
Sample Databases	Produces the Sample Databases submenu with a list of available sample databases that you can use to explore various features of Microsoft Access.
Check for Updates	Activates your browser, which displays a list of updates to Office 2003. These updates can be downloaded and installed to improve the efficiency of Office or to fix an error in one or more of the Office applications.
Detect and Repair	Detects and repairs errors in the Access program.
Activate Product	Activates Access if it has not already been activated.
Customer Feedback Options	Gives or denies Microsoft permission to collect anonymous information about your hardware.
About Microsoft Office Access	Displays the About Microsoft Access dialog box. The dialog box lists the owner of the software and the product identification. You need to know the product identification if you call Microsoft for assistance. The three buttons below the OK button are the System Info button, the Tech Support button, and the Disabled Items button. The System Info button displays system information, including hardware resources, components, software environment, and applications. The Tech Support button displays technical assistance information. The Disabled Items button displays a list of disabled items that prevents Access from functioning properly.

Use Help

1 Using the Type a Question for Help Box

Instructions: Perform the following tasks using the Access Help system.

1. Use the Type a question for help box on the menu bar to get help on lookup fields.
2. Click About creating a field that looks up or list values in tables (MDB) in the list of links in the Search Results task pane. Tile the windows. Double-click the Microsoft Access Help window title bar to maximize it. Click the Show All button. Read and print the information. At the top of the printout, write down the number of links the Access Help system found.
3. One at a time, click two additional links in the Search Results task pane and print the information. Hand in the printouts to your instructor. Use the Back and Forward buttons to return to the original page.
4. Use the Type a question for help box to search for information on calculated fields. Click the About calculations in a query (MDB) link in the Search Results task pane. When the Microsoft Access Help window is displayed, maximize the window. Read and print the information. One at a time, click the links on the page and print the information for any new page that displays. Close the Microsoft Access Help window.
5. For each of the following words and phrases, click one link in the Search Results task pane, click the Show All link, and then print the page: table; record; field; database design; primary key; foreign key; and referential integrity.

2 Expanding on the Access Help System Basics

Instructions: Use the Access Help system to understand the topics better and answer the questions listed below. Answer the questions on your own paper, or hand in the printed Help information to your instructor.

1. Show the Office Assistant. Right-click the Office Assistant and then click Animate! on the shortcut menu. Repeat invoking the Animate command to see various animations. Right-click the Office Assistant, click Options on the shortcut menu, click the Reset my tips button, and then click the OK button. Click the lightbulb above the Office Assistant. If you see the lightbulb, it indicates that the Office Assistant has a tip to share with you.
2. Use the Office Assistant to find help on filtering records. Print the help information for three links in the Search Results task pane. Close the Microsoft Access Help window. Hand in the printouts to your instructor. Hide the Office Assistant.
3. Press the F1 key. Search for information on Help. Click the first two links in the Search Results task pane. Read and print the information for both.
4. One at a time, invoke the first three commands in Table A-1 on the previous page. Print each page. Click two links on one of the pages and print the information. Hand in the printouts to your instructor.
5. Click About Microsoft Access on the Help menu. Click the Tech Support button and print the resulting page. Click the System Info button. Below the Components category, print the CD-ROM and Display information. Hand in the printouts to your instructor.

Appendix B

Speech and Handwriting Recognition

Introduction

This appendix discusses the Office capability that allows users to create and modify databases using its alternative input technologies available through **text services**. Office provides a variety of text services, which enable you to speak commands and enter text in an application. The most common text service is the keyboard. Other text services include speech recognition and handwriting recognition.

The Language Bar

The **Language bar** allows you to use text services in the Office applications. You can utilize the Language bar in one of three states: (1) in a restored state as a floating toolbar in the Access window (Figure B-1a or Figure B-1b if Text Labels are enabled); (2) in a minimized state docked next to the notification area on the Windows taskbar (Figure B-1c); or (3) hidden (temporarily closed and out of the way). If the Language bar is hidden, you can activate it by right-clicking the Windows taskbar, pointing to Toolbars on the shortcut menu (Figure B-1d), and clicking Language bar on the Toolbars submenu. If you want to close the Language bar, right-click the Language bar and then click Close the Language bar on the shortcut menu (Figure B-1e).

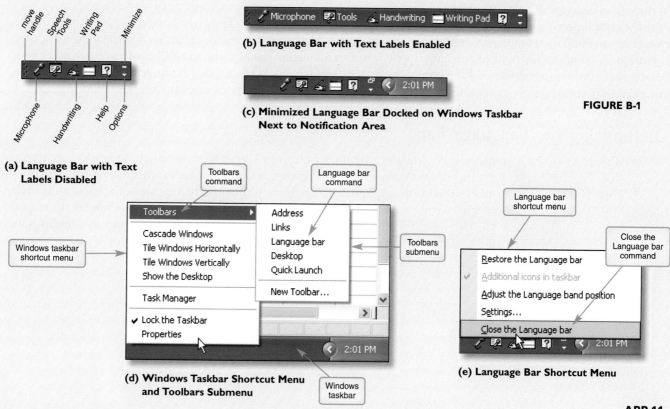

FIGURE B-1

When Windows was installed on your computer, the installer specified a default language. For example, most users in the United States select English (United States) as the default language. You can add more than 90 additional languages and varying dialects such as Basque, English (Zimbabwe), French (France), French (Canada), German (Germany), German (Austria), and Swahili. With multiple languages available, you can switch from one language to another while working in Access. If you change the language or dialect, then text services may change the functions of the keys on the keyboard, adjust speech recognition, and alter handwriting recognition. If a second language is activated, then a Language icon appears immediately to the right of the move handle on the Language bar. This appendix assumes that English (United States) is the only language installed. Thus, the Language icon does not appear in the examples in Figure B-1 on the previous page.

Buttons on the Language Bar

The Language bar shown in Figure B-2a contains seven buttons. The number of buttons on your Language bar may be different. These buttons are used to select the language, customize the Language bar, control the microphone, control handwriting, and obtain help.

The first button on the left is the Microphone button, which enables and disables the microphone. When the microphone is enabled, text services adds two buttons and a balloon to the Language bar (Figure B-2b). These additional buttons and the balloon will be discussed shortly.

The second button from the left is the Speech Tools button. The Speech Tools button displays a menu of commands (Figure B-2c) that allow you to hide or show the balloon on the Language bar; train the Speech Recognition service so that it can interpret your voice better; add and delete words from its dictionary, such as names and other words not understood easily; and change the user profile so more than one person can use the microphone on the same computer.

The third button from the left on the Language bar is the Handwriting button. The Handwriting button displays the Handwriting menu (Figure B-2d), which lets you choose the Writing Pad (Figure B-2e), Write Anywhere (Figure B-2f), or the on-screen keyboard (Figure B-2g). The On-Screen Symbol Keyboard command on the Handwriting menu displays an on-screen keyboard that allows you to enter special symbols that are not available on a standard keyboard. You can choose only one form of handwriting at a time.

The fourth button indicates which one of the handwriting forms is active. For example, in Figure B-2a, the Writing Pad is active. The handwriting recognition capabilities of text services will be discussed shortly.

The fifth button from the left on the Language bar is the Help button. The Help button displays the Help menu. If you click the Language Bar Help command on the Help menu, the Language Bar Help window appears (Figure B-2h). On the far right of the Language bar are two buttons stacked above and below each other. The top button is the Minimize button and the bottom button is the Options button. The Minimize button minimizes the Language bar so that it appears on the Windows taskbar. The next section discusses the Options button.

Customizing the Language Bar

The down arrow icon immediately below the Minimize button in Figure B-2a is called the Options button. The Options button displays a menu of text services options (Figure B-2i). You can use this menu to hide the Speech Tools, Handwriting, and Help buttons on the Language bar by clicking their names to remove the check mark to the left of each button. The Settings command on the Options menu displays a dialog box that lets you customize the Language bar. This command will be discussed shortly. The Restore Defaults command redisplays hidden buttons on the Language bar.

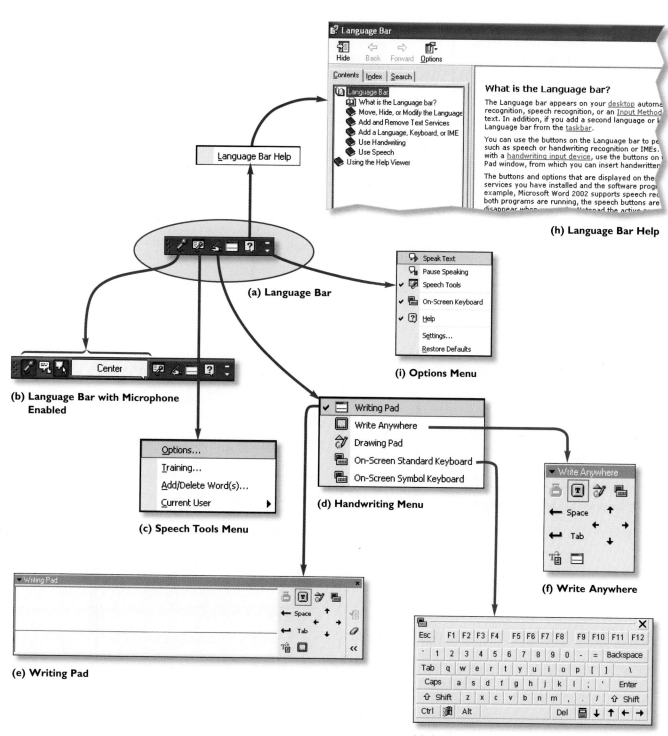

(a) Language Bar

(b) Language Bar with Microphone Enabled

(c) Speech Tools Menu

(d) Handwriting Menu

(e) Writing Pad

(f) Write Anywhere

(g) On-Screen Standard Keyboard

(h) Language Bar Help

(i) Options Menu

FIGURE B-2

If you right-click the Language bar, a shortcut menu appears (Figure B-3a on the next page). This shortcut menu lets you further customize the Language bar. The Minimize command on the shortcut menu docks the Language bar on the Windows taskbar. The Transparency command in Figure B-3a toggles the Language bar between being solid and transparent. You can see through a transparent Language bar (Figure B-3b on the next page). The Text Labels command toggles on text labels on the Language bar (Figure B-3c on the next page) and off (Figure B-3b).

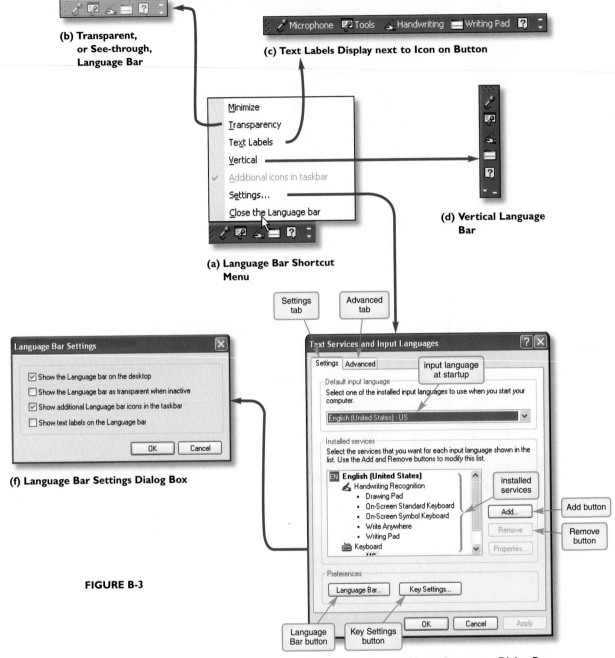

(b) Transparent,
or See-through,
Language Bar

(c) Text Labels Display next to Icon on Button

(a) Language Bar Shortcut
Menu

(d) Vertical Language
Bar

(f) Language Bar Settings Dialog Box

FIGURE B-3

(e) Text Services and Input Languages Dialog Box

The Settings command in Figure B-3a displays the Text Services and Input Languages dialog box (Figure B-3e). The Text Services and Input Languages dialog box allows you to add additional languages, add and remove text services, modify keys on the keyboard, modify the Language bar, and extend support of advanced text services to all programs, including Notepad and other programs that normally do not support text services (through the Advanced tab). If you want to remove any one of the services in the Installed services list, select the service, and then click the Remove button. If you want to add a service, click the Add button. The Key Settings button allows you to modify the keyboard. If you click the Language Bar button in the Text Services and Input Languages dialog box, the Language Bar Settings dialog box appears (Figure B-3f). This dialog box contains Language bar options, some of which are the same as the commands on the Language bar shortcut menu shown in Figure B-3a.

The Close the Language bar command on the shortcut menu shown in Figure B-3a closes or hides the Language bar. If you close the Language bar and want to redisplay it, see Figure B-1d on page APP 11.

Speech Recognition

The **Speech Recognition service** available with Office enables your computer to recognize human speech through a microphone. The microphone has two modes: dictation and voice command (Figure B-4). You switch between the two modes by clicking the Dictation button and the Voice Command button on the Language bar. These buttons appear only when you turn on Speech Recognition by clicking the Microphone button on the Language bar (Figure B-5a on the next page). If you are using the Microphone button for the very first time in Access, it will require that you check your microphone settings and step through voice training before activating the Speech Recognition service.

The Dictation button places the microphone in Dictation mode. In **Dictation mode**, whatever you speak is entered as text in the active cell. The Voice Command button places the microphone in Voice Command mode. In **Voice Command mode**, whatever you speak is interpreted as a command. If you want to turn off the microphone, click the Microphone button on the Language bar or in Voice Command mode say, "Mic off" (pronounced mike off). It is important to remember that minimizing the Language bar does not turn off the microphone.

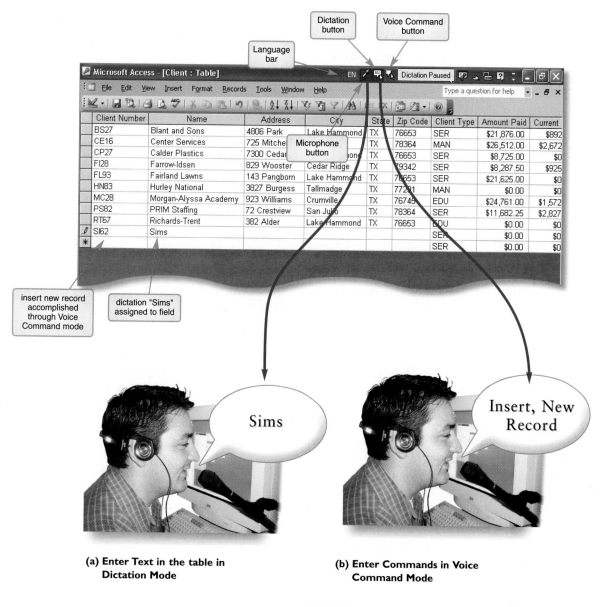

(a) **Enter Text in the table in Dictation Mode**

(b) **Enter Commands in Voice Command Mode**

FIGURE B-4

The Language bar speech message balloon shown in Figure B-5b displays messages that may offer help or hints. In Voice Command mode, the name of the last recognized command you said appears. If you use the mouse or keyboard instead of the microphone, a message will appear in the Language bar speech message balloon indicating the word you could say. In Dictation mode, the message, Dictating, usually appears. The Speech Recognition service, however, will display messages to inform you that you are talking too soft, too loud, too fast, or to ask you to repeat what you said by displaying, What was that?

Getting Started with Speech Recognition

For the microphone to function properly, you should follow these steps:

1. Make sure your computer meets the minimum requirements.
2. Start Access. Activate Speech Recognition by clicking Tools on the menu bar, pointing to Speech, and then clicking Speech Recognition on the Speech submenu.
3. Set up and position your microphone, preferably a close-talk headset with gain adjustment support.
4. Train Speech Recognition.

The following sections describe these steps in more detail.

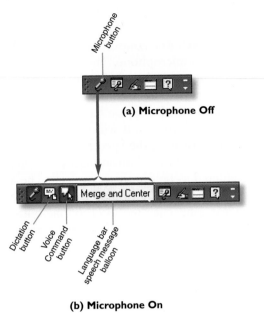

(a) Microphone Off

(b) Microphone On

FIGURE B-5

SPEECH RECOGNITION SYSTEM REQUIREMENTS For Speech Recognition to work on your computer, it needs the following:

1. Microsoft Windows 98 or later or Microsoft Windows NT 4.0 or later
2. At least 128 MB RAM
3. 400 MHz or faster processor
4. Microphone and sound card

SETUP AND POSITION YOUR MICROPHONE Set up your microphone as follows:

1. Connect your microphone to the sound card in the back of the computer.
2. Position the microphone approximately one inch out from and to the side of your mouth. Position it so you are not breathing into it.
3. On the Language bar, click the Speech Tools button, and then click Options on the Speech Tools menu (Figure B-6a).
4. When text services displays the Speech input settings dialog box (Figure B-6b), click the Advanced Speech button. When text services displays the Speech Properties dialog box (Figure B-6c), click the Speech Recognition tab.
5. Click the Configure Microphone button. Follow the Microphone Wizard directions as shown in Figures B-6d, B-6e, and B-6f. The Next button will remain dimmed in Figure B-6e until the volume meter consistently stays in the green area.
6. If someone else installed Speech Recognition, click the New button in the Speech Properties dialog box and enter your name. Click the Train Profile button and step through the Voice Training dialog boxes. The Voice Training dialog boxes will require that you enter your gender and age group. It then will step you through voice training.

You can adjust the microphone further by clicking the Settings button in the Speech Properties dialog box (Figure B-6c). The Settings button displays the Recognition Profile Settings dialog box that allows you to adjust the pronunciation sensitivity and accuracy versus recognition response time.

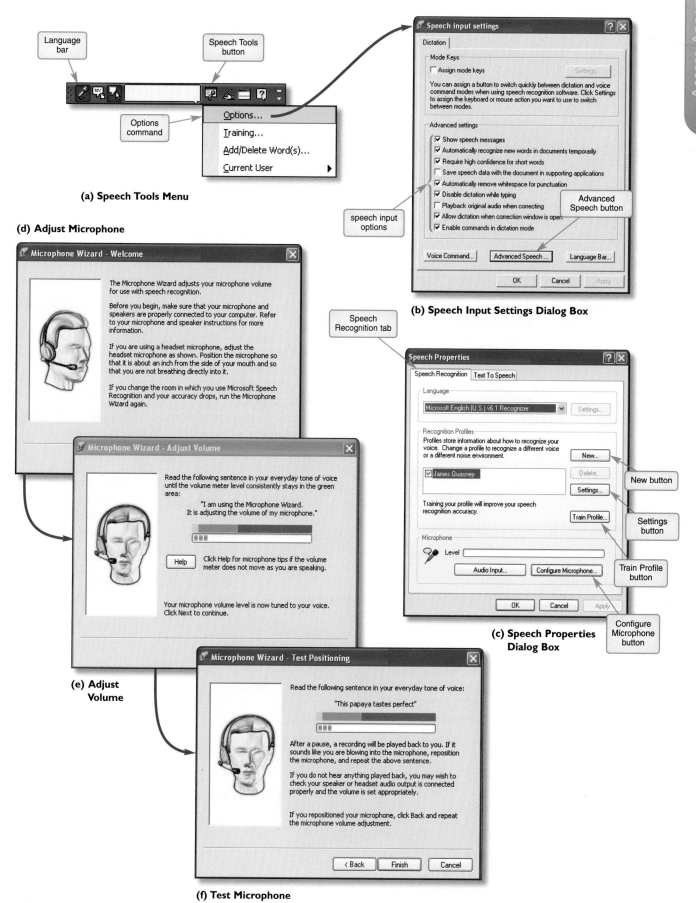

(a) Speech Tools Menu

(b) Speech Input Settings Dialog Box

(c) Speech Properties Dialog Box

(d) Adjust Microphone

(e) Adjust Volume

(f) Test Microphone

FIGURE B-6

TRAIN THE SPEECH RECOGNITION SERVICE   The Speech Recognition service will understand most commands and some dictation without any training at all. It will recognize much more of what you speak, however, if you take the time to train it. After one training session, it will recognize 85 to 90 percent of your words. As you do more training, accuracy will rise to 95 percent. If you feel that too many mistakes are being made, then continue to train the service. The more training you do, the more accurately it will work for you. Follow these steps to train the Speech Recognition service:

1. Click the Speech Tools button on the Language bar and then click Training (Figure B-7a).
2. When the Voice Training dialog box appears (Figure B-7b), click one of the sessions and then click the Next button.
3. Complete the training session, which should take less than 15 minutes.

If you are serious about using a microphone to speak to your computer, you need to take the time to go through at least three of the eight training sessions listed in Figure B-7b.

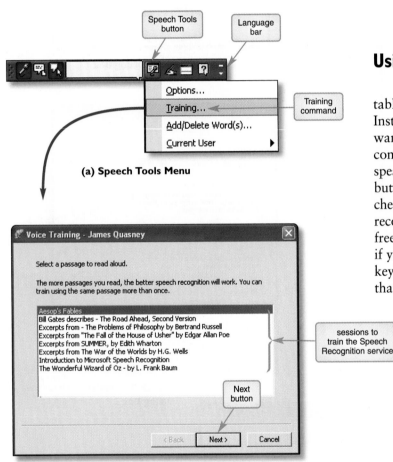

(a) Speech Tools Menu

(b) Voice Training Dialog Box

FIGURE B-7

Using Speech Recognition

Speech recognition lets you enter text into a table similarly to speaking into a tape recorder. Instead of typing, you can dictate text that you want to assign to fields, and you can issue voice commands. In Voice Command mode, you can speak menu names, commands on menus, toolbar button names, and dialog box option buttons, check boxes, list boxes, and button names. Speech recognition, however, is not a completely hands-free form of input. Speech recognition works best if you use a combination of your voice, the keyboard, and the mouse. You soon will discover that Dictation mode is far less accurate than Voice Command mode. Table B-1 lists some tips that will improve the Speech Recognition service's accuracy considerably.

Table B-1   Tips to Improve Speech Recognition

NUMBER	TIP
1	The microphone hears everything. Though the Speech Recognition service filters out background noise, it is recommended that you work in a quiet environment.
2	Try not to move the microphone around once it is adjusted.
3	Speak in a steady tone and speak clearly.
4	In Dictation mode, do not pause between words. A phrase is easier to interpret than a word. Sounding out syllables in a word will make it more difficult for the Speech Recognition service to interpret what you are saying.
5	If you speak too loudly or too softly, it makes it difficult for the Speech Recognition service to interpret what you said. Check the Language bar speech message balloon for an indication that you may be speaking too loudly or too softly.
6	If you experience problems after training, adjust the recognition options that control accuracy and rejection by clicking the Settings button shown in Figure B-6c on page APP 17.
7	When you are finished using the microphone, turn it off by clicking the Microphone button on the Language bar or in Voice Command mode, say "Mic off." Leaving the microphone on is the same as leaning on the keyboard.
8	If the Speech Recognition service is having difficulty with unusual words, then add the words to its dictionary by using the Add/Delete Word(s) command on the Speech Tools menu (Figure B-8a). The last names of individuals and the names of companies are good examples of the types of words you should add to the dictionary.
9	Training will improve accuracy; practice will improve confidence.

The last command on the Speech Tools menu is the Current User command (Figure B-8a). The Current User command is useful for multiple users who share a computer. It allows them to configure their own individual profiles, and then switch between users as they use the computer.

For additional information on the Speech Recognition service, enter speech recognition in the Type a question for help box on the menu bar.

Handwriting Recognition

Using the Office **Handwriting Recognition service**, you can enter text and numbers into Access by writing instead of typing. You can write using a special handwriting device that connects to your computer or you can write on the screen using your mouse. Four basic methods of handwriting are available by clicking the Handwriting button on the Language bar: Writing Pad; Write Anywhere; Drawing Pad; and On-Screen Keyboard. Although the on-screen keyboard does not involve handwriting recognition, it is part of the Handwriting menu and, therefore, will be discussed in this section.

If your Language bar does not include the Handwriting button, then for installation instructions, enter install handwriting recognition in the Type a question for help box on the menu bar.

(a) Speech Tools Menu

(b) Add/Delete Word(s) Dialog Box

FIGURE B-8

Writing Pad

To display the Writing Pad, click the Handwriting button on the Language bar and then click Writing Pad (Figure B-9). The **Writing Pad** resembles a notepad with one or more lines on which you can use freehand to print or write in cursive. With the Text button enabled, you can form letters on the line by moving the mouse while holding down the mouse button. To the right of the notepad is a rectangular toolbar. Use the buttons on this toolbar to adjust the Writing Pad, select cells, and activate other handwriting applications.

Consider the example in Figure B-9. With the insertion point in the City field, the word, Lee, is written in cursive on the **Pen line** in the Writing Pad. As soon as the word is complete, the Handwriting Recognition service automatically assigns the word to the City field.

FIGURE B-9

You can customize the Writing Pad by clicking the Options button on the left side of the title bar and then clicking the Options command (Figure B-10a). Invoking the Options command causes the Handwriting Options dialog box to display. The Handwriting Options dialog box contains two sheets: Common and Writing Pad. The Common sheet lets you change the pen color and pen width, adjust recognition, and customize the toolbar area of the Writing Pad. The Writing Pad sheet allows you to change the background color and the number of lines that are displayed in the Writing Pad. Both sheets contain a Restore Default button to restore the settings to what they were when the software was installed initially.

(a) **Writing Pad Options Menu**

(b) **Handwriting Options Dialog Box with Common Sheet Active**

(c) **Handwriting Options Dialog Box with Writing Pad Sheet Active**

FIGURE B-10

When you first start using the Writing Pad, you may want to remove the check mark from the Automatic recognition check box in the Common sheet in the Handwriting Options dialog box (Figure B-10b). With the check mark removed, the Handwriting Recognition service will not interpret what you write in the Writing Pad until you click the Recognize Now button on the toolbar (Figure B-9 on page APP 20). This allows you to pause and adjust your writing.

The best way to learn how to use the Writing Pad is to practice with it. Also, for more information, enter handwriting recognition in the Type a question for help box on the menu bar.

Write Anywhere

Rather than use Writing Pad, you can write anywhere on the screen by invoking the Write Anywhere command on the Handwriting menu (Figure B-11) that appears when you click the Handwriting button on the Language bar. In this case, the entire window is your writing pad.

In Figure B-11, the word, TX, is written in cursive using the mouse button. Shortly after the word is written, the Handwriting Recognition service interprets it, assigns it to the State field, and erases what was written.

It is recommended that when you first start using the Writing Anywhere service that you remove the check mark from the Automatic recognition check box in the Common sheet in the Handwriting Options dialog box (Figure B-10b on the previous page). With the check mark removed, the Handwriting Recognition service will not interpret what you write on the screen until you click the Recognize Now button on the toolbar (Figure B-11).

Write Anywhere is more difficult to use than the Writing Pad, because when you click the mouse button, Access may interpret the action as selecting a field rather than starting to write. For this reason, it is recommended that you use the Writing Pad.

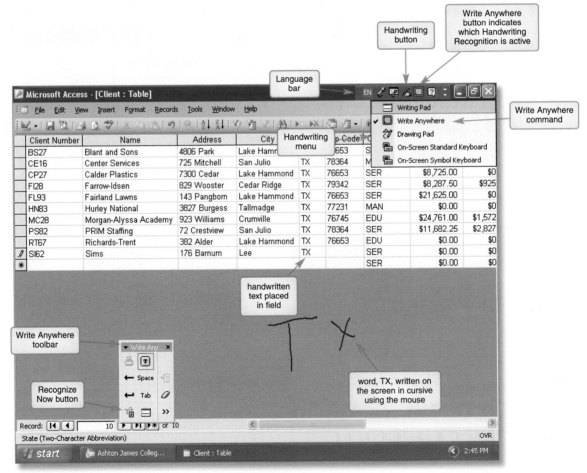

FIGURE B-11

On-Screen Keyboard

The On-Screen Standard Keyboard command on the Handwriting menu (Figure B-12) displays an on-screen keyboard. The **on-screen keyboard** lets you enter data into a field by using your mouse to click the keys. The on-screen keyboard is similar to the type found on handheld computers.

The On-Screen Symbol Keyboard command on the Handwriting menu (Figure B-12) displays a special on-screen keyboard that allows you to enter symbols that are not on your keyboard, as well as Unicode characters. **Unicode characters** use a coding scheme capable of representing all the world's current languages.

FIGURE B-12

Appendix C

Publishing Office Web Pages to a Web Server

With the Office applications, you use the Save as Web Page command on the File menu to save the Web page to a Web server using one of two techniques: Web folders or File Transfer Protocol. A **Web folder** is an Office shortcut to a Web server. **File Transfer Protocol** (**FTP**) is an Internet standard that allows computers to exchange files with other computers on the Internet.

You should contact your network system administrator or technical support staff at your ISP to determine if their Web server supports Web folders, FTP, or both, and to obtain necessary permissions to access the Web server. If you decide to publish Web pages using a Web folder, you must have the Office Server Extensions (OSE) installed on your computer.

Using Web Folders to Publish Office Web Pages

When publishing to a Web folder, someone first must create the Web folder before you can save to it. If you are granted permission to create a Web folder, you must obtain the URL of the Web server, a user name, and possibly a password that allows you to access the Web server. You also must decide on a name for the Web folder. Table C-1 explains how to create a Web folder.

Office adds the name of the Web folder to the list of current Web folders. You can save to this folder, open files in the folder, rename the folder, or perform any operations you would to a folder on your hard disk. You can use your Office program or Windows Explorer to access this folder. Table C-2 explains how to save to a Web folder.

Using FTP to Publish Office Web Pages

When publishing a Web page using FTP, you first must add the FTP location to your computer before you can save to it. An FTP location, also called an **FTP site**, is a collection of files that reside on an FTP server. In this case, the FTP server is the Web server.

To add an FTP location, you must obtain the name of the FTP site, which usually is the address (URL) of the FTP server, and a user name and a password that allows you to access the FTP server. You save and open the Web pages on the FTP server using the name of the FTP site. Table C-3 explains how to add an FTP site.

Office adds the name of the FTP site to the FTP locations list in the Save As and Open dialog boxes. You can open and save files using this list. Table C-4 explains how to save to an FTP location.

Table C-1 Creating a Web Folder

1. Click File on the menu bar and then click Save As (or Open).
2. When the Save As dialog box (or Open dialog box) appears, click My Network Places on the My Places bar, and then click the Create New Folder button on the toolbar.
3. When the Add Network Place Wizard dialog box appears, click the Next button. If necessary, click Choose another network location. Click the Next button. Click the View some examples link, type the Internet or network address, and then click the Next button. Click Log on anonymously to deselect the check box, type your user name in the User name text box, and then click the Next button. Enter the name you want to call this network place and then click the Next button. Click the Finish button.

Table C-2 Saving to a Web Folder

1. Click File on the menu bar and then click Save As.
2. When the Save As dialog box appears, type the Web page file name in the File name text box. Do not press the ENTER key.
3. Click My Network Places on the My Places bar.
4. Double-click the Web folder name in the Save in list.
5. If the Enter Network Password dialog box appears, type the user name and password in the respective text boxes and then click the OK button.
6. Click the Save button in the Save As dialog box.

Table C-3 Adding an FTP Location

1. Click File on the menu bar and then click Save As (or Open).
2. In the Save As dialog box, click the Save in box arrow and then click Add/Modify FTP Locations in the Save in list; or in the Open dialog box, click the Look in box arrow and then click Add/Modify FTP Locations in the Look in list.
3. When the Add/Modify FTP Locations dialog box appears, type the name of the FTP site in the Name of FTP site text box. If the site allows anonymous logon, click Anonymous in the Log on as area; if you have a user name for the site, click User in the Log on as area and then enter the user name. Enter the password in the Password text box. Click the OK button.
4. Close the Save As or the Open dialog box.

Table C-4 Saving to an FTP Location

1. Click File on the menu bar and then click Save As.
2. When the Save As dialog box appears, type the Web page file name in the File name text box. Do not press the ENTER key.
3. Click the Save in box arrow and then click FTP Locations.
4. Double-click the name of the FTP site to which you wish to save.
5. When the FTP Log On dialog box appears, enter your user name and password and then click the OK button.
6. Click the Save button in the Save As dialog box.

Appendix D

Changing Screen Resolution and Resetting the Access Toolbars and Menus

This appendix explains how to change your screen resolution in Windows to the resolution used in this book. It also describes how to reset the Access toolbars and menus to their installation settings.

Changing Screen Resolution

The **screen resolution** indicates the number of pixels (dots) that your system uses to display the letters, numbers, graphics, and background you see on your screen. The screen resolution usually is stated as the product of two numbers, such as 800 × 600. An 800 × 600 screen resolution results in a display of 800 distinct pixels on each of 600 lines, or about 480,000 pixels. The figures in this book were created using a screen resolution of 800 × 600.

The screen resolutions most commonly used today are 800 × 600 and 1024 × 768, although some Office specialists operate their computers at a much higher screen resolution, such as 2048 × 1536. The following steps show how to change the screen resolution from 1024 × 768 to 800 × 600.

To Change the Screen Resolution

1

• **If necessary, minimize all applications so that the Windows desktop appears.**

• **Right-click the Windows desktop.**

Windows displays the Windows desktop shortcut menu (Figure D-1).

FIGURE D-1

2

• **Click Properties on the shortcut menu.**

• **When Windows displays the Display Properties dialog box, click the Settings tab.**

Windows displays the Settings sheet in the Display Properties dialog box (Figure D-2). The Settings sheet shows a preview of the Windows desktop using the current screen resolution (1024 × 768). The Settings sheet also shows the screen resolution and the color quality settings.

FIGURE D-2

3

• **Drag the slider in the Screen resolution area to the left so that the screen resolution changes to 800 × 600.**

The screen resolution in the Screen resolution area changes to 800 × 600 (Figure D-3). The Settings sheet shows a preview of the Windows desktop using the new screen resolution (800 × 600).

FIGURE D-3

4

- **Click the OK button.**
- **If Windows displays the Monitor Settings dialog box, click the Yes button.**

Windows changes the screen resolution from 1024 × 768 to 800 × 600 (Figure D-4).

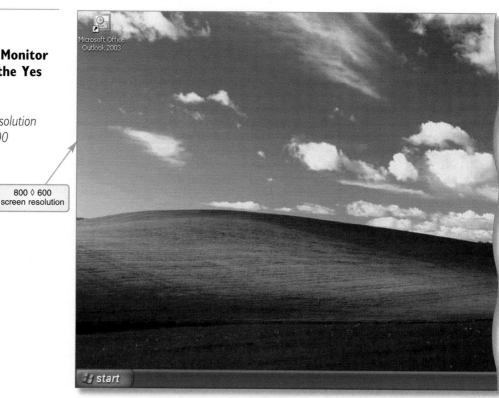

800 ◊ 600 screen resolution

FIGURE D-4

As shown in the previous steps, as you decrease the screen resolution, Windows displays less information on your screen, but the information increases in size. The reverse also is true: as you increase the screen resolution, Windows displays more information on your screen, but the information decreases in size.

Resetting the Access Toolbars and Menus

In Microsoft Access, you can personalize toolbars and menus. You can change the toolbar or toolbars that appear by using the Toolbars command on the View menu, and then selecting the toolbars you want to appear. You also can change the buttons that appear on a particular toolbar by using the Toolbar Options button (see Figure D-5 on the next page). In addition, Access personalizes the commands on the menus based on their usage. Each time you start Access, the toolbars and menus have the same settings as the last time you used the application. This appendix shows you how to reset usage data, that is, how to clear menu and toolbar settings. Resetting usage data does not affect the location of the toolbars, nor does it change any buttons you might have added using the Customize dialog box. To reverse these changes, you need to reset the toolbar. The steps on the next page show how to reset the usage data and also the Database toolbar.

To Reset Menu and Toolbar Usage Data

1

• **Start Access following the steps outlined at the beginning of Project 1.**

• **Click View on the menu bar, and then point to Toolbars.**

The View menu and Toolbars submenu appear (Figure D-5).

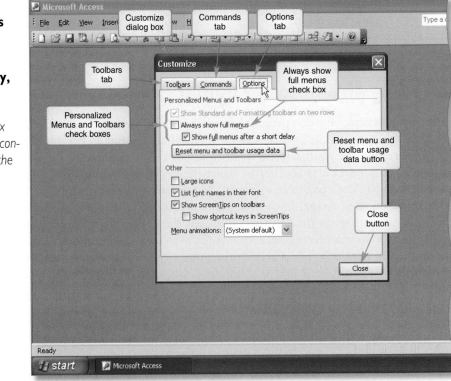

FIGURE D-5

2

• **Click Customize on the Toolbars submenu.**

• **When Access displays the Customize dialog box, if necessary, click the Options tab.**

Access displays the Customize dialog box (Figure D-6). The Customize dialog box contains three sheets used for customizing the Access toolbars and menus.

FIGURE D-6

3

• **Click the Reset menu and toolbar usage data button.**

The Microsoft Office Access dialog box displays a message indicating the actions that will be taken and asks if you are sure you want to proceed (Figure D-7).

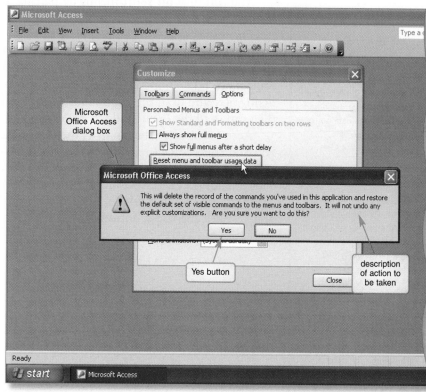

FIGURE D-7

4

• **Click the Yes button in the Microsoft Office Access dialog box.**

• **Click the Toolbars tab in the Customize dialog box and then click Database (the word Database and not the check box in front of it) in the Toolbars list.**

The Customize dialog box displays the Toolbars sheet with Database highlighted in the Toolbars list (Figure D-8).

5

• **Click the Reset button.**

• **When the Microsoft Office Access dialog box appears, asking if you are sure you want to reset the changes made to the Database toolbar, click the OK button.**

• **Repeat the process for any other toolbar you want to reset.**

6

• **Click the Close button in the Customize dialog box.**

Access resets the Database toolbar to its installation settings.

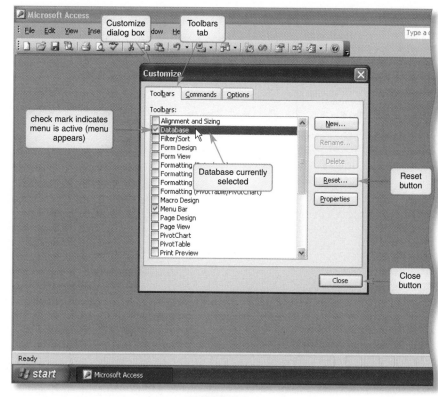

FIGURE D-8

You can turn off short menus by placing a check mark in the Always show full menus check box in the Customize dialog box (see Figure D-6 on page APP 28).

One other task you can complete through the Customize dialog box in Figure D-6 is to add buttons to toolbars and commands to menus. To add buttons, click the Commands tab in the Customize dialog box and drag the commands to a toolbar. To add commands to a menu, click the Commands tab in the Customize dialog box and drag the commands to the menu name. When the menu appears, you then can drag the commands to the desired menu location.

Access considers the menu at the top of the Access window to be a toolbar. If you add commands to menus as described in the previous paragraph and want to reset them to their installation settings, do the following: (1) Click Toolbars on the View menu; (2) click Customize; (3) click the Toolbars tab; (4) scroll down in the Toolbars list and click Menu Bar; (5) click the Reset button; (6) click the OK button; and (7) click the Close button.

Other Ways

1. Click Toolbar Options button on Database toolbar, point to Add or Remove Buttons, click Customize, click Options tab, click Reset menu and toolbar usage data button to reset usage data, click Yes button, click Close button

2. Click Toolbar Options button on Database toolbar, point to Add or Remove Buttons, click Customize, click Toolbars tab, click toolbar name, click Reset button to reset toolbar to installation settings, click OK button, click Close button

3. Right-click toolbar, click Customize, click Options tab, click Reset menu and toolbar usage data button to reset usage data, click Yes button, click Close button

4. Right-click toolbar, click Customize on shortcut menu, click Toolbars tab, click toolbar name, click Reset button to reset toolbar to installation settings, click OK button, click Close button

5. In Voice Command mode, say "View, Toolbars, [desired toolbar name], Reset, OK, Close"

Appendix E

Microsoft Office Specialist Certification

What Is Microsoft Office Specialist Certification?

Microsoft Office Specialist certification provides a framework for measuring your proficiency with the Microsoft Office 2003 applications, such as Microsoft Office Word 2003, Microsoft Office Excel 2003, Microsoft Office Access 2003, Microsoft Office PowerPoint 2003, and Microsoft Office Outlook 2003. The levels of certification are described in Table E-1.

Table E-1 Levels of Microsoft Office Specialist Certification

LEVEL	DESCRIPTION	REQUIREMENTS	CREDENTIAL AWARDED
Microsoft Office Specialist	Indicates that you have an understanding of the basic features in a specific Microsoft Office 2003 application	Pass any ONE of the following: Microsoft Office Word 2003 Microsoft Office Excel 2003 Microsoft Office Access 2003 Microsoft Office PowerPoint 2003 Microsoft Office Outlook 2003	Candidates will be awarded one certificate for each of the Specialist-level exams they have passed: Microsoft Office Word 2003 Microsoft Office Excel 2003 Microsoft Office Access 2003 Microsoft Office PowerPoint 2003 Microsoft Office Outlook 2003
Microsoft Office Expert	Indicates that you have an understanding of the advanced features in a specific Microsoft Office 2003 application	Pass any ONE of the following: Microsoft Office Word 2003 Expert Microsoft Office Excel 2003 Expert	Candidates will be awarded one certificate for each of the Expert-level exams they have passed: Microsoft Office Word 2003 Expert Microsoft Office Excel 2003 Expert
Microsoft Office Master	Indicates that you have a comprehensive under-standing of the features of four of the five primary Microsoft Office 2003 applications	Pass the following: Microsoft Office Word 2003 Expert Microsoft Office Excel 2003 Expert Microsoft Office PowerPoint 2003 And pass ONE of the following: Microsoft Office Access 2003 or Microsoft Office Outlook 2003	Candidates will be awarded the Microsoft Office Master certificate for fulfilling the requirements.

Why Should You Be Certified?

Being Microsoft Office certified provides a valuable industry credential — proof that you have the Office 2003 applications skills required by employers. By passing one or more Microsoft Office Specialist certification exams, you demonstrate your proficiency in a given Office 2003 application to employers. With more than 400 million people in 175 nations and 70 languages using Office applications, Microsoft is targeting Office 2003 certification to a wide variety of companies. These companies include temporary employment agencies that want to prove the expertise of their workers, large corporations looking for a way to measure the skill set of employees, and training companies and educational institutions seeking Microsoft Office 2003 teachers with appropriate credentials.

The Microsoft Office Specialist Certification Exams

You pay $50 to $100 each time you take an exam, whether you pass or fail. The fee varies among testing centers. The **Microsoft Office Expert** exams, which you can take up to 60 minutes to complete, consist of between 40 and 60 tasks that you perform on a personal computer in a simulated environment. The tasks require you to use the application just as you would in doing your job. The **Microsoft Office Specialist** exams contain fewer tasks, and you will have slightly less time to complete them. The tasks you will perform differ on the two types of exams. After passing designated Expert and Specialist exams, candidates are awarded the **Microsoft Office Master** certificate (see the requirements in Table E-1 on the previous page).

How to Prepare for the Microsoft Office Specialist Certification Exams

The Shelly Cashman Series offers several Microsoft-approved textbooks that cover the required objectives of the Microsoft Office Specialist certification exams. For a listing of the textbooks, visit the Shelly Cashman Series Microsoft Office Specialist Center at scsite.com/winoff2003/cert. Click the link Shelly Cashman Series Microsoft Office 2003-Approved Microsoft Office Textbooks (Figure E-1). After using any of the books listed in an instructor-led course, you should be prepared to take the indicated Microsoft Office Specialist certification exam.

How to Find an Authorized Testing Center

To locate a testing center, call 1-800-933-4493 in North America, or visit the Shelly Cashman Series Microsoft Office Specialist Center at scsite.com/winoff2003/cert. Click the link Locate an Authorized Testing Center Near You (Figure E-1). At this Web site, you can look for testing centers around the world.

Shelly Cashman Series Microsoft Office Specialist Center

The Shelly Cashman Series Microsoft Office Specialist Center (Figure E-1) lists more than 15 Web sites you can visit to obtain additional information about certification. The Web page (scsite.com/winoff2003/cert) includes links to general information about certification, choosing an application for certification, preparing for the certification exam, and taking and passing the certification exam.

FIGURE E-1

Index

⬜ Quick Reference Summary

In Microsoft Office Access 2003, you can accomplish a task in a number of ways. The following table provides a quick reference to each task presented in this textbook. The first column identifies the task. The second column indicates the page number on which the task is discussed in the book. The subsequent four columns list the different ways the task in column one can be carried out. You can invoke the commands listed in the MOUSE, MENU BAR, and SHORTCUT MENU columns using Voice commands.

Microsoft Office Access 2003 Quick Reference Summary

TASK	PAGE NUMBER	MOUSE	MENU BAR	SHORTCUT MENU	KEYBOARD SHORTCUT
Add Field	AC 129	Insert Rows button	Insert | Rows	Insert Rows	INSERT
Add Group of Records	AC 139	Query Type button arrow | Append Query	Query | Append Query	Query Type | Append Query	
Add Record	AC 23, AC 116	New Record button	Insert | New Record		
Add Table to Query	AC 92	Show Table button	Query | Show Table	Show Table	
Advanced Filter/Sort	AC 124		Records | Filter | Advanced Filter Sort		
Apply Filter	AC 121, AC 123	Filter By Selection or Filter By Form button	Records | Filter		
Calculate Statistics	AC 100	Totals button	View | Totals	Totals	
Change Group of Records	AC 136	Query Type button arrow | Update Query	Query | Update Query	Query Type | Update Query	
Clear Query	AC 75		Edit | Clear Grid		
Close Database	AC 26	Close Window button	File | Close		
Close Form	AC 39	Close Window button	File | Close		
Close Query	AC 73	Close Window button	File | Close		
Close Table	AC 21	Close Window button	File | Close		
Collapse Subdatasheet	AC 153	Expand indicator (-)			
Create Calculated Field	AC 96			Zoom	SHIFT+F2
Create Database	AC 10	New button	File | New		CTRL+N
Create Form	AC 38	New Object button arrow | AutoForm	Insert | AutoForm		
Create Index	AC 161	Indexes button	View | Indexes		
Create Query	AC 68	New Object button arrow | Query	Insert | Query		
Create Report	AC 43	New Object button arrow | Report	Insert | Report		
Create Snapshot	AC 184		File | Export, select SNP as file type	Export, select SNP as file type	
Create Table	AC 17	Tables object | Create table in Design view or Create table by using wizard	Insert | Table		

TASK	PAGE NUMBER	MOUSE	MENU BAR	SHORTCUT MENU	KEYBOARD SHORTCUT
Crosstab Query	AC 104	New Object button arrow | Query	Insert | Query		
Default Value	AC 142	Default Value property box			
Delete Field	AC 130	Delete Rows button	Edit | Delete	Delete Rows	DELETE
Delete Group of Records	AC 138	Query Type button arrow | Delete Query	Query | Delete Query	Query Type | Delete Query	
Delete Record	AC 125	Delete Record button	Edit | Delete Record	Delete Record	DELETE
Exclude Duplicates	AC 87	Properties button	View | Properties | Unique Values Only	Properties | Unique Values Only	
Exclude Field from Query Results	AC 78	Show check box			
Expand Subdatasheet	AC 153	Expand indicator (+)			
Export Using Drag-and-Drop	AC 182	Drag object, then drop			
Export Using Export Command	AC 183		File | Export	Export	
Field Size	AC 19, AC 127	Field Size property box			
Field Type	AC 20	Data Type box arrow | appropriate type			Appropriate letter
Filter Records	AC 121, AC 123	Filter By Selection or Filter By Form button	Records | Filter		
Font in Datasheet	AC 133		Format | Font	Font	
Format	AC 144	Format property box			
Format a Calculated Field	AC 98	Properties button	View | Properties	Properties	
Format Datasheet	AC 134		Format | Datasheet	Datasheet	
Group in Query	AC 103	Totals button	View | Totals		
Import	AC 177		File | Get External Data | Import	Import	
Include All Fields in Query	AC 74	Double-click asterisk in field list			
Include Field in Query	AC 71	Double-click field in field list			
Join Properties	AC 94		View | Join Properties	Join Properties	
Key Field	AC 19	Primary Key button	Edit | Primary Key	Primary Key	
Link	AC 180		File | Get External Data | Link Table	Link Tables	
Lookup Field	AC 147	Text box arrow | Lookup Wizard			
Move to First Record	AC 27	First Record button			CTRL+UP ARROW
Move to Last Record	AC 27	Last Record button			CTRL+DOWN ARROW
Move to Next Record	AC 27	Next Record button			DOWN ARROW
Move to Previous Record	AC 27	Previous Record button			UP ARROW
Open Database	AC 26	Open button	File | Open		CTRL+O
Open Form	AC 116	Forms object | Open button		Open	Use ARROW keys to move highlight to name, then press ENTER key
Open Table	AC 26	Tables object | Open button		Open	Use ARROW keys to move highlight to name, then press ENTER key

Microsoft Office Access 2003 Quick Reference Summary

TASK	PAGE NUMBER	MOUSE	MENU BAR	SHORTCUT MENU	KEYBOARD SHORTCUT
Preview Table	AC 30	Print Preview button	File | Print Preview	Print Preview	
Print Relationships	AC 151		File | Print Relationships		
Print Report	AC 47	Print button	File | Print	Print	CTRL+P
Print Results of Query	AC 72	Print button	File | Print	Print	CTRL+P
Print Table	AC 30	Print button	File | Print	Print	CTRL+P
Quit Access	AC 50	Close button	File | Exit		ALT+F4
Relationships (Referential Integrity)	AC 150	Relationships button	Tools | Relationships		
Remove Filter	AC 122	Remove Filter button	Records | Remove Filter/Sort		
Resize Column	AC 131	Drag right boundary of field selector	Format | Column Width	Column Width	
Restructure Table	AC 126	Tables object | Design button		Design View	
Return to Select Query Window	AC 72	View button arrow	View | Design View		
Run Query	AC 71	Run button	Query | Run		
Save Form	AC 39	Save button	File | Save		CTRL+S
Save Query	AC 80	Save button	File | Save		CTRL+S
Save Table	AC 21	Save button	File | Save		CTRL+S
Search for Record	AC 117	Find button	Edit | Find		CTRL+F
Select Fields for Report	AC 44	Add Field button or Add All Fields button			
Simple Query Wizard	AC 34	New Object button arrow | Query	Insert | Query		
Sort Data in Query	AC 86	Sort row | Sort row arrow | type of sort			
Sort Records	AC 155	Sort Ascending or Sort Descending button	Records | Sort | Sort Ascending or Sort Descending	Sort Ascending or Sort Descending	
Switch Between Form and Datasheet Views	AC 41, AC 120	View button arrow	View | Datasheet View		
Top-Values Query	AC 89	Top Values button	View | Properties	Properties	
Use AND Criterion	AC 84				Place criteria on same line
Use OR Criterion	AC 85				Place criteria on separate lines
Validation Rule	AC 141	Validation Rule property box			
Validation Text	AC 141	Validation Text property box			